D0104444

PROJECT CENSORED'S
STATE OF THE FREE PRESS 2021

EDITED BY **Mickey Huff** AND **Andy Lee Roth**

FOREWORD BY
Matt Taibbi

PROJECT CENSORED'S

STATE OF THE FREE PRESS | 2021

The Top Censored Stories and Media Analysis of 2019–20

EDITED BY **Mickey Huff** AND **Andy Lee Roth**
WITH **Project Censored**

FOREWORD BY **Matt Taibbi**

Seven Stories Press
New York • Oakland • Liverpool

Seven Stories Press
140 Watts Street
New York, NY 10013
www.sevenstories.com

ISBN 978-1-64421-026-0 (paperback)
ISBN 978-1-64421-027-7 (electronic)
ISSN 1074-5998

9 8 7 6 5 4 3 2 1

Book design by Jon Gilbert

Printed in the USA

DEDICATION

To Ernesto Carmona Ulloa,
and journalists everywhere who
break down blockades on the
free flow of information.

Ernesto Carmona—Chilean author and journalist, executive secretary of the Latin American Federation of Journalists' Investigation Commission on Attacks Against Journalists, Project Censored judge, esteemed colleague, and dear friend.

Contents

Foreword

MATT TAIBBI

Don't blame the mirror if your mug is crooked.
—RUSSIAN SAYING

The American news landscape is changing, rapidly. Forty years ago Americans watched the same three network news programs and read the same handful of daily newspapers. Today the industry is divided along partisan lines, and media companies avoid challenging audiences with depressing or politically uncomfortable news, for fear of losing market share.

The news is now like sports or pro wrestling: a fan engagement business, heavily influenced by commercial considerations that have little to do with truth and untruth. This is the case with conservative outlets like Fox News and the Daily Caller, but also with traditionally liberal outlets like MSNBC and even the *New York Times*. This new landscape of competing political hot takes, mutating quickly around a ratings supernova named Donald Trump, has also changed our conception of what is meant by a "censored" news story.

Project Censored was founded in 1976 by a college professor named Carl Jensen, who wanted students at Sonoma State University to learn to look at news media more critically. Most famous for its annual Top 25 list of the most important news stories ignored or covered up by popular media sources, Project Censored became part watchdog agency, part quietly effective shaming mechanism. Working reporters like myself learned to peek at the list (often wincing first) for a glimpse into work we probably should be doing, instead of delivering clicks or ratings for bosses.

The "Censored" list was once dominated by a few themes: regulatory indulgences for corporate malefactors (for example, "Twenty-One States Offer Corporations Immunity from Violating Environmental Laws," story #12 in *Censored 1998*), atrocities abroad ("United States' Policies in Colombia Support Mass Murder," story #3 in *Censored 2003*), corruption in the financial services sector ("US Congress Sells Out to Wall Street," #1 in *Censored 2010*), and abuses in the criminal justice system ("Inmates and Activists Protest Chemical Weapons in US Prisons and Jails," #19 in *Censored 2018*).[1] Pollution, war, banking, and policing: all rackets, all poor fits for American commercial media, in which corporate advertisers are coddled, twin narratives of American beneficence abroad and the self-correcting market at home are sacrosanct, and white middle-class audiences don't want to know what is being done in their name in "those" neighborhoods.

The press still has trouble with these themes, as reflected in this year's list, which tells us about the US military's role in spreading environmental disaster (#3), the human trafficking scourge in Yemen, a country devastated by US-backed policies (#21), profiteering in plasma markets (#17), and an ignored public banking revolution (#8). In some ways the modern corporate press is worse than it ever has been in taking on powerful interests, and less interested than ever in addressing wealth inequality or the problems of poor people.

News companies hate stories about inequality for a variety of reasons, but especially because they're a bummer: advertisers know images of deprivation and suffering depress the urge to buy, which is why we typically don't see poverty on TV unless it's being chased by police. Hard to sell Buicks to guilt-ridden audiences. There are larger political considerations: the ideology underpinning most modern news coverage assumes poverty is the fault of the poor. Go all the way back to *The Jeffersons* and we've always been told "Movin' On Up" is just a matter of pulling up those bootstraps, and even if you fail—no problem, family and a sense of humor can turn even being poor into *Good Times*.

Another major problem is complexity. Quick-hitting modern news formats make it difficult to explain knotty topics. In banking, for instance, the difference between perceiving the subprime mortgage crisis as corruption or bad luck has a lot to do with whether one understands how instruments like the Collateralized Debt Obligation were used by banks to disguise risk in mortgage investments. But you can't explain a CDO in a tweet. In this landscape the advantage always goes to the outlet willing to reduce crises to one-line takes: the still-widespread notion that the 2008 crash was caused by irresponsible (and largely minority) home-borrowers had a lot to do with it being the simpler explanation.

In today's cleaved media, however, there are additional complications. Conservative outlets are happy to show urban despair, but to sell it as the fault of Democratic Party mayors and "poverty pimps." Outlets that cater to blue-state audiences, meanwhile, openly demonize the "economic insecurity" of the white rural poor, cast as disingenuous Trump-lovers whose "perception" of declining opportunity was driven by hatred of Barack Obama. Similarly, the Bernie Sanders message about the effects of corporate greed on working people was sold in the popular press as an affectation of upper-class college students.

In the atomized media landscape, neither "side" of the media is much interested in poverty, but the cover-up is different depending on which channel you watch. The modern media consumer has been trained to worry first and foremost about assigning blame, and to perceive the world as a vast left–right battleground in which problems only exist because (circle one) the Democrats/Republicans allow it.

In other words, the news media is now not merely in the business of ignoring the kinds of stories Project Censored has long worried about, it's now actively engaged in teaching audiences to disbelieve in the very existence of such stories—typically, perpetual, systemic social problems with bipartisan causes. Modern audiences often have an easier time believing in outlandish conspiracy theories (birtherism, Russiagate) than in certain kinds of systemic corruption.

Take story #4 on this year's list, "Congressional Investments and Conflicts of Interest." As someone who's covered the problem of members of Congress trading on non-public information, and the inadequacy of the STOCK Act legislation designed to prevent it, I know this is the very definition of a bipartisan problem. Members in both parties have taken shameless advantage to use their offices for profiteering purposes (Republicans

Richard Burr and Kelly Loeffler made most of the headlines this year, but Dianne Feinstein and Nancy Pelosi have had their own issues here).

The absence of a clear partisan angle makes this story a tough sell in today's media landscape. Same with the exploding military budget, warrantless surveillance, drone warfare, regulatory capture, police brutality, and a host of other problems whose causes reach beyond the awfulness of Donald Trump.

Also, modern news companies have long understood that the winningest commercial formula involves breeding an air of superiority among viewers, for whom social horrors must be extensively contextualized, to prevent any hint that the viewer holds any culpability of his or her own. A lot of stories today are just diatribes about the iniquity of "those people," which can mean just about anything. Fox cashed in by running decades of stories about the Association of Community Organizations for Reform Now (ACORN), leftist academics, and immigrant criminals, and the last four years of blue-state press has basically been one long program about the evils of Donald Trump.

Even when the critical posture is warranted—I think this is the case a lot with Trump—we're raising audiences of finger-pointers who won't or can't hear certain kinds of bad news.

This new reality makes the mission of Project Censored more important than ever. It's hard enough to challenge the Pentagon, Wall Street, Big Pharma, the intelligence community, or the prison–industrial complex. On top of that, we have a new foe, in the increasingly closed mind of the news consumer. We're headed toward a future in which the commercial press seems determined to forget that a major portion of journalism's mission is to hold a mirror to our uglier selves.

The war in Vietnam was slowed when Americans were told about My Lai, or shown pictures of Phan Thi Kim Phuc, the "napalm girl." That tradition was continued in Iraq with Abu Ghraib and the *Collateral Murder* video. Today we mostly shut out news about our darker side, which is why we need Project Censored. Someone has to remind us to look in the mirror.

MATT TAIBBI is an author and journalist who has contributed to dozens of publications. He began his career in the former Soviet Union, where he wrote in English and in Russian for more than ten years for papers like *The Moscow Times*, *The eXile*, *Komsomolskaya Pravda*, *Trud*, *Stringer*, and *Kommersant*. After returning to the United States in 2002, he wrote for outlets like *The Nation*, the *New York Press*, and *Rolling Stone*, specializing in campaign trail reporting and coverage of Wall Street. He earned the National Magazine Award for commentary in 2008 and the Izzy Award for outstanding independent journalism in 2020. Taibbi has authored ten books, four of which were *New York Times* bestsellers: *Griftopia*, *The Divide*, *Insane Clown President*, and *The Great Derangement*. He lives with his wife and three children in New Jersey.

Notes

1. Robin Stovall, Brian Foust, and Ellen Krebs, "Twenty-One States Offer Corporations Immunity from Violating Environmental Laws," in *Censored 1998: The News That Didn't Make the News*, eds. Peter Phillips and Project Censored (New York: Seven Stories Press, 1998), 54–56, https://www.projectcensored.org/12-states-offer-corporations-immunity-from-violating-environmental-laws/; Lauren Renison, Adam Cimino, Erik Wagle, Gabrielle Mitchell, Jorge Porras, and Fred Fletcher, "United States' Policies in Colombia Support Mass Murder," in *Censored 2003:*

Media Democracy in Action, eds. Peter Phillips and Project Censored (New York: Seven Stories Press, 2002), 41–45, https://www.projectcensored.org/3-united-states-policies-in-columbia-support-mass-murder/; Jocelyn Rapp, Caitlin Ruxton, Samual Mikhail, and Chip McAuley, "US Congress Sells Out to Wall Street," in *Censored 2010: The Top 25 Censored Stories of 2008–09*, eds. Peter Phillips and Mickey Huff with Project Censored (New York: Seven Stories Press, 2009), 12–16, https://www.projectcensored.org/1-us-congress-sells-out-to-wall-street-sources/; and Cynthia Alvarez, Veronica Esquivez, William Ha, and Andy Lee Roth, "Inmates and Activists Protest Chemical Weapons in US Prisons and Jails," in *Censored 2018: Press Freedoms in a "Post-Truth" World*, eds. Andy Lee Roth and Mickey Huff with Project Censored (New York: Seven Stories Press, 2017), 86–88, https://www.projectcensored.org/19-inmates-activists-protest-chemical-weapons-us-prisons-jails/.

The Pandemic and the State of the Free Press

ANDY LEE ROTH with MICKEY HUFF

Will the COVID-19 pandemic be the end of the free press?

The COVID-19 pandemic has functioned like an X-ray, starkly exposing fateful compound fractures in American society. Beyond its terrible toll on human life, the pandemic has made clearer than ever before structural weaknesses in fundamental US institutions and the nationwide malignancy of chronic racial prejudices and economic inequalities.

The pandemic has not spared journalism, and any contemporary assessment of the free press must necessarily begin with the coronavirus and its impacts. The pandemic has accelerated two trends that imperil journalism and the free flow of information upon which the profession depends.

As the *New York Times* reported in May 2020, approximately 36,000 employees of news media companies in the United States have been "laid off, furloughed or had their pay reduced since the arrival of the coronavirus."[1] One news industry analyst told BuzzFeed that, due to plummeting advertising revenues, the pandemic would likely amount to a "full extinction event" for many news organizations.[2]

Even venerable independent news outlets are not escaping unscathed. For example, in May 2020 *The Atlantic* laid off 68 employees, comprising 17 percent of its staff.[3] News industry layoffs, furloughs, and closures have become so frequent during the pandemic that the Poynter Institute reports having to update its online record of these events "almost daily."[4]

Under the pandemic, intensified censorship and a "global crackdown" on press freedoms constitute a second existential threat to journalism.

An April 2020 *Foreign Policy* article observed that the coronavirus had initiated a "censorship pandemic," with governments around the world "cracking down on their critics" under the pretext of banning fake news about the crisis.[5] As of May 14, 2020, the Index on Censorship had documented more than 150 incidents in which journalists were physically or verbally assaulted, detained, or arrested—a figure the Index wrote was likely just "the very tip of the iceberg."[6]

In a separate article, the Index on Censorship reported that governments throughout the world, from Brazil to Scotland, have used the pandemic to justify revamping or curtailing freedom of information laws, which journalists (and the general public) in 126 countries depend on to obtain government records and documents.[7] As Amnesty International's director of law and policy, Ashfaq Khalfan, stated, "There is no hope of containing this virus if people can't access accurate information."[8]

In the United States, Index on Censorship noted, President Donald Trump maintained his habit of attacking reporters' credentials and terminating press conferences when journalists' questions about his administration's handling of the crisis displeased him.[9] In late May of 2020

Trump issued an executive order to impose new regulatory pressures on social media companies after Twitter placed warnings on two misleading tweets he made about mail-in balloting, notifying Trump's readership that his claims were unsubstantiated by facts.[10]

Will a consolidated, corporate "free press" be the end of independent journalism?

Even as establishment news outlets such as the *New York Times* and the *Washington Post* cover the pandemic and its impacts on other news outlets, they also run features that deny credit to—or, worse yet, *discredit*—legitimate independent news outlets.

For example, the *Washington Post* and the *New York Times* were quick to report on evidence that US senators Richard Burr (R-NC) and Kelly Loeffler (R-GA) each sold significant shares of their personal stock holdings immediately after attending a Senate Health Committee meeting in which they were briefed on the coronavirus. Burr and Loeffler sold their shares in hotels and other companies that stood to be hit hard by the pandemic, while publicly expressing confidence in the government's ability to fight the virus and forestall a national crisis. Their transactions were "not only unethical but almost certainly illegal," the *New York Times* editorial board wrote, noting that, under the STOCK Act of 2012, lawmakers and their aides are "explicitly barred from using nonpublic information for trades."[11]

Notably, however, the story of Burr and Loeffler's potentially illegal transactions was originally broken not by the *Times* or the *Post*, but by a pair of independent news outlets: ProPublica reported on Burr's market transactions and the Daily Beast reported on Loeffler's stock sales on March 19, 2020, a day before the first print reports in the *Times* or the *Post*.[12] ProPublica and the Daily Beast received no credit for breaking the stories—they were not mentioned at all—in the *New York Times's* first report on the topic.[13] *The Washington Post's* first story credited the Daily Beast, but not ProPublica.[14]

As an organization that highlights the crucial contributions of *independent* journalism, we at Project Censored noted these omissions with dismay. In the classrooms where we teach, students learn to credit their sources appropriately or risk receiving a failing grade for academic dishonesty.

But there are more glaring problems with establishment news media coverage of the pandemic than failing to give credit where credit is due. As Anthony DiMaggio noted in an April 2020 *CounterPunch* article about right-wing protests against public health restrictions in Ohio, Idaho, Michigan, and other states, "News outlets like the *New York Times* are repeating clichés about how right-wing shutdown protests are another manifestation of working-class resentment against the system."[15]

This narrative endures, DiMaggio noted, despite a substantial body of research demonstrating that Trump's so-called "working-class" base is "not motivated by concerns with poverty and economic vulnerabilities," while the reportedly grassroots protests have in fact been orchestrated by "national pro-business groups" (including Freedom-Works and Americans for Prosperity) and "quasi-fascist and white nationalist groups" (such as the Proud Boys).

The Washington Post for its part has taken advantage of fears and misapprehensions about the pandemic to run a series of articles that effectively echo President Trump's call for a tough stance against China, while on May 24, 2020, the *Post* featured a lead article that Melvin Goodman described as "a chauvinist attack on Iran that had the rare attribute of being both counterfactual and counter-instinctive."[16] For more evidence of how corporate news media have distorted the public's understanding of the pandemic, see Robin Andersen's chapter on News Abuse in this volume.

Even more alarming, perhaps, in a May 2020 "Here to Help" feature on recognizing false information in online feeds, the *New York Times* audaciously advised its readers that, if they have never heard of the outlet that published an article, "there's a good chance that it exists solely to publish fake news."[17] The feature further advised that, if a questionable story's contents were "legitimately out-rageous," then "plenty of other news outlets would have written about it, too."

We encourage editors and reporters at the *Times* to consider the first chapter of this book, the Project's annual listing of the year's 25 most important but underreported news stories—nearly all of which were factually reported by legitimate *independent* news outlets, but systematically ignored by the *New York Times* and other "trustworthy" establishment outlets. Given the *Times*'s apparent inability to acknowledge high-quality, transparently-sourced jour-nalism produced by independent news organizations, its counsel on "obscure news outlets" reveals more about its own hegemonic stance as the self-appointed arbiter of legitimate news and journalism than it does to help readers effectively distinguish valid stories from bogus ones.

Part of the Project's mission is to expand the public's awareness of important news stories and topics that fall outside the corporate news media's narrow definition of who and what are newsworthy. This mission derives from the Project's guiding principles.

Guiding Principles

Guiding principles function like a compass, providing direction. Although guiding principles cannot dictate what to do at every step in a journey, without them it is harder to assess when the path taken strays from the goal.

Guiding principles are even more important in times of crisis, when it is even easier—and more dire—to lose one's bearings.

This year's Media Democracy in Action chapter includes a contribution by the Society of Professional Journalists, the oldest organization currently representing US journalists, whose mission is to promote and defend freedom of speech and freedom of the press. In Chapter 6, Fred Brown introduces the SPJ's guiding principles for ethical journalism: Seek truth and report it; minimize harm; act independently; and be accountable and transparent. If more corporate news outlets rigorously adhered to these principles, the chapters in this book on Junk Food News and News Abuse would be shorter than they are—or perhaps altogether unnecessary.

What, then, are Project Censored's guiding principles? Based on the belief that a free press and an informed public are cornerstones of democratic self-government, Project Censored's work is guided by the following tenets:

1. We champion and promote independent investigative journalism.

2.   We hold corporate media to account when they fail to provide news coverage that adequately informs the public as community members and global citizens.

3.   We provide hands-on critical media literacy education to students—and we make their work public.

4.   We believe that increasing public awareness of, trust in, and support for independent journalism is one essential dimension of every movement for social justice.

These four principles define the Project, and—because we are a small organization with a lean budget—they help us choose how to focus our efforts.

Project Censored's "52/12" News Cycle

Unlike the news organizations whose work we track and evaluate, Project Censored does not report breaking news, and we do not work on a 24/7 news cycle. In fact, Project Censored might be better described as following a 52/12 news cycle.

In each yearbook, we track underreported news topics and important story themes over the course of a 52-week, 12-month year. Candidly, this means the Project is not an ideal source for daily, breaking news stories—though we also produce a weekly syndicated radio program and maintain an active online presence through our website and social media.

As *State of the Free Press | 2021* goes to print, we are actively monitoring news coverage of developing stories, including the police killing of George Floyd in Minneapolis and subsequent protests across the United States and around the world, and the responses of Twitter, Facebook, and other social media sites to President Trump's executive order targeting social media platforms. In covering protests against police violence, journalists in the United States have been subjected to increasing attacks, arrests, and other threats to their personal safety and their profession.[18] In response to Trump's executive order regarding social media censorship, the Center for Democracy & Technology is bringing a lawsuit against the president, arguing that Trump's order violates the First Amendment.[19] The world does not stop for us to take its temperature.

Nevertheless, we credit our 52/12 orientation for helping us to identify and analyze systemic patterns and subsurface trends in news coverage that otherwise remain invisible or taken for granted amidst the unceasing stream of breaking news. The kind of insight that comes with stepping back from the squalls of the 24/7 news cycle is evident, we contend, in the Project's analysis and clearing away of what we have previously described as "the black smoke of fake news."[20]

Fake News: Who Checks the Fact-Checkers?

Since the tragic 2016 presidential election, politicians, pundits, and pollsters have latched onto "fake news" as a hot issue. So too have the corporate news media, which have found in this topic an endless source of content that is not just "newsworthy" but also a ratings-winning lure for audience attention.

Thus, for example, the establishment media dutifully report on each new statement by Facebook's Mark Zuckerberg about his company's role in policing (or perpetuating) the online spread of misinformation, while other corporate news reports uncritically endorse fact-checking organizations such as NewsGuard and Snopes.[21]

But is anyone checking the fact-checkers?

Corporate news organizations tend to sidestep this important question. A deeper examination suggests why this might be so. The corporate press appears to assume that NewsGuard is a trustworthy judge of fake news because it has partnered with major corporate entities—such as Microsoft—and because its advisory board includes a number of former government officials—such as Tom Ridge, the first director of Homeland Security, and Michael Hayden, who ran the Central Intelligence Agency when George W. Bush was president—who tidily fit the establishment news media's standard if narrow criteria of newsworthy actors and sources.[22]

If corporate news coverage of NewsGuard followed the Society of Professional Journalists's guidelines—act independently, be transparent—it would highlight these essential considerations, which call into question the fact-checking organization's credibility and ultimate purpose.

Deeper investigative analysis of fact-checking operations promoted by NewsGuard, Facebook, and others demonstrates how formulaic news reporting of complex issues fails to promote genuine understanding.[23] At best, quickly produced news reports based on the typical corporate and government sources serve to provide the appearance of vigorous public debate while doing little if anything to resolve the public's doubts and fears regarding fake news.

Pico Iyer articulated a more extreme version of this problem when he described how pollsters, pundits, and other popular sources of "news" frequently attempt "to persuade us that hearsay + opinion + guesswork = truth."[24] Iyer likened our contemporary media politics to *Othello*, Shakespeare's tragedy in which the villain Iago coaxes noble Othello "away from the realm of knowledge and into the adjacent territories of inference and rumor," with tragic, fatal consequences.

Shifting from Shakespeare's Venice to our contemporary media culture, Project Censored and the contributors to the inaugural edition of the Project's *State of the Free Press* eschew hearsay and guesswork (though not *informed* opinion) to ground us firmly in the realm of knowledge, where claims to truth and expressions of opinion are validated by transparently-sourced and verifiable facts.

Inside *State of the Free Press* / *2021*

State of the Free Press launches a new version of the Project's long-running *Censored* yearbook series. The book's streamlined format distills the core components of previous *Censored* volumes. We continue to publish case studies of specific news themes, as presented in previous yearbooks, via the Project's online "Censored Notebook," where we can cover a wider range of topics in a more timely fashion than is possible with each year's book.[25]

Chapter 1 of *State of the Free Press* presents the 25 most important but underreported news stories of 2019–2020 as determined by Project Censored. This list is the final result of a yearlong process of identifying and vetting candidate stories undertaken by several hundred college and university students and faculty members who participate in the Project's Campus Affiliates Program. This review process culminates with the Project's panel of 28 expert judges voting to determine which stories make the list and how they are ranked.[26]

The resulting 25 stories expose the corporate news media's blind spots when it comes to reporting on systemic social problems, including the disappearance or murder of a disproportionately large number of Indigenous women and girls (this year's #1 story), the deadly consequences of enduring economic inequality, and attacks on freedom of expression—as well as important solutions-oriented reporting on voting, banking, and access to affordable medicines. The Top 25 list honors independent journalists and news outlets, and it highlights how their coverage of otherwise untold stories informs the public and bolsters democracy.

In Chapter 2, Steve Macek and Zach McNanna revive the Project's Déjà Vu News chapter. Last presented in *Censored 2017*, Déjà Vu News tracks news stories featured in previous *Censored* yearbooks to update those stories and to assess whether they have subsequently received any more widespread substantive news coverage. Macek and McNanna provide updates on five past stories, including the Project's 2018 report on global internet shutdowns, its 2011 report on Pentagon pollution, and developments in coverage of the government's $21 trillion in unaccounted-for spending, as first detailed in *Censored 2019*.

Izzy Snow and Susan Rahman partner with a team of College of Marin students to present Chapter 3, "Capitalism, Celebrity, and Consuming Corona," their analysis of the year's most distasteful Junk Food News. "Junk Food News" is the term Carl Jensen coined to explain how, all too often, profit-driven corporate news outlets peddle cheaply produced, soft-serve "news" stories focused on celebrityhood, the latest trending craze, and other cultural meringue in place of the nutrients provided by substantive investigative journalism. This year Snow, Rahman, and their research team assess the corporate news media's coverage of the death of professional basketball star Kobe Bryant, Trump's antic pandemic prescriptions, and the quarantined inspiration we are supposed to derive from Tom Hanks and other Hollywood favorites. Importantly, in each case, the chapter juxtaposes the corporate media's fixation on "junk food" stories with vital stories from the same time that hardly received any news coverage.

While Junk Food News avoids covering substantial stories by wallowing in trivia, "News Abuse" is the term Project Censored uses to identify genuinely important news topics that have been subject to distorted coverage by corporate news outlets. In Chapter 4, "Establishment Media's War Metaphors Obscure Injustices and Block Global Healing," Robin Andersen offers a scathing assessment of corporate media News Abuse in 2019–2020. Andersen identifies how double standards and skewed framing served to mystify the public about the COVID-19 pandemic, the debate over healthcare during the 2020 Democratic primary campaigns, and the mass demonstrations in Hong Kong and Chile. Examined with scrutiny, Andersen suggests, News Abuse makes it clear how far the corporate news media stray from representing the "mainstream" interests and values of most Americans.

Adam Bessie and Peter Glanting's "Going Remote:

Flattening the Curriculum" illustrates how the shift to remote, online "classrooms" in response to the COVID-19 pandemic has introduced new, exclusionary educational standards that further marginalize historically disadvantaged students and consolidate corporate influence in higher education. Their feature's vivid imagery and lucid text show that the 'Zoomified' corporate vision of education "doesn't have to pass"—instead, educators can develop "expansive" classrooms that re-center students as "imaginative creators" and "critical citizens."

The union of imagination and critical thinking is a hallmark of the type of contributions that comprise each year's Media Democracy in Action chapter. From a platform for whistleblowers, *The Whistleblower Newsroom*, and Citizen Lab's work to track links between developing technologies and digital censorship, to critical media literacy education programs in classrooms at UCLA and in programs linked with California's juvenile justice system, to guiding principles for ethical journalism and organizing for truly democratic, publicly owned news media, the Media Democracy in Action chapter aptly concludes the 2021 edition of *State of the Free Press* by presenting six inspired exemplars in the struggle to build a more inclusive and civil society.

From Difficult Questions to Decisive Actions

How to sum up Project Censored's assessment of the state of the free press in 2021? The question demands a multifaceted response, as this introduction attempts to delineate and artist Anson Stevens-Bollen's cover illustrates.

From a critical perspective, when we scrutinize the corporate news media's track record during the previous twelve months, there is plenty to warrant pessimism, if not grave concern.

From an affirmative standpoint, there remains cause for optimism—as documented not only by the forward-thinking contributors to the book's concluding chapter on Media Democracy in Action, but also by the robust reporting in the public interest by the intrepid independent journalists and news outlets whose work Chapter 1 highlights.

We want you, our readers, to dig into this year's book in search of your own assessments of the state of the free press in the United States. Even more, we hope that what you find here will galvanize you to action, engaging your imagination and critical thinking skills in service of strengthening independent journalism and revitalizing the democratic institutions that depend on it.

As the COVID-19 pandemic and the recent uprisings against police brutality make clear, our health—as individuals and as a community—depends crucially on a commitment to truth, even when this entails reckoning with harsh realities that challenge cherished beliefs about who we are and what we stand for. Our shared future depends on being media literate, critically savvy, and imaginatively organized. Drawing upon a rich heritage of path-breaking teachers, activists, muckrakers, whistleblowers, and dreamers, we must dare to seek out facts, dispel myths and inaccuracies, and share and act upon the truths that bind us responsibly, effectively, and democratically.

Andy Lee Roth, Seattle
Mickey Huff, Sonoma County
May 2020

Notes

Many thanks to Elizabeth Boyd for helpful comments on earlier versions of this introduction, and to Sarah Brooks for encouraging the discussion of guiding principles.

1. Marc Tracy, "News Media Outlets Have been Ravaged by the Pandemic," *New York Times*, April 10, 2020, updated May 1, 2020, https://www. nytimes.com/2020/04/10/business/media/news-media-coronavirus-jobs. html.

2. Ken Doctor, quoted in Craig Silverman, "The Coronavirus is a Media Extinction Event," BuzzFeed, March 23, 2020, https://www.buzzfeed-news.com/article/craigsilverman/coronavirus-news-industry-layoffs.

3. Laura Hazard Owen, "The Atlantic's Layoffs May Sound the Death Knell for Two Media Revenue Hopes: Video and In-Person Events," Nieman Lab, May 22, 2020, https://www.niemanlab.org/2020/05/ the-atlantics-layoffs-sound-the-death-knell-for-two-media-revenue-hopes-video-and-events/.

4. Kristen Hare, "Here are the Newsroom Layoffs, Furloughs and Closures Caused by the Coronavirus," Poynter Institute, April 6, 2020, last updated June 22, 2020, https://www.poynter.org/business-work/2020/ here-are-the-newsroom-layoffs-furloughs-and-closures-caused-by-the-coronavirus/.

5. Jacob Mchangama and Sarah McLaughlin, "Coronavirus Has Started a Censorship Pandemic," *Foreign Policy*, April 1, 2020, https://foreignpolicy. com/2020/04/01/coronavirus-censorship-pandemic-disinforma-tion-fake-news-speech-freedom/.

6. Mark Frary, "150 Attacks on Media Freedom Reported in 50 Days," Index on Censorship, May 14, 2020, https://www.indexoncensorship. org/2020/05/150-attacks-on-media-freedom-reported-in-50-day/.

7. Mark Frary, "How FOI Laws are being Rewritten during the COVID-19 Crisis," Index on Censorship, May 1, 2020, https://www. indexoncensorship.org/2020/05/how-foi-laws-are-being-rewritten-during-the-covid-19-crisis/.

8. "Crackdown on Journalists Weakens Efforts to Tackle COVID-19," Amnesty International, May 1, 2020, https://www.amnesty.org/en/latest/ news/2020/05/global-crackdown-on-journalists-weakens-efforts-to-tackle-covid19/.

9. Frary, "150 Attacks."

10. Jeff Mason and Nandita Bose, "Trump to Sign Executive Order on Social Media on Thursday: White House," Reuters, May 27, 2020, https://www. reuters.com/article/us-twitter-trump-idUSKBN2331NK.

11. The Editorial Board, "Did Richard Burr and Kelly Loeffler Profit from the Pandemic?" *New York Times*, March 20, 2020, https://www.nytimes. com/2020/03/20/opinion/coronavirus-burr-loeffler-stocks.html. Senator Burr, the *Times*'s editors noted, was one of three senators who voted against the STOCK Act. In May 2020 the *Wall Street Journal* reported that the Justice Department was closing its investigations of Loeffler and two other senators—James Inhofe (R-OK) and Dianne Feinstein

(D-CA)—suspected of insider trading, while Burr's case remained under investigation. Aruna Viswanatha, "Justice Department Closing Insider-Trading Investigations into Three U.S. Senators," *Wall Street Journal*, May 26, 2020, https://www.wsj.com/articles/justice-department-closing-insider-trading-investigations-into-three-u-s-senators-11590520934.

12. Robert Faturechi and Derek Willis, "Senator Dumped up to $1.7 Million of Stock after Reassuring Public about Coronavirus Preparedness," ProPublica, March 19, 2020, https://www.propublica.org/article/senator-dumped-up-to-1-7-million-of-stock-after-reassuring-public-about-coronavirus-preparedness; and Lachlan Markay, William Bredderman, and Sam Brodey, "Sen. Kelly Loeffler Dumped Millions in Stock after Coronavirus Briefing," Daily Beast, March 19, 2020, updated March 20, 2020, https://www.thedailybeast.com/sen-kelly-loeffler-dumped-millions-in-stock-after-coronavirus-briefing.

13. Shane Goldmacher, "Kelly Loeffler and Richard Burr were Briefed on Coronavirus. Then They Sold Stocks. What Now?" *New York Times*, March 20, 2020, updated May 14, 2020, https://www.nytimes.com/2020/03/20/us/politics/kelly-loeffler-richard-burr-insider-trading.html. The *New York Times*'s failure to acknowledge ProPublica's original reporting seems especially noteworthy, because the *Times* and ProPublica regularly collaborate on investigative reports—though the *Times*'s subsequent editorial, cited above, did acknowledge the original reporting by ProPublica and the Daily Beast.

14. Michelle Ye Hee Lee, John Wagner, and Teo Armus, "Sen. Richard Burr, Head of Powerful Committee, Sold Large Amount of Stocks before Sharp Declines in Market," *Washington Post*, March 20, 2020, https://www.washingtonpost.com/politics/sen-richard-burr-r-nc-head-of-powerful-committee-sold-large-amount-of-stocks-before-sharp-declines-in-market/2020/03/19/6cf4b25a-6a31-11ea-9923-57073adce27c_story.html.

15. Anthony DiMaggio, "Coronavirus and Rightwing Rebellion: Retreading a Tired Narrative," *CounterPunch*, April 21, 2020, https://www.counterpunch.org/2020/04/21/coronavirus-and-rightwing-rebellion-retreading-a-tired-narrative/.

16. Melvin Goodman, "Trump Administration and the Washington Post: Picking Fights Together," *CounterPunch*, May 26, 2020, https://www.counterpunch.org/2020/05/26/trump-administration-and-the-washington-post-picking-fights-together/.

17. Brian X. Chen, "Here to Help: How to Recognize False Information in Online Feeds," *New York Times*, May 23, 2020, A3.

18. Scott Nover, "160 Threats to Press Freedom in the United States—This Week (Part I)," Pressing (Substack newsletter), June 2, 2020, https://pressing.substack.com/p/160-threats-to-press-freedom-in-the.

19. Daniel Uria, "Center for Democracy and Technology Challenges Trump Social Media Executive Order," United Press International (UPI), June 2, 2020, https://www.upi.com/Top_News/US/2020/06/02/Center-for-Democracy-and-Technology-challenges-Trump-social-media-executive-order/5211591139691/.

20. Andy Lee Roth and Mickey Huff, "Introduction," *Censored 2019: Fighting the Fake News Invasion*, eds. Mickey Huff and Andy Lee Roth with

Project Censored (New York: Seven Stories Press, 2018), 17–35. The image of black smoke comes from H.G. Wells's 1898 novel, *The War of the Worlds*.

21. For in-depth coverage of this topic by Project Censored, see Emil Marmol and Lee Mager, "'Fake News': The Trojan Horse for Silencing Alternative News and Reestablishing Corporate News Dominance," in *Censored 2020: Through the Looking Glass*, eds. Andy Lee Roth and Mickey Huff with Project Censored (New York: Seven Stories Press, 2019), 221–53, available online at https://www.projectcensored.org/fake-news-the-trojan-horse-for-silencing-alternative-news-and-reestablishing-corporate-news-dominance/.

22. See, for example, Igor Ogorodnev, "No Need to Install: Microsoft Has Controversial Fake News Filter NewsGuard Built into Mobile Browser," RT, January 23, 2019, updated May 2020, https://www.rt.com/news/449530-newsguard-edge-browser-media-integrated/.

23. Indeed, Project Censored's own analysis has revealed that, far from combatting "fake news," fact-checking initiatives involving collaboration among corporate, military, and governmental organizations frequently promote propaganda favorable to US foreign policy, reduce traffic to progressive websites that provide critical reporting and historical context, and functionally censor any news media that they deem to represent "foreign influence." See Mikhaela Alcasabas, Cem Ismail Addemir, Troy Patton, Peter Phillips, Steve Macek, and Mickey Huff, "Think Tank Partnerships Establish Facebook as Tool of US Foreign Policy," in *Censored 2020: Through the Looking Glass*, eds. Andy Lee Roth and Mickey Huff with Project Censored (New York: Seven Stories Press, 2019), 25–30, https://www.projectcensored.org/2-think-tank-partnerships-establish-facebook-as-tool-of-us-foreign-policy/.

24. Pico Iyer, "What Do We Know?" *New York Times*, December 31, 2016, https://www.nytimes.com/2016/12/31/opinion/sunday/what-do-we-know.html.

25. See https://www.projectcensored.org/category/press-release/ [continuously updated].

26. For more detailed information about the Project's process of reviewing and ranking underreported news stories, see "A Note on Research and Evaluation of *Censored* News Stories" in Chapter 1 of this volume.

The Top *Censored* Stories and Media Analysis of 2019–20

Compiled and edited by
ANDY LEE ROTH, STEVE MACEK,
and ZACH MCNANNA

Introduction by ANDY LEE ROTH

INTRODUCTION

ANDY LEE ROTH

Story selection is essentially composed of two processes: one determines the availability of news and relates journalists to sources; the other determines the suitability of news, which ties journalists to audiences.
—HERBERT J. GANS, *Deciding What's News*[1]

Availability and suitability. This elementary pair of factors shapes whether an event gets reported as news or not, sociologist Herbert Gans wrote in *Deciding What's News*, his groundbreaking 1979 study of the professional values, daily routines, and competitive pressures that shape journalists' news judgments.[2]

Inaccessible or inappropriate. Each of the 25 independent news stories presented here evidently failed, one way or another, to rise to the attention of the corporate news media or to meet their criteria for newsworthiness.

Nevertheless, a rich mix of fiercely independent news

outlets—punching well above their weight, when compared to the staff size and operational budgets of their corporate counterparts—managed to identify and cover these events and issues as newsworthy, thus informing the public about several dozen crucial but otherwise marginalized or ignored news stories.

Story Availability

In what ways were such stories available to independent journalists but not so for their corporate counterparts? Due to constraints on budgets and staff as well as a lack of time, establishment news outlets often employ what Gans described as "quickly and easily applied methods of empirical inquiry."[3] By contrast, the exemplars of independent investigative journalism highlighted here often depended on time-consuming, labor-intensive public records requests to unlock or substantiate important news stories—as in the case of Benjamin Neimark, Oliver Belcher, and Patrick Bigger's report for The Conversation on the US military's contribution to the climate crisis, which constitutes the basis for story #3 in this year's Top 25 list.

In other instances, the stories celebrated here depend on research studies and policy documents produced by nongovernmental organizations (NGOs), which corporate news outlets perhaps dismissed—mistakenly—as bit players or prejudiced advocates. By contrast, as featured in story #14, Fran Quigley's Common Dreams article covers an extensive report, "Medicine for All," produced by the Democracy Collaborative; while story #20, on transforming the criminal-legal system, draws on a fourteen-point "Vision for Justice" platform advocated by 117 rights groups, including the American Civil Liberties Union (ACLU), Color of Change, and the Prison Policy Initiative.

Still other stories in this year's Top 25 list may have seemed inaccessible to corporate news outlets due to geographical or social distance. This is almost certainly the case in the pair of stories focused on efforts by First Nations and Native American communities to counter the living legacy of colonial trauma, as covered here in story #1 ("Missing and Murdered Indigenous Women and Girls") and story #15 ("Indigenous Trauma and Suicide an Enduring Legacy of Colonialism"). Nevertheless, independent news organizations consistently manage to span these geographical and social distances, to center the stories of communities and issues that have been marginalized or ignored by corporate news—as exemplified by Devon Heinen's *New Statesman* article "Nobody to Call," a harrowing, intimate account of Indigenous suicide as a public health issue, highlighted here in story #15.

Independent news coverage of violence against people of color, including, especially, women of color—as featured in stories about Indigenous women and girls, and also in story #7, on the underreporting of missing and victimized Black women and girls—makes it obvious that there is more to story selection than story availability. As institutions, US newsrooms are not removed from, or immune to, the structural racism that underlies the social problems addressed by these stories.

Story Suitability

Direct, detailed reporting on missing, murdered, or victimized women and girls of color places demands on audiences to reckon with the living legacies of colonial conquest and slavery, including institutionalized racism, sexism, and economic inequality. As Matt Taibbi notes in this book's foreword, "News companies hate stories about inequality," in part because "images of deprivation and suffering depress the urge to buy." Such stories make for ideologically unsuitable news.

In some cases, this is reinforced by conventional journalism's orientation to *events* rather than to *issues*, as Gaye Tuchman pointedly observed in her pioneering 1978 study, *Making News*.[4] Thus, story #5, on the deadly consequences of the widening gap between the richest and poorest Americans, likely seemed unsuitable to corporate news outlets—even despite the readymade news hook of an August 2019 Government Accountability Office report on that topic. The deep-rooted processes and myriad institutions that drive increasing inequality in the United States (and around the world) resist simple descriptive reporting.

As both Gans and Tuchman found in their studies of US news organizations, establishment journalists also typically shy away from critiques of capitalism.[5] Thus, Gans's conception of "built-in anticipatory avoidance" helps to explain corporate news outlets' reticence to cover economic inequality (story #5), the movement to establish public banks (story #8), and reports that, under the existing economic order, many of the poorest are now selling their own blood to survive (story #17).[6] Anticipatory avoidance may also explain the corporate media's silence on story #24, about independent journalist Abby Martin's court case to challenge a Georgia state law that restricts advocacy of BDS (Boycott, Divestment and Sanctions), the movement to persuade Israel to obey international law and respect the human rights of Palestinians. Just as the corporate news media skirted covering the censorship of an Al Jazeera documentary that exposed the influence of the pro-Israel lobby in the United States, so they decline to report on Martin's First Amendment case against Georgia.[7] As Tuchman wrote, "The power to keep an occurrence out of the news is power over the news."[8]

From this perspective, Project Censored's annual Top 25 list can be read as an index of the corporate news media's power to set an agenda that includes some stories as suitable while invisibly excluding others as non-news. As Tuchman emphasized, "ideology prevents knowledge by limiting inquiry," and many standard reporting procedures work to hide "the socioeconomic structure of contemporary society" and to obscure "structural linkages between events."[9]

But there is more to the Project's annual Top 25 story list than a condemnation of the establishment media's shortcomings in story selection, its daily—even hourly—framing for the public of "all the news that's fit to print," as stipulated by the *New York Times*'s daring but dubious slogan. The Top 25 story list can and should also be read as evidence of how inquiry can lead to knowledge that challenges conventional news frames and official narratives.

Inquiry and Knowledge

The journalists and news outlets whose work this chapter highlights exemplify how independent investigative reporting hinges on alternative, more inclusive conceptions of story availability and story suitability—Gans called this "multiperspectival news"—that, in turn, enhance the public's knowledge. In some cases, as noted in the story summaries that follow, independent news coverage has spurred subsequent corporate news coverage—a type of "agenda setting" that has not received adequate attention from scholars of news production, but which, nonetheless, underscores how independent news outlets play a crucial role in informing the public, whether directly or indirectly.

Inquiry and knowledge are also cornerstones of Project Censored's Campus Affiliates Program, which coordinates students and faculty from colleges and universities in a collective effort to identify, vet, and publicize independent news reports on topics and issues that the corporate news media have obscured or ignored. This year, 308 students under the guidance of 32 faculty members from 19 college and university campuses across the United States and Canada participated in this process, identifying and reviewing several hundred independent news stories, from which this year's top 25 stories have been selected. These students' direct, hands-on development of their critical thinking and media literacy skills contributes to Project Censored's ongoing, collective effort to invigorate the public's knowledge of—and demand for—high-quality, independent alternatives to the corporate version of news that otherwise sets a narrow agenda for what and who counts as important and newsworthy in the United States.

ACKNOWLEDGMENTS: Geoff Davidian provided invaluable assistance and effervescent camaraderie in helping to prepare this year's slate of several hundred Validated Independent News stories for the voting process. Troy Patton, Matthew Phillips, and Veronica Vasquez provided keen research assistance during the final vetting of this year's top *Censored* stories. John Roth offered helpful comments on the chapter's introduction.

A NOTE ON RESEARCH AND EVALUATION OF *CENSORED* NEWS STORIES

How do we at Project Censored identify and evaluate independent news stories, and how do we know that the Top 25 stories that we bring forward each year are not only relevant and significant but also trustworthy? The answer is that every candidate news story undergoes rigorous review, which takes place in multiple stages during each annual cycle. Although adapted to take advantage of both the Project's expanding affiliates program and current technologies, the vetting process is quite similar to the one Project Censored founder Carl Jensen established more than forty years ago.

Candidate stories are initially identified by Project Censored professors and students, or are nominated by members of the general public, who bring them to the Project's attention.[10] Together, faculty and students vet each candidate story in terms of its importance, timeliness, quality of sources, and corporate news coverage. If it fails on any one of these criteria, the story is not included.

Once Project Censored receives the candidate story, we undertake a second round of judgment, using the same criteria and updating the review to include any subsequent, competing corporate coverage. Stories that pass this round of review get posted on our website as Validated Independent News stories (VINs).[11]

In early spring, we present all VINs in the current cycle to the faculty and students at all of our affiliate campuses, and to our panel of expert judges, who cast votes to winnow the candidate stories from several hundred to 25.

Once the Top 25 list has been determined, Project Censored student interns begin another intensive review of each story using LexisNexis and ProQuest databases. Additional faculty and students contribute to this final stage of review.

The Top 25 finalists are then sent to our panel of judges, who vote to rank them in numerical order. At the same time, these experts—including media studies professors, professional journalists and editors, and a former commissioner of the Federal Communications Commission—offer their insights on the stories' strengths and weaknesses.[12]

Thus, by the time a story appears in the pages of *Censored*, it has undergone at least five distinct rounds of review and evaluation.

Although the stories that Project Censored brings forward may be socially and politically controversial—and sometimes even psychologically challenging—we are confident that each is the result of serious journalistic effort, and therefore deserves greater public attention.

THE TOP *CENSORED* STORIES AND MEDIA ANALYSIS OF 2019–20

1.

Missing and Murdered Indigenous Women and Girls

Danielle McLean, "Missing and Murdered Women is a Grim, Unsolved Problem. Native Communities are Demanding Action," ThinkProgress, August 24, 2019, https://archive.thinkprogress.org/missing-and-murdered-women-is-a-grim-unsolved-problem-native-communities-are-demanding-action cdde640e38b3/.

Abaki Beck, "Why Aren't Fossil Fuel Companies Held Accountable for Missing and Murdered Indigenous Women?" *YES! Magazine*, October 5, 2019, https://www.yesmagazine.org/planet/native-fossil-fuel-missing-murdered-indigenous-women-mmiwg-20191004.

Hallie Golden, "'Sister, Where Did You Go?': The Native American Women Disappearing from US Cities," *The Guardian*, May 1, 2019, https://www.theguardian.com/us-news/2019/apr/30/missing-native-american-women-alyssa-mclemore.

Carrie N. Baker, "Making Missing and Murdered Indigenous Women and Girls Visible," *Ms. Magazine*, December 2, 2019, https://msmagazine.com/2019/12/02/making-missing-and-murdered-indigenous-women-and-girls-visible/.

Student Researchers: Jeramy Dominguez (Sonoma State University), Katrina Tend (Diablo Valley College), and James Byers (Frostburg State University)

Faculty Evaluators: Ashley Hall (Sonoma State University), Mickey Huff (Diablo Valley College), and Andy Duncan (Frostburg State University)

Indigenous women and girls face physical violence—including murder, kidnapping, sexual trafficking, and rape—with a "shocking regularity" that amounts to an "epidemic" of violence, according to an August 2019 report from ThinkProgress.[13] From tribal reservations and rural communities to urban areas, the scope of the problem is "almost impossible to put into context," the *Guardian* reported in May 2019, because no single federal government database consistently tracks how many Native women and girls go missing each year. Due to negligence and incapacity, combined with the complexity of criminal jurisdiction on tribal lands limiting which crimes tribal courts can prosecute, law enforcement and the justice system seldom identify the perpetrators of these crimes, much less charge or convict them.

With some notable exceptions, the cases of missing and murdered Indigenous women and girls receive little to no major news coverage: A January 2020 article in the *New Republic* described one *New York Times* report on the subject as "a small recognition in a sea of loss."[14] Both the crisis and Native responses to it—epitomized by the burgeoning Missing and Murdered Indigenous Women (MMIW) movement—are dramatically underreported.

As ThinkProgress reported, the Urban Indian Health Institute (UIHI) found 5712 reports of murdered or missing Native women and girls throughout the United States in 2016—but only 116 of these were logged in the Department of Justice's database.[15] According to Federal Bureau of Investigation (FBI) data, Native Americans disappear at twice the per capita rate of white Americans, while research funded by the Department of Justice found that on some tribal lands Indigenous women were murdered at more than ten times the national average, the *Guardian* reported. A 2016 Department of Justice report, based on 2010 data, found that "more than 4 in 5 American Indian and Alaska Native women (84.3 percent) have experienced violence in their lifetime," and more than one in three (34.1 percent) have experienced rape.[16]

"I wouldn't say we're more vulnerable," Annita Lucchesi,

a Southern Cheyenne descendant and executive director of the Sovereign Bodies Institute, told the *Guardian*, "I'd say we're targeted."

Campaigners, including the Sovereign Bodies Institute, the Brave Heart Society, and the Urban Indian Health Institute, identify aspects of systemic racism—including the indelible legacies of settler colonialism, issues with law enforcement, a lack of reliable and comprehensive data, and flawed policymaking—as deep-rooted sources of the crisis.[17]

As *YES! Magazine* reported, tribal communities in the United States often lack jurisdiction to respond to crimes: The Major Crimes Act of 1885 restricted the crimes that tribal courts could prosecute, and in a 1978 case, *Oliphant v. Suquamish*, the Supreme Court determined that tribal

---

"I wouldn't say we're more vulnerable, I'd say we're targeted."

Annita Lucchesi, Sovereign Bodies Institute

---

courts cannot prosecute non-Native offenders, even if they live on tribal lands. Although the 2013 reauthorization of the Violence Against Women Act empowered tribal courts to handle some cases related to domestic violence, dating violence, and violations of protection orders, it left sex trafficking and other forms of sexual violence outside tribal jurisdiction, *YES! Magazine* reported.[18]

In the absence of tribal jurisdiction, in many cases the FBI or county sheriffs are officially responsible for investigating crimes against women and girls. However, county sheriffs and local FBI offices are typically "understaffed and underfunded," Lucchesi told *YES! Magazine*.

The impacts of inadequate staffing and funding are evident in a 2010 Government Accountability Office report, which found that, from 2005 to 2009, federal prosecutors declined to prosecute 67 percent of the 2594 cases involving sexual violence in Indian Country.[19] As noted in a report from the Sovereign Bodies Institute and the Brave Heart Society, "lack of accountability helps to maintain a culture of violence, where Indigenous women and girls are made to be easy targets."[20]

Nearly three-quarters of American Indian and Alaska Natives live in urban areas, but the plight of missing and murdered Indigenous women and girls in US cities is not necessarily any better reported.[21] In a 2018 report, the Urban Indian Health Institute documented 506 cases of missing and murdered American Indian and Alaska Native women and girls across 71 cities. The report found 280 cases of murder (56 percent), 128 missing persons cases (25 percent), and 98 cases with unknown status (19 percent). The UIHI report emphasized that, due to the Institute's limited resources and "poor data collection by numerous cities," the 506 cases its report identified are "likely an undercount" of missing and murdered Indigenous women and girls in urban areas.[22] As the *Guardian* reported, more than 60 percent of the police departments in the 71 cities studied either failed to "demonstrate that they were accurately tracking disappearances, or provided [UIHI] with compromised data." Despite incomplete data, the UIHI report documented cases tied to domestic violence, sexual assault, police brutality, and lack of safety for sex workers—all underscored by "institutional and structural racism, gaps in law enforcement response and prosecution, along with lack of data," the *Guardian* reported.

ThinkProgress reported how Native organizations, such as the Global Indigenous Council, have taken the initiative to draw attention to the epidemic of violence: In collaboration with regional tribal leadership groups, the Global Indigenous Council has placed "Invisible No More" billboards, depicting a Native woman with a giant red hand painted over her mouth, along state highways in Minnesota, North Dakota, South Dakota, Michigan, Montana, New Mexico, Arizona, and Oklahoma.

The MMIW movement has also focused attention on connections between the fossil fuel industry—including "man camps," the temporary housing facilities for crews working on pipeline projects like Keystone XL—and violence against Native women. A production boom in oil fields in northeastern Montana, for example, has led to surges in violent crime, sex trafficking, and rape cases, according to tribal police and local activists, *YES! Magazine* reported. The Sovereign Bodies Institute has documented 529 cases of missing and murdered Indigenous women in Montana, North Dakota, South Dakota, and Nebraska, states that would be further impacted by extensions to the controversial Keystone XL Pipeline. Nearly 80 percent of those cases, *YES! Magazine* reported, are either unsolved or without an identified perpetrator, and 30 percent are active missing persons cases.

From the White House, a world apart from both tribal lands and most Native people living in cities, Donald Trump issued an executive order in November 2019 to establish a task force—comprised exclusively of federal officials—on missing and murdered Indigenous people.[23] A report in the *New Republic* characterized Trump's order as "a meager offering from a violent administration."[24] Although a number of Native leaders joined in the announcement and thanked the president, other prominent leaders were more circumspect.[25] Suzan Harjo—a member of the Cheyenne and Hodulgee Muscogee Tribe and a Presidential Medal of Freedom recipient—described the task force as coopting the efforts of Native activists at the tribal, community, and state levels; Congresswoman Deb Holland (D-NM), a member of the Pueblo of Laguna, released a statement condemning "lack of consultation with Tribes, which is a pattern of this Administration on all Indian Country issues."[26]

The New York Times and the *Seattle Times* deserve recognition for their reporting on the crisis of murdered and missing Indigenous women and girls in the United States, but the failure of other major news outlets on this issue is striking.[27]

In June 2019 the Canadian National Inquiry into Missing and Murdered Indigenous Women and Girls released its final report, which received widespread news coverage in the United States.[28] *The Washington Post* and *Time* magazine reported on the Inquiry's conclusion, that the crisis constituted genocide.[29] In a segment that featured Annita Lucchesi of the Sovereign Bodies Institute, NPR compared the situations in the United States and Canada.[30] *The New York Times* noted that, "even before its release, the inquiry has been forcing a national reckoning."[31]

But coverage from major outlets such as the *Washington Post*, *Time* magazine, and others might well have left US audiences with the impression that the crisis of murdered and missing Indigenous women is primarily a Canadian issue. Beyond coverage of Canada's National Inquiry, US corporate news outlets have provided nearly nothing in the way of reporting on missing and murdered

Indigenous women in the United States. When corporate news outlets do cover this topic, reporting has tended to focus on congressional legislation and divisive party politics.[32] Although numerous news outlets reported in late 2019 on Senate Majority Leader Mitch McConnell's efforts to block reauthorization of the Violence Against Women Act, corporate news outlets mostly ignored how amendments to it would address the crisis of missing and murdered Indigenous women.[33]

With few exceptions, major news outlets like NPR and the *Washington Post* have limited their coverage to other important but secondary matters, such as Native women organizing self-defense classes, the symbolism of the clothing worn by the gay Indigenous couple who won Canada's *Amazing Race*, and book reviews.[34]

As a result of limited news coverage, the United States is far from a national reckoning on its crisis of missing and murdered Indigenous women and girls.[35]

2.
Monsanto "Intelligence Center" Targeted Journalists and Activists

Sam Levin, "Revealed: How Monsanto's 'Intelligence Center' Targeted Journalists and Activists," *The Guardian*, August 8, 2019, https://www.theguardian.com/business/2019/aug/07/monsanto-fusion-center-journalists-roundup-neil-young.

Student Researcher: Sarah Ghiorso (Sonoma State University)

Faculty Evaluator: Kyla Walters (Sonoma State University)

The agricultural giant Monsanto—which the German pharmaceutical corporation Bayer acquired in 2018—created an "intelligence fusion center" in order to "monitor and discredit" journalists and activists, Sam Levin reported for the *Guardian* in August 2019.

Levin wrote that Monsanto "adopted a multi-pronged strategy" to target Carey Gillam, a Reuters journalist who had reported on the likelihood of Monsanto's Roundup weed killer causing cancer. Monsanto also monitored a nonprofit organization focused on the food industry, US Right to Know, and the Twitter account of musician Neil Young, a prominent critic of Monsanto. An ongoing legal case over the dangers of Monsanto's Roundup weed killer led to disclosure of the internal documents. As Levin reported, company communications "add fuel to the ongoing claims that Monsanto has 'bullied' critics and scientists and worked to conceal the dangers of glyphosate, the world's most widely used herbicide."

Monsanto's internal communications documented how the company planned a series of "actions" to attack the credibility of Gillam's 2017 book, *Whitewash: The Story of a Weed Killer, Cancer, and the Corruption of Science*, by providing "talking points" for "third parties" and explaining to "industry and farmer customers" how to post negative book reviews; how the company paid Google to promote search results for "Monsanto Glyphosate Carey Gillam" that criticized her work; and how it considered placing pressure on Reuters, where Gillam had worked for seventeen years, to "push back on her editors" in hopes that she would be "reassigned."

After musician Neil Young released a 2015 album titled *The Monsanto Years*, Monsanto's fusion center also produced reports on Young's public criticism of the company, and the center evaluated the album's lyrics "to develop a list of 20+ potential topics he may target."

The revealed documents show that Monsanto considered legal action against Young.

According to the LinkedIn page of one person identified as a manager of Monsanto's "global intelligence and investigations," the fusion center included a team "responsible for the collection and analysis of criminal, activist/extremist, geo-political and terrorist activities affecting company operations across 160 countries," the *Guardian* reported.

Noting that government-run fusion centers have "increasingly raised privacy concerns surrounding the way law enforcement agencies collect data, surveil citizens and share information," the *Guardian* quoted Dave Maass, a senior investigative researcher at the Electronic Frontier Foundation, who distinguished between corporations monitoring legitimate criminal threats, such as cyberattacks, and "corporations levering their money to investigate people who are engaging in their first amendment rights."

A Bayer spokesperson, Christopher Loder, told the *Guardian* that Monsanto's activities were "intended to ensure there was a fair, accurate and science-based dialogue about the company and its products in response to significant misinformation."

As the *Guardian* reported, Bayer "has continued to assert that glyphosate is safe," but three US court cases, in 2018 and 2019, resulted in verdicts against Monsanto, holding the company liable for plaintiffs' non-Hodgkin lymphoma, a blood cancer.[36] In August 2019, The Hill reported that, in response to more than 18,000 people having filed suit against Monsanto, alleging cases of non-Hodgkin lymphoma caused by exposure to Roundup, Bayer was offering $8 billion to settle all outstanding claims.[37]

Monsanto's campaign to monitor and discredit journalists and other critics has received almost no corporate news coverage. In June 2019, ABC News reported that Monsanto had "started contacting journalists, politicians and activists it was keeping tabs on and documenting via 'watch lists,'" according to Monsanto's parent company, Bayer.[38] ABC's coverage was noteworthy—not only as a rare instance of corporate news coverage on this topic, but also for how it consistently emphasized the perspective of Monsanto and Bayer. ABC quoted a statement made by the PR firm FleishmanHillard that sought to normalize Monsanto's actions and its own business relationship with Monsanto: "Corporations, NGOs and other clients rightfully expect our firm to help them understand diverse perspectives before they engage. To do so, we and every other professional communications agency gather relevant information from publicly available sources." These planning documents, FleishmanHillard asserted, "help our clients best engage in the dialogue relevant to their business and societal objectives." Other than the PR firm Fleishman-Hillard, the ABC News report quoted only Bayer officials, including the company's head of corporate communications and its chairman of the board of management.

In September 2019, HuffPost published a substantial article on Monsanto's history of using "shady tactics to attack critics and influence the media."[39] Paul D. Thacker's report included a summary of the *Guardian*'s August 2019 report as "the latest example of Monsanto's efforts to track journalists," and it provided additional detail about how Monsanto avoided undertaking direct responses to its critics by engaging a network of third-party supporters, including the Genetic Literacy Project and the American Council on Science and Health.

3.

US Military—A Massive, Hidden Contributor to Climate Crisis

Benjamin Neimark, Oliver Belcher, and Patrick Bigger, "US Military is a Bigger Polluter Than as Many as 140 Countries—Shrinking This War Machine is a Must," The Conversation, June 24, 2019, https://theconversation.com/us-military-is-a-bigger-polluter-than-as-many-as-140-countries-shrinking-this-war-machine-is-a-must-119269.

Student Researcher: Fabiola Gregg (City College of San Francisco)

Faculty Evaluator: Jennifer Levinson (City College of San Francisco)

The US military is "one of the largest polluters in history, consuming more liquid fuels and emitting more climate-changing gases than most medium-sized countries," Benjamin Neimark, Oliver Belcher, and Patrick Bigger reported for The Conversation in June 2019. By burning fossil fuels, the US military emitted more than 25,000 kilotons of carbon dioxide in 2017. If the US military were a country, Neimark, Belcher, and Bigger wrote, its fuel usage would make it "the 47th largest emitter of greenhouse gases in the world."[40]

Noting that studies of greenhouse gas emissions usually focus on how much energy and fuel civilians use, Neimark, Belcher, and Bigger wrote that US military emissions "tend to be overlooked in climate change studies." Nevertheless, they reported, "Significant reductions to the Pentagon's budget and shrinking its capacity to wage war would cause a huge drop in demand from the biggest consumer of liquid fuels in the world."

Neimark, Belcher, and Bigger's report for The Conversation summarized key findings from a research article they wrote with Cara Kennelly and published in the *Transactions of the Institute of British Geographers*, a peer-reviewed academic journal, in June 2019.[41] In the study, they examined how US military supply chains impact the world's climate, by analyzing bulk fuel purchases, as documented by the US Defense Logistics Agency–Energy (DLA-E). A sub-agency of the US Department of Defense, the DLA-E manages "the US military's supply chains, including its hydrocarbon fuel purchases and distribution." The authors obtained data on US military fuel purchases through multiple Freedom of Information Act requests to the DLA-E.

"It's very difficult to get consistent data from the Pentagon and across US government departments," Neimark, Belcher, and Bigger wrote. A loophole in the 1997 Kyoto Protocol exempted the United States from reporting military emissions. Although the Paris Accord closed this loophole, Neimark, Belcher, and Bigger noted that, "with the Trump administration due to withdraw from the accord in 2020, this gap . . . will return."

Nevertheless, based on the data they were able to analyze, the authors in the *Transactions* article concluded that if "the US military were a country, it would nestle between Peru and Portugal in the global league table of fuel purchasing," going on to observe that the military's carbon emissions for 2014 were "roughly equivalent to total—not just fuel—emissions from Romania."[42]

Moreover, Neimark, Belcher, and Bigger found that US "forward operating bases" (FOBs) located in Afghanistan and other overseas theaters of operations have enormous fuel requirements and spew huge amounts of carbon into the atmosphere. They wrote that "a single US Marine Corp brigade operating across . . . a network of FOBs requires over 500,000 gallons of fuel per day."[43]

Noting that "action on climate change demands shut-tering vast sections of the military machine," Neimark, Belcher, and Bigger recommended that "money spent procuring and distributing fuel across the US empire" be reinvested as "a peace dividend, helping to fund a Green New Deal in whatever form it might take."

As of May 2020, the original report by Neimark, Belcher, and Bigger appears to have received little to no corporate news coverage, with the exception of the republication of their Conversation piece by news aggregator Yahoo! News and *Newsweek*, a report in the British newspaper *The Daily Mail*, and a brief summary in ScienceDaily.[44] Independent news outlets, including *YES! Magazine*, The Ecologist, and Quartz, also republished the original article from The Conversation.[45]

4.
Congressional Investments and Conflicts of Interest

Peter Cary, "Republicans Passed Tax Cuts—Then Profited," Center for Public Integrity, January 24, 2020, https://publicintegrity.org/inequality-poverty-opportunity/taxes/trumps-tax-cuts/republicans-profit-congress/; also published as "How Republicans Made Millions on the Tax Cuts They Pushed through Congress," Vox, January 24, 2020, https://www.vox.com/policy-and-politics/2020/1/24/21078559/republicans-tax-cuts-congress-profits.

Donald Shaw, "Facing Climate Crisis, Senators Have Millions Invested in Fossil Fuel Companies," Sludge, September 24, 2019, https://readsludge.com/2019/09/24/facing-climate-crisis-senators-have-millions-invested-in-fossil-fuel-companies.

Student Researchers: Cale Carpenter (North Central College), Chris Valenzuela (College of Western Idaho), and Christopher Rodriguez (Sonoma State University)

Faculty Evaluators: Steve Macek (North Central College), Anna Gamboa (College of Western Idaho), and Peter Phillips (Sonoma State University)

In January 2020 the Center for Public Integrity and Vox reported that the 2017 Tax Cuts and Jobs Act, which granted corporations a 14 percent reduction in taxes, also helped Republicans in Congress who own shares in those corporations reap huge financial rewards. Although Republicans "sold the bill as a package of business and middle-class tax cuts that would not help the wealthy, the cuts likely saved members of Congress hundreds of thousands of dollars in taxes collectively, while the corporate tax cut hiked the value of their holdings," Peter Cary of the Center for Public Integrity reported. Democrats in Congress also benefited, but none of them voted for the legislation.

The Act doled out nearly $150 billion in corporate tax savings in 2018 alone.[46] Because the tax cuts were not "paid for" with corresponding reductions in government spending, the move will likely cause an increase of some $1.9 trillion in the national debt over the next decade.

In the months after the tax cuts were passed, stock prices soared. As a result, congressional Republicans saw a significant boost to the value of their portfolios. For example, Apple's stock prices rose in October 2018, jumping 37 percent. Representative Mike Kelly of Pennsylvania and his wife own stock in the tech giant and many other companies; the total value of their investments is at least $439,000. Likewise, Representative Orrin Hatch of Utah and his spouse's assets are worth between $562,000 and $1.43 million, and include ownership of mutual funds and a limited liability corporation (as well as a "blind trust" worth between $1 million and $5 million). All but one of the 47 Republicans on the three key congressional committees that controlled the drafting of the tax bill own stocks and mutual funds.

Adding to the congressional Republicans' windfall was what Cary called the Act's "crown jewel," a newly created

20 percent deduction for income from "pass-through" businesses, or smaller, single-owner corporations. These businesses do not pay corporate taxes and they shift profits to investors and shareholders, who are only taxed at lower, individual rates. At least 22 of the 47 members of the House and Senate tax-writing committees have investments in pass-through businesses.

Real estate developers and investors also benefited greatly from the Tax Cuts and Jobs Act. Cary quoted Ed Kleinbard, the former chief of staff of the Congress's Joint Committee on Taxation, as saying "[i]f you are a real estate developer, you never pay tax." An addition to the bill featured a provision that allows real estate companies with relatively few employees to take the 20 percent deduction usually reserved for larger business with a sizeable number of employees. Out of the 47 Republicans responsible for drafting the bill, at least 29 held real estate interests at the time of its passage.

Over the past year, taxes were not the only legislative issue in which decisions were potentially influenced by the financial interests of members of Congress.

Members of the US Senate are heavily invested in the fossil fuel companies that drive the current climate crisis, creating a conflict between those senators' financial interests as investors and their responsibilities as elected representatives. According to a September 2019 Sludge investigation by Donald Shaw, 29 senators and their spouses hold between $3.5 million and $13.9 million worth of stock in 86 fossil fuel companies, including well-known giants like ExxonMobil and Royal Dutch Shell and "a range of lesser known companies that specialize in pipeline operations, natural gas exports, and oilfield services."

Shaw's report was based on the senators' personal financial filings as of August 16, 2019. According to the US Energy Information Administration, fossil fuel combustion accounted for about 76 percent of the greenhouse gases emitted in 2017.[47]

Joe Manchin, a Democratic senator from West Virginia, where coal mining is a major business, has millions invested in coal. Shaw found that Manchin owns between $1 million and $5 million worth of non-public stock in a family coal business, Enersystems. Manchin's 2018 financial disclosure reported that he earned between $100,001 and $1 million in dividends and interest from Enersystems, in addition to $470,000 in "ordinary business income."

Manchin is the senior Democrat on the Senate's Energy and Natural Resources Committee, which oversees legislation on energy resources and development, nuclear energy, federal coal, oil, and gas, and other mineral leasing, among other issues. If Democrats take control of the Senate in 2020, Manchin is in line to chair the Committee.

Manchin was the only Democrat to vote against protecting the Arctic National Wildlife Refuge from oil drilling in 2017. Manchin also voted to approve construction of the Keystone XL oil pipeline.

Jerry Moran, the Republican junior senator from Kansas, is likely the largest senatorial investor in ExxonMobil. Moran owns between $102,003 and $280,000 worth of ExxonMobil stock. He has stated that he does not believe that human activity has any effect on climate change.

ExxonMobil has known since at least 1977 that burning fossil fuels contributes to global warming, but the company suppressed that information for decades and worked to sow confusion over the scientific evidence for climate change in service of its bottom line, as Shaw's report documented in detail and as Project Censored has previously reported.[48]

Although the corporate media, including CBS News, have provided some critical coverage of the 2017 Tax Cuts and Jobs Act and its impacts, the report by the Center for Public Integrity and Vox is distinctive in having analyzed the financial disclosure forms of the lawmakers who drafted and voted for the legislation to show how they profited from it personally.[49] Corporate news outlets have not covered this important aspect of the story.

In addition, despite the significant conflicts of interest exposed by Donald Shaw's reporting for Sludge, the alarming facts about US senators' massive investments in the fossil fuel industry appear to have gone completely unreported in the corporate press.

5.
"Inequality Kills": Gap between Richest and Poorest Americans Largest in 50 Years

Fernando De Maio, "We Must Address the Roots of Inequality to Keep It from Killing Us," Truthout, December 21, 2019, https://truthout.org/articles/we-must-address-the-roots-of-inequality-to-keep-it-from-killing-us.

Patrick Martin, "US Study Shows: Poverty and Social Inequality are Killers," World Socialist Web Site, September 12, 2019, https://www.wsws.org/en/articles/2019/09/12/pers-s12.html.

María José Carmona, "Stress, Overwork, and Insecurity are Driving the Invisible Workplace Accident Rate," Inequality.org (Institute for Policy Studies), September 13, 2019, https://inequality.org/research/invisible-workplace-accident-rate/.

Student Researchers: Maria Meyer (San Francisco State University) and Marco Gonzales (Sonoma State University)

Faculty Evaluators: Kenn Burrows (San Francisco State University) and Peter Phillips (Sonoma State University)

COVID-19 has made clear the crucial links between inequality and poor health.[50] But in December 2019, well before the United States began to grapple with the pandemic, Fernando De Maio reported for Truthout that the "true root causes of illness extend beyond the health care system" to the social determinants of health. As documented in several recent research studies, some of those social determinants can be clearly discerned in the links between income inequality and life expectancy and between racial segregation and premature mortality.

As the World Socialist Web Site reported, an August 2019 Government Accountability Office (GAO) report concluded that poor Americans are nearly twice as likely as their rich counterparts to die before reaching old age;[51] while Truthout reported on 2018 data from the US Census Bureau that showed the gap between the richest and poorest households in the United States is now the largest it has been in more than fifty years, with wealth more concentrated than ever before.[52] "Democrats and Republicans may have different interpretations of these facts," De Maio wrote, "but in public health, decades of research are coming to a consensus: Inequality kills."

Understanding the links between inequality and poor health requires examining data at the levels of cities and communities, De Maio reported. "Without this kind of data," he wrote, we maintain the "mirage" that "the economy is great because macroeconomic indicators say so." Across the five hundred largest cities in the United States, income inequality correlates with premature mortality. For example, the Chicago Health Atlas has documented a nine-year gap between the life expectancy of Chicago's Black and white residents, where the Black residents have a higher degree of economic hardship than their white counterparts.[53] As De Maio reported, this gap in life expectancy results in more than 3000 "excess deaths"— deaths that likely would not have occurred if Black residents had similar incomes to white residents. Heart disease, cancer, stroke, diabetes, and kidney disease account for premature mortality among Chicago's Black residents, researchers determined. "All of these are conditions that an equitable health care system would address," De Maio noted.

A separate 2018 study of Chicago, which De Maio co-authored, found a "strong relationship" between racial and economic segregation and premature mortality.[54] As

---

"Democrats and Republicans may have different interpretations of these facts, but in public health, decades of research are coming to a consensus: Inequality kills."

Fernando De Maio, co-director, Center for Community Health Equity

---

he wrote for Truthout, "decades of disinvestment" provide the foundation for current patterns of segregation, which public health experts identify as one form of "structural violence," a term for social and political arrangements that harm populations. From this perspective, lowering premature mortality requires more than healthcare reform; "it requires concerted action to limit the concentration of wealth and power," De Maio wrote.

In Chicago, West Side United (WSU), a coalition of healthcare institutions, residents, community-based and nonprofit organizations, and government agencies, has formed to tackle the sixteen-year life expectancy gap that exists between the city's downtown Loop and West Side communities. Focused on healthcare, neighborhood and physical environment, economic vitality, and education, WSU works to address the root causes of poor health by increasing hiring from West Side neighborhoods, supporting business development, and expanding the use of community health workers, De Maio reported.

As Patrick Martin noted in his report for the World Socialist Web Site, the damning GAO report "was not actually commissioned ... to expose the connection between poverty and premature death." Instead, Congress called for the GAO to examine how changes in life expectancy might affect Social Security and Medicare programs, "to assist congressional efforts, supported by both parties, to cut spending on these 'entitlement' programs," Martin wrote. He noted that, with stagnant incomes and the disappearance of traditional pension plans, Social Security and other safety net programs "are increasingly the lifeline on which millions depend," and politicians' efforts to shrink or eliminate them "could run into widespread opposition."

The poorest Americans are also more likely than their rich counterparts to face illness or premature death due to the inherent dangers of low-wage work. From delivery drivers to home care providers, low-paid workers face increasing pressures to work faster and longer, making their jobs more stressful—and, ultimately, deadly, María José Carmona reported for Inequality.org in September 2019. Carmona reported on a 2019 International Labour Organization (ILO) study, which found that less than 14 percent of the 7500 people who die "due to unsafe and unhealthy working conditions every day" die from occupational accidents. Instead, the ILO determined, the vast majority of work-related deaths are due to stress-related illnesses or accidents that take place when workers are off-duty.[55]

"Today's greatest workplace risk isn't falling or infectious agents … but increasing pressure, precarious contracts, and working hours incompatible with life, which, bit by bit, continue to feed the invisible accident rate that does not appear in the news," Carmona wrote.

The ILO report noted that excessive working hours are associated with "chronic effects of fatigue which can lead to cardiovascular disease and gastrointestinal disorders, as well as poorer mental health status, including higher rates of anxiety, depression and sleeping disorders."[56] Workers employed on temporary or casual bases are most vulnerable, Carmona reported; temporary and casual workers "have a harder time asserting their rights" and they consistently face having to choose between health and work, "between enduring pain [and] running the risk of not being called back."

When focusing on work-related stress, "we have to be careful with labels," José Antonio Llosa, a professor of psychology based in Spain, warned. "It's not the fault of the worker who doesn't know how to deal with the stress," Llosa told Inequality.org, and the solutions are not individual anti-anxiety drug prescriptions, exercise programs, or meditation routines, but rather "changing the way that work is organized."

While noting that protecting workers is "impossible in a market that is unrestrained and insecure," Carmona concluded that curbing competition, better regulating work hours, and slowing down work processes could all help to improve workers' health and safety, on and off the job.

As of May 2020, Project Censored has not been able to identify any corporate news coverage on the GAO or Census Bureau reports on inequality and premature mortality, or on the ILO report about work-related illnesses, accidents, and deaths that take place when workers are off-duty.

6.

Shadow Network of Conservative Outlets Emerges to Exploit Faith in Local News

Priyanjana Bengani, "Hundreds of 'Pink Slime' Local News Outlets are Distributing Algorithmic Stories and Conservative Talking Points," *Columbia Journalism Review*, December 18, 2019, https://www.cjr.org/tow_center_reports/hundreds-of-pink-slime-local-news-outlets-are-distributing-algorithmic-stories-conservative-talking-points.php.

Katherina Sourine and Dominick Sokotoff, "Pseudo Local News Sites in Michigan Reveal Nationally Expanding Network," *Michigan Daily*, November 1, 2019, https://www.michigandaily.com/section/community-affairs/pseudo-local-news-sites-michigan-reveal-nationally-expanding-network.

Carol Thompson, "Dozens of New Websites Appear to be Michigan Local News Outlets, but with Political Bent," *Lansing State Journal*, October 20, 2019, updated October 22, 2019, https://www.lansingstatejournal.com/story/news/local/2019/10/21/lansing-sun-new-sites-michigan-local-news-outlets/3984689002/.

Student Researcher: Troy Patton (Diablo Valley College)

Faculty Evaluator: Mickey Huff (Diablo Valley College)

A December 2019 report by the *Columbia Journalism Review* (*CJR*) highlighted how a network of 450 websites operated by five corporate organizations in twelve states "mimic the appearance and output of traditional news organizations" in order to "manipulate public opinion by exploiting faith in local media." These sites "co-opt the language, design and structure of news organizations," Priyanjana Bengani reported, to "cover certain candidates and topics, including limited government, tort reform, and labour unions, with a conservative bias."

The story of "[d]ozens of websites branded as local news outlets" in Michigan, a crucial swing state in the 2016 election, was originally reported by Carol Thompson for the *Lansing State Journal* in October 2019. The *CJR* report expanded on previous investigations conducted by Thompson, the *Michigan Daily*, and others, which had identified around two hundred sites in several states posing as local news outlets while publishing politically biased content.

Thompson's original report for the *Lansing State Journal* noted that the network of websites in Michigan shared a common "About Us" section, identifying Metric Media as the publisher and describing its plans to launch thousands of such sites nationwide. The sites' privacy policies pages indicated that they were all operated by Locality Labs. Thompson reported that Locality Labs ran similar networks of sites in Illinois and Maryland, and identified Brian Timpone as Locality Labs's CEO.

The Michigan Daily's November 2019 report provided further detail on the intricate relationships between Brian Timpone, Metric Media, Locality Labs, and other outlets. Although the web of interconnected sites is difficult to follow, the *CJR* highlighted five corporate bodies with 21 news networks that are connected through a complex web of shared IP addresses, backend web IDs, and the involvement of Timpone. As *CJR* reported, "In 2012, Timpone's company Journatic, an outlet known for its low-cost automated story generation (which became known as 'pink slime journalism'), attracted national attention and outrage for faking bylines and quotes, and for plagiarism."[57] In 2013, Journatic rebranded as Locality Labs. Brian Timpone is also the co-founder of Local Government

Information Services (LGIS), a network of more than thirty print and web publications in Illinois that feature conservative news and share the same layout as Metric Media's websites. And, as *CJR* reported, in 2015 Timpone incorporated Newsinator, a firm that the *Chicago Tribune* described as having a history of "doing paid political work and offer[ing] marketing services to companies under the name Interactive Content Services."[58] The CEO of Franklin Archer, which operates the single largest network of these faux-local publications, is Michael Timpone, Brian's brother.

Based on *CJR*'s network analysis of Metric Media, Franklin Archer, Newsinator, LGIS, and Locality Labs (also known as Local Labs), Priyanjana Bengani concluded, "Typically, creating entities that focus on communities, local news, and single issues important to the general public would be a worthwhile endeavour. But, the partisan material present on the more established networks along with the ideological leanings of some of the key personnel give us pause."

Since October 2019 at least three significant scholarly books have been published that address the topic of growing control over local media outlets by conservative owners with ties to right-wing organizations, but during the past year major corporate news outlets have provided minimal coverage of this topic.[59] In October 2019 the *New York Times* published an article that credited the *Lansing State Journal* with breaking the story on pseudo-local news organizations in Michigan, and drew significantly from Carol Thompson's original report.[60] Corporate coverage has been lacking in regard to this Sinclair-like network of right-leaning news sites filling the holes left by the demise of many local news outlets. The *Columbia Journalism Review*'s piece expands on the breadth and scope of previous coverage, but its findings do not appear to have been reported by any of the major establishment news outlets.

7.
Underreporting of Missing and Victimized Black Women and Girls

Carma Henry, "There are 64,000 Missing Black Women and Girls in the United States and No One Seems to Care," *Westside Gazette*, February 21, 2019, https://thewestsidegazette.com/there-are-64000-missing-black-women-and-girls-in-the-united-states-and-no-one-seems-to-care/.

Tanasia Kenney, "'693 Bodies . . . All Black': White S.C. Man Accused of Trafficking, Kidnapping Underage Girls for Sex Withdraws Request for Bond, May Have More Victims," Atlanta Black Star, October 17, 2019, https://atlantablackstar.com/2019/10/17/693-bodies-all-black-white-s-c-man-accused-of-trafficking-kidnapping-underage-girls-for-sex-withdraws-request-for-bond-may-have-more-victims/.

Paula Rogo, "South Carolina DJ Accused of Trafficking and Sexual Crimes Against Black Girls," *Essence*, October 19, 2019, https://www.essence.com/news/south-carolina-dj-human-trafficking-black-girls/.

"Everything to Know about the White Man Who May Have Sex Trafficked Nearly 700 Black Girls," NewsOne, October 18, 2019, https://newsone.com/3890531/jason-roger-pope-dj-kid-sex-trafficking/.

Student Researchers: Zakeycia Briggs (Indian River State College) and Melissa Harden (North Central College)

Faculty Evaluators: Elliot D. Cohen (Indian River State College) and Steve Macek (North Central College)

The rate at which Black women and girls go missing in the United States is higher than that of their white counterparts. As Carma Henry reported for the *Westside Gazette*, "What's even more alarming is that the media coverage and legislation that missing Black girls are getting seems to be lacking compared to missing white girls." As of 2014 there are 64,000 missing Black women and girls, most of whom have not been found, due in part to the lack of coverage their stories garner.

As Henry explained, a 2010 study of US media coverage of missing children found that "only 20 percent of reported stories focused on missing Black children despite [their disappearances] corresponding to 33 percent of the overall missing children cases."[61] The study concluded that missing persons stories involving Black children, and specifically missing Black girls, are reported on by corporate media less frequently than other missing children cases.

A 2015 study discussed in the *William & Mary Journal of Race, Gender, and Social Justice* found that the disparity listed in the 2010 study between the reportage and the reality of missing Black children had increased substantially.[62] As of 2015, Black children accounted for 35 percent of missing children cases, while only representing a dismal 7 percent of media reports on missing children. Media coverage is often vital in missing person cases because it raises community awareness and can drive funding and search efforts that support finding those missing persons.

The Atlanta Black Star shed light on perhaps the most prolific offender against Black women and girls in recent history, Jason Roger Pope, who has been indicted on charges relating to human trafficking and child sex crimes. Pope, a white South Carolina promoter and popular disc jockey better known as DJ Kid, has made claims suggesting he may have participated in the trafficking, assault, and/or rapes of nearly seven hundred African American girls—primarily under-aged—right up until his arrest in

August 2019. Victims as young as thirteen years old testified that Pope coerced them into performing sex acts in exchange for items such as money and drugs.

On his active Facebook page, Pope wrote, "I'm 36 with 693 BODIES (All Black females), WBU?" In a photo album called "DJ KID (PARTIES & GIRLS—Part 1)" there are numerous photographs depicting Pope in inappropriate, sexually-charged poses with under-aged African American girls. A relative of Pope's reportedly contacted police in mid-2018, claiming that Pope would pay underage girls to perform sex acts and later post about the encounters online, but their concerns were ignored. Pope has police records going as far back as 2011 relating to sexual misconduct with minors. Yet outside of a few local news outlets, the corporate media has been silent on Pope's crimes.

Human trafficking relies on an expansive underground market that frequently goes unnoticed and underreported. According to the Bureau of Justice Statistics, it is estimated that, globally, 94 percent of humans trafficked for sex consist of women and girls.[63] The Human Trafficking Search also notes that African Americans are affected by sex trafficking disproportionately in the United States, accounting for more than 40 percent of confirmed sex trafficking victims despite only representing 13.1 percent of the population.[64]

The corporate media's failure to report on Pope's egregious acts is reflective of their larger pattern of ignoring crimes against Black women and girls, whether they are trafficked, abused, or disappeared. House Majority Leader Nancy Pelosi has spoken out against the widespread problem of missing Black women and girls in the United

States, hoping to call attention to the often-ignored issue, yet the little coverage she received on the issue ironically tended to obscure the fact that a disproportionate number of the women and girls missing in the United States are Black.[65]

Apart from small independent sources, many of which report primarily on the Black community, this gap in coverage of missing Black women and girls has gone widely underreported. An ABC News article discussed the fact that many Black families have to fight to get the attention of media and police for their missing person cases.[66] CNN detailed the many factors that contribute to higher rates of missing Black children in America and identified inadequate media coverage as a source of the disparity.[67] But, broadly, US corporate media are not willing to discuss their own shortcomings or to acknowledge the responsibilities they neglect by failing to provide coverage on the search for missing and victimized Black women and girls.

8.
The Public Banking Revolution

Ellen Brown, "The Public Banking Revolution is upon Us," Common Dreams, April 18, 2019, https://www.commondreams.org/views/2019/04/18/public-banking-revolution-upon-us.

Ananya Garg, "California Just Legalized Public Banks. Will the Rest of the Nation Follow Suit?" *YES! Magazine*, October 4, 2019, https://www.yesmagazine.org/economy/2019/10/04/california-public-banking-law.

Mario Koran, "California Just Legalized Public Banking, Setting the Stage for More Affordable Housing," *The Guardian*, October 4, 2019, https://www.theguardian.com/us-news/2019/oct/03/california-governor-public-banking-law-ab857.

Eric Heath, "Public Banking Can Fund Green Investment," The Hill, July 22, 2019, https://thehill.com/opinion/energy-environment/454075-public-banking-can-fund-green-investment.

Oscar Perry Abello, "To Keep the Economy Afloat, the Fed Turns to North Dakota," *YES! Magazine*, April 29, 2020, https://www.yesmagazine.org/economy/2020/04/29/coronavirus-economy-public-banking/.

Student Researcher: Matthew Ascano (San Francisco State University)

Faculty Evaluator: Kenn Burrows (San Francisco State University)

In October 2019, California governor Gavin Newsom signed the Public Banking Act, authorizing city and county governments to create or sponsor public banks. As *YES! Magazine* reported, though establishing the charters for such banks will likely take several years, public banks like the Bank of North Dakota, which was established in 1919, provide a robust alternative to the "big for-profit banks that the government uses to invest public money into Wall Street, rather than local communities." Public banks will provide "public agencies access to loans at interest rates much lower than they could find at private banks," the *Guardian* reported. Run like nonprofits, public banks are not legally obligated to maximize profits, as private banks are; instead, public banks are mandated to serve their communities. As Ellen Brown, the founder of the Public Banking Institute, had previously reported for Common Dreams, "a growing public banking movement is picking up momentum across the U.S." More than 25 public bank bills were "currently active, and dozens of groups are promoting the idea," Brown wrote in April 2019.

After California legislators enacted the state's Public Banking Act, the cities of Los Angeles and San Francisco announced plans to establish public banks.[68] In November 2019, New Jersey governor Phil Murphy established a task force to create a business and operations plan for how a public bank could help meet the capital needs of the state's small businesses, nonprofits, students, and afford-able housing projects.[69]

From efforts to divest public employee pension funds from the fossil fuel industry and private prisons, to funding the proposed Green New Deal, and counteracting the massive, rapid shutdown of the economy caused by the COVID-19 pandemic, public banking has never seemed more relevant.

The year 2019 marked the 100th anniversary of the United States's first publicly-owned state bank, the Bank of North Dakota (BND), which was established in response to a farmers' revolt against out-of-state banks that were unfairly foreclosing on their farms. As *YES! Magazine*'s Ananya Garg reported, in 2018 the BND "recorded its 15th consecutive year of record profit," with $159 million in income, $7 billion in assets, and an investment portfolio of $1.9 billion. As Ellen Brown told *YES! Magazine*, North Dakota was the only state that escaped the 2008 finan-cial crisis: "It never went in the red" and it had the lowest unemployment and foreclosure rates at that time.

One aim of the Standing Rock movement—which in 2016 brought together Indigenous activists from across the nation to oppose the Dakota Access Pipeline—was public and personal divestment from the big bank funding the pipeline's development, Wells Fargo. As Ananya Garg reported for *YES! Magazine*, at the time of the Standing Rock protests, "many individuals were able to switch their personal accounts to nonprofit credit unions." But credit unions typically lack "the capacity to handle the large gov-ernment accounts of cities and states." Garg described how, in 2017, the Seattle City Council voted to divest its banking services from Wells Fargo, because of the bank's ties to the

Dakota Access Pipeline. But when Seattle officials could not find an alternative institution to process the city's $3 billion in annual revenues, Seattle was forced to return to Wells Fargo for its banking. A public bank would have provided the necessary alternative, thus bolstering divestment efforts in Seattle and throughout the nation.

In July 2019, The Hill reported on how public banking could help fund the Green New Deal, the policy proposal to address climate change and environmental deterioration. Skeptics have argued that strapped federal and state governments lack the financial resources to take on the Green New Deal's multi-trillion-dollar costs. However, as Eric Heath explained, state banks, such as the BND, "free the financial resources needed to fund vital investments in the planet's future." Public banks' mission to serve the public interest could allow them "to extend financing to projects that other banks would not consider"—not because green investments are unprofitable, but because "their profits slowly accumulate and are widely shared across a community." A September 2019 study, published by the Northeast-Midwest Institute, recommended the adoption of public banks by all Northeast and Midwestern states, not as "a panacea" but as one important move for "addressing critical investment gaps and realigning state resources with state interests."[70]

The COVID-19 pandemic's extraordinary impact on the economy has led to somewhat wider discussion about the desirability of public banks. With the pandemic, news outlets such as The Hill and even News Corp's Market-Watch are beginning to join pioneering outlets like YES! Magazine in covering public banking.[71]

With the congressional bailout package including an

initial disbursement of $349 billion in forgivable loans to small businesses through the Small Business Administration's Paycheck Protection Program, the CEO of the Bank of North Dakota, Eric Hardmeyer, told *YES! Magazine*, "The Fed seems to be thinking of everything we were thinking about two or three weeks ago."

Recalling how President Franklin D. Roosevelt used the Reconstruction Finance Corporation—"a special-purpose public bank"—not only to bail out private banks, but also to finance "massive public-works and social programs, which transformed America," Timothy Knowles and Ameya Pawar advocated following Roosevelt's example and launching "a network of national, state and local public banks to forge a 21st-century New Deal."[72]

"If cities had public banks, they would be much better equipped" to deal with budget shortfalls caused by the COVID-19 pandemic and to maintain the services and staff vital to cities' economic recovery, Isaiah Poole and Rick Girling wrote in an editorial for The Hill. They went on to call for state and local political leaders to "use emergency powers to rapidly create public banks that can serve as key engines of a just and sustainable economic recovery."[73]

No major corporate media outlets appear to have devoted recent coverage to this important and timely topic.

9.
Rising Risks of Nuclear Power
Due to Climate Change

Christina Chen, "Nuclear vs. Climate Change: Rising Seas," Natural Resources Defense Council (NRDC), September 16, 2019, https://www.nrdc.org/experts/christina-chen/nuclear-vs-climate-change-rising-seas.

Karen Charman, "Can Nuclear Power's Deadly Waste be Contained in a Warming World?" Truthout, September 23, 2019, https://truthout.org/articles/can-nuclear-powers-deadly-waste-be-contained-in-a-warming-world/.

Student Researcher: Ryan Gopar Ramírez (Sonoma State University)

Faculty Evaluators: Peter Phillips (Sonoma State University) and Daniel Kammen (UC Berkeley)

Nuclear power plants are unprepared for climate change. Rising sea levels and warmer waters will impact power plants' infrastructure, posing increased risks of nuclear disasters, according to reports from the Natural Resources Defense Council (NRDC) and Truthout from September 2019.

"[I]f nuclear power is going to have a role in addressing climate change," Christina Chen wrote in the second of a two-part NRDC report, "stronger safety and environmental regulations will be needed." Chen's report highlighted problems stemming from a January 2019 decision by the US Nuclear Regulatory Commission (NRC) to weaken recommendations from its own staff to reassess the adequacy of preparations for seismic and flooding hazards at nuclear sites.

In a dissent to the NRC's decision, one of its commissioners, Jeff Baran, wrote, "Instead of requiring nuclear power plants to be prepared for the actual flooding and earthquake hazards that could occur at their sites, NRC will allow them to be prepared only for the old, outdated hazards typically calculated decades ago when the science of seismology and hydrology was far less advanced than it is today."

NRC staff had recommended raising safety standards in response to the ongoing Fukushima disaster, which began in 2011 when an earthquake and tsunami destroyed the Fukushima Daiichi Nuclear Power Plant.

Writing for Truthout, Karen Charman reported that "nuclear reactors need an uninterrupted electricity supply to run the cooling systems that keep the reactors from melting down." However, this requirement may be "increasingly difficult to guarantee in a world of climate-fueled megastorms and other disasters."

As Charman noted, in the late 1980s Hans Blix, chairman of the International Atomic Energy Agency, promoted the role of nuclear energy as a means to combat climate change. Since then advocates for nuclear energy—including 2020 Democratic presidential hopefuls Cory Booker and Andrew Yang—have promoted nuclear power as a clean energy source because it does not produce carbon emissions.

However, as Charman wrote, "the fact that reactors don't emit carbon while operating doesn't mean nuclear energy is 'clean.'" Nuclear disasters such as the meltdown and explosion at Chernobyl in 1986, the partial meltdown at Three Mile Island in Pennsylvania in 1979, and the successive meltdowns and explosions at Fukushima in 2011—all of which resulted in radioactive contamination—are stark examples of what can go wrong.

Many of the world's estimated 442 nuclear power plants operating in 2019 are located near sea level because, as Christina Chen's article explained, "Nuclear power plants require huge amounts of water to prevent fission products in the core and spent nuclear fuel from overheating."[74] This makes nuclear power the most water-intensive energy source in terms of consumption and withdrawal per unit of energy delivered.

As Ensia, a solutions-focused media outlet, reported in 2018, more than one hundred US, European, and Asian nuclear power stations positioned just a few meters above sea level may be vulnerable to serious flooding caused by accelerating sea-level rise and increasingly frequent storm surges.[75] In the United States, nine nuclear plants are located within two miles of the ocean, and a team of researchers at Stanford identified four of those reactors as vulnerable to storm surges and rising sea levels, John Vidal reported for Ensia. David Lochbaum, a former director of the nuclear safety project at the Union of Concerned Scientists, told Ensia that, since the early 1980s, there have been more than twenty incidents of flooding recorded at US nuclear plants.

In 2019, as Greenland's ice sheet lost an estimated 600 billion tons of water—the biggest drop in its surface mass since recordkeeping began in 1948—scientists predicted that sea levels could rise by as much as two meters by 2100.[76]

Tracking back to 2013, corporate news media have only sporadically addressed the potential for climate change to impact nuclear power plants. In 2013, for example, the *New York Times* reported that the US Department of Energy had concluded that the nation's entire energy system was vulnerable to increasingly severe and costly weather events driven by climate change.[77] However, the article did not address how rising sea levels would affect nuclear power plants. More recently, a July 2019 *U.S. News & World Report* article noted that, although the nuclear power sector is often depicted as being relatively resistant to unpredictable weather associated with climate change, heat waves are "punching holes in that narrative."[78] Although this report stressed the threats of rising water and air temperatures, it did not address rising sea levels.

10.
Revive Journalism with a Stimulus Package and Public Option

Craig Aaron, "Journalism Needs a Stimulus. Here's What It Should Look Like," *Columbia Journalism Review*, March 24, 2020, https://www.cjr.org/analysis/journalism-stimulus. php.

Victor Pickard, "We Need a Media System That Serves People's Needs, Not Corporations," *Jacobin*, January 27, 2020, https://jacobinmag.com/2020/01/corporate-media-system-democracy.

Victor Pickard, "American Journalism is Dying. Its Survival Requires Public Funds," *The Guardian*, February 19, 2020, https://www.theguardian.com/commentisfree/2020/feb/19/american-journalism-press-publishing-mcclatchy.

Student Researcher: Veronica Vasquez (Diablo Valley College)

Faculty Advisor: Mickey Huff (Diablo Valley College)

In response to the coronavirus pandemic, in March 2020 President Trump authorized a $2.2 trillion rescue package, which included direct payments of $1200 per adult plus $500 per child to millions of Americans, and more than $500 billion for large corporations, including the airline industry.[79] Anticipating President Trump's approval of the landmark Coronavirus Aid, Relief, and Economic Security (CARES) Act, Craig Aaron, the president of Free Press, wrote that the United States urgently needs a stimulus package for journalism. "In the face of this pandemic," Aaron wrote in the *Columbia Journalism Review*, "the public needs good, economically secure journalists more than ever." Aaron's organization, Free Press, determined that US journalism needs $5 billion in immediate emergency funds, and his article presented a three-pronged plan for the recovery of journalism, including a doubling of federal funds for public media, direct support for newsrooms, and new investments in journalism.

Doubling the annual federal appropriations for public media over the next two years would require an additional $930 million. "This money isn't for *Downton Abbey* reruns," Aaron wrote. Instead, for example, it could be used to extend the successful model of using public media as an educational resource while students are home from school. In California, the Los Angeles Unified School District and the local PBS affiliate, KCET, have partnered "to offer instruction over the airwaves while kids are out of school, with separate channels focused on different ages," Aaron noted.[80] A congressional appropriation of at least $200 million could expand public media's "Ready to Learn" initiative to cover all school-aged children. Any recovery package should also include direct support for daily and weekly newsrooms, including jobs at newspapers, community papers, and alt-weeklies committed to local news coverage. Just $625 million could help retain 25,000 newsroom jobs, Aaron reported. Congress could facilitate this investment by offering deferred or no-interest business loans and tax credits, such as Aaron's proposed Emergency Jobs for Journalism Tax Credit, which would provide outlets with $40,000 per newsroom employee hired during 2020. COVID-19, Aaron wrote, provides an opportunity to "revive and reimagine journalism's future." Thus, as Aaron advocated, a future stimulus bill could include $2 billion for a "First

Amendment Fund" that would support "new positions, outlets, and approaches to newsgathering."

Arguing that a "resilient and community-centered media system" is necessary to get through the pandemic, Aaron concluded, "Now is the time to act. We need significant public investments in all corners of the economy, and journalism is no exception."

In an article published by *Jacobin*, media scholar Victor Pickard argued that the current US media system "naturalizes the powerful and profitable while defunding adversarial journalism." For a media system to be "democratically governed and accessible to all," Pickard wrote, we must "stop grasping for a technological fix or a market panacea" and "acknowledge that no entrepreneurial solution lies just around the bend." Instead we must seek non-market alternatives. A public option for journalism, establishing permanent support for a well-funded national public media service, "could help guarantee universal access to quality news," he wrote.

Drawing on the late sociologist Erik Olin Wright's model for building alternatives to capitalism, Pickard wrote that "the most surefire way to tame and erode commercial media is to create a truly publicly owned system." A robust public media system would require an annual budget of approximately $30 billion, Pickard reported. "That may seem large, but relative to the problem—and compared to the outlays for recent tax cuts and military expenditures—it's actually a modest proposal," he wrote. (Pickard's *Jacobin* article appeared before Trump's authorization of the CARES Act; the $30 billion necessary to create a truly public media system would cost less than 1.4 percent of the CARES Act expenditures.)

Without incessant commercial pressures, journalists could "practice the craft that led them to the profession in the first place." This kind of journalism, Pickard wrote, "could devote unwavering attention to combatting social injustice," laying bare the "social costs of policy failure and the structural roots of inequality."

While corporate news outlets have reported the ongoing demise of newspapers and especially local news sources, they have rarely covered proposals such as Aaron's and Pickard's to revitalize journalism through public funding—and when they have, the coverage has tended to be slight or belittling. For example, among the very few establishment news articles to address Aaron's piece,

---

"Now is the time to act. We need significant public investments in all corners of the economy, and journalism is no exception."

Craig Aaron, president, Free Press

---

the *Washington Post*'s Margaret Sullivan offered a relatively tepid endorsement.[81] Though corporate media have perhaps predictably afforded few positive mentions of publicly owned media, in May 2020 the *Washington Post* did run an editorial by Victor Pickard on the history of, and current potential for, municipal newspapers.[82]

11.
New Green Scare: Law Enforcement Crackdown on Environmental Activism

Elizabeth King, "The New Green Scare," *The Progressive*, October 6, 2019, https://progressive.org/magazine/the-new-green-scare-king-191001/.

Student Researcher: Rebecca Noelke (Indian River State College)

Faculty Evaluator: Elliot D. Cohen (Indian River State College)

As scientists warn of imminent climate change, environmental welfare activists in the United States are facing growing legal penalties and a crackdown by law enforcement agencies designed to counteract environmental activism.[83] Dubbed the "New Green Scare," this resurgence of the state siding with corporations that engage in environmental exploitation is leading to mounting legal concerns for activists.

As Elizabeth King explained in an October 2019 *Progressive* magazine article, while the Trump administration's corporate-friendly policies dramatically endanger the health of our environment, those who take direct action in its defense are increasingly being framed as domestic terrorists. The FBI and pro-fossil fuel politicians like Oklahoma senator James Inhofe have identified environmental activism as a significant domestic terrorism threat.

Environmental protesters often risk incarceration and drawn-out legal battles for charges such as trespassing, sabotage, burglary, and terrorism. For example, the Dakota Access Pipeline protests, in which the Standing Rock Sioux Tribe sought to protect their water from the construction of the pipeline, resulted in a total of 836 criminal cases. A number of US states, including Texas and North Dakota, have enacted new laws to target environmental activists, and seven states have even instituted laws that specifically target pipeline protesters. The expansion of "critical infrastructure" laws to include pipelines puts activists who protest against such environmentally dangerous projects at risk of enhanced legal penalties.

Meanwhile, in West Virginia, activist Holden Dometrius was charged in April 2019 with a felony threat of terroristic acts for chaining himself to construction equipment being used to build the Mountain Valley Pipeline, a project that "poses a major threat to the local ecology, including many endangered species," King reported. Since then, other nonviolent Mountain Valley Pipeline protestors—who would have previously been charged with misdemeanors—are now being charged with felonies.

State-level laws to restrict eco-activism are frequently based on model legislation drafted by the American Legislative Exchange Council (ALEC), and have often been introduced by politicians with direct ties to ALEC, King wrote. Funded by conservative billionaire Charles Koch and dozens of other large corporations, ALEC is the driving force behind much of the "critical infrastructure" legislation being passed by state legislatures throughout the country.

In late March 2020, amid the coronavirus outbreak, three Republican-controlled state legislatures—in South Dakota, West Virginia, and Kentucky—passed laws criminalizing fossil fuel protests.[84]

While corporate media outlets are paying increased attention to topics such as climate change and the Green New Deal endorsed by some Democratic candidates in their 2020 primary election campaigns, they have generally disregarded the fact that the government is criminalizing eco-activist protest and direct action. The passage of state legislation in South Dakota, West Virginia, and Kentucky assigning criminal penalties for protests directed at pipelines and other fossil fuel facilities was largely covered by outlets outside the corporate media establishment, including HuffPost, The Hill, and the Weather Channel.[85]

12.

Police Officers Implicated in Online Hate Groups as Facebook Profits

Will Carless and Michael Corey, "To Protect and Slur," Reveal (Center for Investigative Reporting), June 14, 2019, http://www.revealnews.org/article/inside-hate-groups-on-facebook-police-officers-trade-racist-memes-conspiracy-theories-and-islamophobia/ [Part One of a three-part series].

Nick Statt, "Hundreds of Active and Former Police Officers are Part of Extremist Facebook Groups," The Verge, June 14, 2019, https://www.theverge.com/2019/6/14/18679598/facebook-hate-groups-law-enforcement-police-officers-racism-islamaphobia.

Alex Kotch, "Facebook is Making Millions by Promoting Hate Groups' Content," Sludge, September 25, 2019, https://readsludge.com/2019/09/25/facebook-is-making-millions-by-promoting-hate-groups-content/.

Student Researchers: Michelle Ann Stanton and Andrea Hernandez-Chavez (Sonoma State University)

Faculty Evaluator: Erica Tom (Sonoma State University)

According to an investigation by Reveal, the media platform for the nonprofit Center for Investigative Reporting, hundreds of US police officers are members of misogynistic, homophobic, racist, anti-Muslim, Confederate, or anti-government militia groups on Facebook. From a sheriff's deputy in Missouri posting anti-Muslim rants to a Georgia officer who shared Confederate memes, "[h]undreds of active-duty and retired" officers "at every level of American law enforcement" are members of hate groups on Facebook, Will Carless and Michael Corey reported.

As Nick Statt wrote in an article published by The Verge in June 2019, "The unifying thread to all of these Facebook groups is that they are frequented and sometimes founded and operated by active and retired police officers, and that they actively recruit other police officers to join."

This is so despite Facebook hate speech policies that ban content targeting individuals based on their race, ethnicity, or religion. Facebook also has rules against violent incitement by groups that have been known to organize and act offline.

However, as Alex Kotch reported for Sludge in September 2019, Facebook profits from promoting hate groups' content. Based on a Sludge study of Facebook ad data, Kotch reported that, between May 2018 and September 2019, "at least 38 hate groups and hate figures, or their political campaigns, paid Facebook nearly $1.6 million to run 4,921 sponsored ads."

According to the Sludge report, nearly $960,000 of these ad revenues could be traced to anti-immigrant groups, $542,000 was spent by anti-LGBTQ groups, and anti-Muslim groups spent nearly $70,000 on ads.

Corporate media coverage of US police involvement in hate groups has been limited. For example, an article published by the *Washington Post* in July 2019 addressed the topic but effectively defended Facebook by emphasizing the difficulties involved in monitoring so many private groups.[86] Also in July 2019, NBC Philadelphia reported that thirteen city police officers would be removed from the force due to violent, homophobic, or racist posts on their Facebook accounts.[87] These thirteen individuals were determined to be the "worst" of the 328 officers being investigated, according to the NBC Philadelphia report.

13.
Lessons from Colorado's Voting System

Amy Goodman and Juan González, interview with Jena Griswold, "Colorado Has One of the Highest Voter Turnouts in the Country. Here's How They Did It," *Democracy Now!*, November 5, 2019, https://www.democracynow.org/2019/11/5/colorado_mail_in_voting_voter_turnout.

Student Evaluator: Kenzie Parker (Sonoma State University)

Faculty Evaluator: Peter Phillips (Sonoma State University)

Colorado boasts "the highest percentage of eligible citizens registered to vote," and its voter participation rates are "often the first or second for the entire nation," Colorado Secretary of State Jena Griswold told *Democracy Now!* in a November 2019 interview. The state's voting measures include same-day voter registration, automatic registration with driver's license services, the extension of voting rights to people on parole, and allowances for some seventeen-year-olds to vote in primary elections. As a result, Amy Goodman reported, Colorado is "considered an example for states needing to expand voter access at a time when Republican legislatures and statehouses across the country are attempting to suppress the vote."

Colorado's mail-in voting system was established "with bipartisan support" in 2013, Griswold explained. "Republican county clerks pushed [for] these reforms," in part because the mail-in system is more efficient and less expensive than in-person voting. The mail-in voting system also supports the state's commitment "to make sure that every eligible Coloradan's voice is heard," Griswold told *Democracy Now!* Although every registered, eligible voter receives a mail-in ballot, people can vote in person if they prefer to do so.

In 2019 the Colorado legislature passed the Colorado Votes Act—which added polling places and mail-in drop boxes throughout the state, including on the campuses of public universities and, with tribal leadership authorization, on tribal lands—and the Restore Voting Rights Parolees law, which enfranchised nearly 11,500 Coloradans on parole.[88]

Colorado's voting reforms "shine in stark contrast to the voter suppression we see across this country," Secretary of State Griswold told *Democracy Now!*

The COVID-19 pandemic has made mail-in voting a hot topic, especially since President Trump and other Republicans have expressed opposition to it on the spurious grounds that voting by mail is prone to fraud.[89] Without endorsing that stance, the *New York Times* has reported skeptically on mail-in voting. For instance, an April 2020 article noted that "many, if not most, states would face daunting financial, logistical and personnel challenges to making mail balloting the norm."[90]

The Washington Post featured an opinion piece by former Colorado governor John Hickenlooper, advocating for the nation to adopt a mail-in voting system modeled after Colorado's.[91] The nation "can't afford a repeat in November" of the "election chaos" experienced by Wisconsin voters in April, after the state's Republican legislators and Supreme Court forced voters and poll workers "to risk covid-19 infection to participate in American democracy," Hickenlooper wrote. The experience of Colorado, along with Washington and Oregon, which also use mail-in voting, "has laid the groundwork for just this moment, when mail-in voting in a national election could be vital to protecting Americans' health—and the health of our democracy." Responding to concerns of fraud, Hickenlooper touted Colorado's use of "rigorous risk-limiting audits" and a centralized database to verify voters' signatures, as well as perhaps the fundamental advantage of mailed ballots—"paper can't be hacked," he wrote. But beyond this opinion piece, the *Washington Post*—like other establishment media outlets—has not reported on Colorado's example as a model of expanding voter access and making elections more democratic.

14.
The Case for a Public Pharmaceutical System

Fran Quigley, "Removing the Profit from Our Pills: The Case for a Public Pharma System," Common Dreams, September 18, 2019, https://www.commondreams.org/views/2019/09/18/removing-profit-our-pills-case-public-pharma-system.

Dean Baker, "Replace Patent Monopolies with Direct Public Funding for Drug Research," Truthout, July 1, 2019, https://truthout.org/articles/replace-patent-monopolies-with-direct-public-funding-for-drug-research/.

Alan MacLeod, "Economist Dean Baker: Systemic Change Needed to Fight Big Pharma Price Gouging," MintPress News, December 12, 2019, https://www.mintpressnews.com/dean-baker-gilead-hiv-pofits-drug-prices/263412/.

Zain Rizvi, "Blind Spot: How the COVID-19 Outbreak Shows the Limits of Pharma's Monopoly Model," Public Citizen, February 19, 2020, https://www.citizen.org/article/blind-spot/.

Student Researchers: Jennifer Pope (San Francisco State University) and Amber Yang (Sonoma State University)

Faculty Evaluator: Kenn Burrows (San Francisco State University)

A September 2019 report by the Democracy Collaborative outlined a model for a democratic public pharmaceutical system, as Fran Quigley reported for Common Dreams. According to the report, the existing pharmaceutical industry, which depends on government-granted patent monopolies, "operates on an extractive model that contributes to inequality and increasingly produces drug shortages, inefficiency, lagging innovation, misinformation and misuse of medications, and most famously, the world's highest drug prices."[92] Instead of piecemeal reform of existing patent and anti-trust laws or government provisions of health insurance—any of which could later be repealed—public ownership of pharmaceutical development, production, and distribution offers a systemic approach to fixing Big Pharma's most fundamental flaws, according to "Medicine for All," the Democracy Collaborative's report.

The Democracy Collaborative model includes plans for a national public pharmaceutical research and development institute for developing new drugs to meet public health needs; state, local, and regional public pharmaceutical manufacturers; regionally owned and operated public wholesale distributors; and engaging the US Postal Service as a partner for pharmaceutical distribution.[93]

As Fran Quigley wrote for Common Dreams, the foundation for these changes is "already in place" because public funding "has long been the bedrock of pharmaceutical research and development." From 2010 to 2016, "every single one" of 210 newly approved drugs traced their origins back to taxpayer-sponsored research, Quigley reported, based on a study published by *PNAS* in March 2018.[94]

In almost every case, Dean Baker wrote in Truthout in July 2019, drugs are "cheap to manufacture," but government-granted patent monopolies make them expensive for consumers. Both Baker's Truthout article and a report for MintPress News by Alan MacLeod addressed the explanations for high drug prices typically made by defenders of the current system. In the existing model, "it is expensive to develop new drugs" and patent monopolies provide companies incentives to take the risks necessary to do so, Baker related. But, he wrote, there is "nothing natural" about a patent-based system for financing drug research and development. Instead, patent monopolies give drug companies "an enormous incentive to push their drugs as widely as possible." The opioid crisis, he noted, is an extreme case of how drug companies exaggerate their drugs' benefits and conceal their negative side effects. But, Baker wrote, "Purdue Pharma would not have been pushing OxyContin so vigorously if it were selling at generic prices."[95]

The current system also leads to lost government revenues—which could otherwise be directed to healthcare and public services—through tax evasion: As revealed by the Panama Papers, in 2015 ten of the thirty US companies holding the most money offshore were pharmaceutical companies, which together held more than $506 billion in offshore accounts not subject to US taxes.[96]

Publicly-owned pharmaceuticals, freed from the financial demand to appease profit-hungry shareholders, would be able to focus on public health priorities, working hand-in-hand with public health departments, as they do in other countries, to assure an adequate supply of medications, priced to be accessible to the broadest array of

Americans. As Fran Quigley reported for Common Dreams, Sweden, Brazil, Cuba, Thailand, and China (among others) "embrace public ownership in key components of their medicines systems," offering working examples of what could be achieved in the United States.

Although the United States has a reputation for being "politically and culturally suspicious of public systems replacing markets," two-thirds of Americans "support making prescription drugs public goods paid for by the federal government," and eight in ten support "breaking patent monopolies to reduce drug prices," Quigley reported.[97]

In February 2020, Public Citizen published a report showing how the COVID-19 pandemic has exposed the limits of Big Pharma's monopoly model. Public Citizen's "Blind Spot" report determined that, since the 2002 severe acute respiratory syndrome (SARS) outbreak, the National Institutes of Health have invested "nearly $700 million [in taxpayer funding] on coronavirus R&D." Indeed, all six of the coronavirus clinical trials active in 2019 "depended crucially on public funding." Although "more sustained interest in coronaviruses could have provided greater scientific understanding, and a stronger toolkit to inform the latest response," Zain Rizvi wrote, the private sector has lagged behind in developing treatments for infectious diseases because they are "less lucrative" than medicines for chronic conditions and rare diseases. As Rizvi's Public Citizen report concluded, the COVID-19 crisis highlights the "urgent need" for an alternative to the existing "monopoly-based model," which prioritizes short-term corporate profits over public health.

While consistently covering partisan political disputes

over prescription drug prices, corporate news media have been relatively mute in reporting on proposals to develop a public pharmaceutical alternative to Big Pharma. In particular, as of May 2020 no corporate news outlets appear to have covered the Democracy Collaborative's "Medicine for All" report.

15.
Indigenous Trauma and Suicide an Enduring Legacy of Colonialism

Devon Heinen, "Nobody to Call: The Plight of Indigenous Suicide in Alaska," *New Statesman*, January 10, 2020, https://www.newstatesman.com/2019/12/nobody-call-indigenous-suicides-alaska.

"Tribe Faces Suicide Crisis," Mountain West News, July 23, 2019, https://mountainwestnews.org/rockies-today-for-tuesday-july-23-99e8bc80babc.

Claudette Commanda and Louise Bradley, "We Must Not Forget Men When We Talk about Indigenous Trauma," *The Globe and Mail*, June 16, 2019, https://www.theglobeandmail.com/opinion/article-we-must-not-forget-men-when-we-talk-about-indigenous-trauma/.

Allison Martell, "Deaths, Bad Outcomes Elude Scrutiny at Canada's Indigenous Clinics," Reuters, October 24, 2019, https://www.reuters.com/article/us-canada-health-insight/deaths-bad-outcomes-elude-scrutiny-at-canadas-indigenous-clinics-idUSKBN1X3152.

Student Researchers: Danna Henderson (First Nations University of Canada), Olivia Page (College of Marin), and Alicia Morrow (University of Regina)

Faculty Evaluators: Patricia W. Elliott (First Nations University of Canada), Susan Rahman (College of Marin), and Kehinde Olalafe (University of Regina)

From evidence of neglect at government-run clinics in Canada's northern reserves to the tragic loss of lives in remote villages in Alaska and on reservation lands in Montana, independent news coverage helps to frame the otherwise underreported issue of Indigenous mistreatment and suicide in historical terms, against the backdrops of settler colonialism and systemic racism that affect Indigenous people and their communities in Canada and the United States.

Indigenous suicide is a serious public health issue throughout the United States, Devon Heinen reported for the *New Statesman* in January 2020. In 2017 the combined suicide rate for US Indigenous peoples was 22.15 per 100,000 people, compared with an overall national average of 16.3 per 100,000 people, according to the Suicide Prevention Resource Center, Heinen reported. In Alaska—where 229 of the 573 federally-recognized American Indian and Alaska Native tribes and villages in the United States are located—the Indigenous suicide rate from 1999 to 2009 was 42.5 per 100,000 people.

In Montana, Native youths aged 11 to 24 are five times more likely to die by suicide than non-Natives, according to data from the Montana Department of Health and Human Services, Mountain West News reported in July 2019. The suicide rate for Native youths in Montana is 42.82 per 100,000 people, compared with eight suicides per 100,000 people for all people in the same age range. Mountain West News reported that, over a period of three months, the Fort Belknap Reservation had experienced a "suicide contagion," with three suicides and an estimated fifteen additional suicide attempts prompting the Fort Belknap Indian Community Council to declare a state of emergency.

As other reports documented, suicide has devastated First Nations communities in Canada. In June 2019, Claudette Commanda and Louise Bradley reported that suicide and self-inflicted injuries are "the leading cause of death" for First Nations youth and adults up to age 44. In November 2019, the Makwa Sahgaiehcan First

Nation declared a state of emergency after a rash of suicides, and the deaths of four Indigenous men by suicide on Ochapowace First Nation led Ochapowace to declare a state of emergency in December 2019.[98] While affirming "the resiliency and strength of Indigenous peoples," Commanda and Bradley wrote that "high rates of suicide, homicide, incarceration and substance abuse born of colonial trauma illustrate the pain and suffering that Indigenous communities continue to experience." The impacts have been especially stark for First Nations male youth, for whom the suicide rate is 126 per 100,000, they noted.

"The challenge that we face collectively," Commanda and Bradley wrote, "is to draw a narrative thread through numbers that point to pain and hurt and give it a human voice."

Devon Heinen's January 2020 report for the *New Statesman* shows how independent investigative journalism can contribute to this aim. Heinen reported in detail on the experience of one Iñupiaq family in the aftermath of the death by suicide of Rosie Hadley, at age twenty. Drawing on extensive interviews with Hadley's family and those who knew her—Heinen conducted 27 separate interviews over four months with Rosie's father, Nathan Hadley—Heinen's report provided a vivid, detailed account of Rosie's life and the community of Buckland, population 400, in Alaska's remote and sparsely populated Northwest Arctic Borough.[99] Through its intimate investigation of one family's experience in the context of their community, the local lack of necessary social services, and the living legacy of the region's colonial history, Heinen's report provides a stark insight into one aspect of Indigenous suicide as a public health issue—how, in his words, "to help people heal after losing someone close."[100]

An October 2019 report by Reuters documented how government-run or -sponsored health clinics in Canada are failing to provide Indigenous communities with necessary services.

For more than nine years, the Canadian federal government has not consistently tracked, let alone investigated, poor outcomes at clinics on Indigenous reserves, Allison Martell reported. These clinics, known as nursing stations, are charged with providing basic and emergency care to about 115,000 people. Through analysis of documents,

> **"The challenge that we face collectively is to draw a narrative thread through numbers that point to pain and hurt and give it a human voice."**
>
> Claudette Commanda and Louise Bradley

including internal reports and meeting notes obtained through public records requests, Martell reported that record-keeping on deaths and other "critical incidents" at the clinics has been "erratic and fragmented." Reuters documented at least two cases—one in Ontario, and another in Manitoba—in which nursing station officials turned away apparently intoxicated patients who subsequently died. Lack of adequate official records made it "difficult" to determine whether this "has been a widespread practice," Martell reported, but a coroner's verdict on one of the deaths described it as the "northern protocol."

"We are treating members of the First Nations communities as second-class citizens," Emily Hill, a senior staff lawyer with Aboriginal Legal Services, told Reuters. Martell wrote that Reuters's findings on deadly negligence in Canada's nursing stations came as Canada is "in the midst of a public reckoning with the legacy of settler colonization."

Recent corporate news coverage on Indigenous suicide and other trauma associated with the destructive legacies of colonization has not been proportionate to the scope of the crisis—with only a few notable exceptions. In August 2019, for example, *U.S. News & World Report* published a brief Associated Press report on the Fort Belknap community's response to suicides.[101] This seven-sentence article drew heavily from previous, more substantial local reporting by the *Billings Gazette*. In June 2019 *USA Today* reported, in more detail, on Native Americans' "increased risk of suicide," in light of the experience of Shelby Rowe, the executive director of the Arkansas Crisis Center, after she experienced a suicide crisis herself.[102] In April 2018 the *New York Times* published a powerful, detailed story about the Arlee Warriors, a state championship high school basketball team from Montana's Flathead Indian Reservation, and its team members' efforts to help their community deal with suicide.[103]

16.

International Law Could Hold US Accountable for Violating Detained Immigrant Children's Rights

Michael Garcia Bochenek and Warren Binford, "The U.S. is Mistreating Children in Its Custody. Can International Law Help?" *American Prospect*, August 15, 2019, https://prospect.org/article/us-mistreating-children-its-custody-can-international-law-help.

Student Researcher: Christina Chacon Sanchez (City College of San Francisco)

Faculty Evaluator: Jennifer Levinson (City College of San Francisco)

After a host of media outlets' front-page headlines reported that thousands of immigrant children had been forcibly separated from their families by US officials, in June 2018 the Trump administration announced an end to its family separation policy, and a federal court ordered the reunification of separated families. However, as Michael Garcia Bochenek and Warren Binford reported for the *American Prospect* in August 2019, when they investigated US Border Patrol facilities in El Paso, Texas, in June 2019, "child after child sat before us describing when and how U.S. officials forcibly separated them from their families this year." The report documented the deplorable conditions and emotional abuse that detained children endured—but also how international law could help to hold US officials to account for violations of children's rights. The UN Convention on the Rights of the Child—which the United States helped draft between 1979 and 1989, and which it officially signed in 1995—could mobilize international pressure on the United States to address these violations, Bochenek and Binford reported.

Under US law, children should not be held in custody by Border Patrol for more than 72 hours. Beyond that time, detained children are supposed to be transferred to the custody of the Department of Health and Human Services, and either reunified with family in the United States or placed in the custody of another caregiver. However, Bochenek and Binford reported that, earlier in 2019, the Border Patrol "was detaining children for more than 90 days on average, in violation of both these legal limits and the children's rights."

The UN Convention on the Rights of the Child is the "most widely ratified human rights treaty in the world," Bochenek and Binford wrote, and some of its specific terms are "now norms of customary international law," indicative of a "global consensus" regarding all countries' obligations to respect children's rights. But, they also noted, "no president has ever sent [the treaty] to the Senate for ratification, the formal agreement to be bound by its terms," making the United States the only signatory among UN member countries not to have done so.

What steps could be taken to make a strong argument that US violations of children's rights violated US obligations under international law? One possible avenue, as Bochenek and Binford considered, is "the regular accounting every U.N. member has to make at the Human Rights Council, a process known as Universal Periodic Review."[104] In 2006 the UN General Assembly mandated the United Nations's newly formed Human Rights Council to undertake "a universal periodic review, based on objective and reliable information, of the fulfilment by each State of its human rights obligations and commitments in a manner which ensures universality of coverage and equal treatment with respect to all States."[105]

In November 2020, when the United States is next up for review, every other UN member will "be able to ask questions and make comments and recommendations on U.S. respect for the Universal Declaration of Human Rights, its voluntary commitments, and its treaty and customary international law obligations," Bochenek and Binford wrote.[106] Furthermore, during that review process, NGOs can submit information—including statements from detained children themselves—to inform those discussions.[107]

While noting that Universal Periodic Review is "not a court process" and that "real change" will likely have to come through domestic strategies (such as the lawsuits being brought against the US government by the American Civil Liberties Union), Bochenek and Binford nonetheless asserted that there is "real value in the political pressure of regular review by other countries." Member states of the United Nations and NGOs submitting statements could invoke the UN Convention on the Rights of the Child to pressure the United States to act.

Reports of abuse of immigrant children in US detention have made headlines in the best-known US news media. For example, in July 2019, Fox News reported on inhospitable detention center conditions for migrant children.[108] The article reported that, "[o]f the 2,669 children detained by the Border Patrol, 826 had been held longer than 72 hours"—though the 72-hour maximum timeframe was described by Fox News not as binding law but as "generally permitted under Customs and Border Protection standards." Bochenek and Binford's *American Prospect* article remains distinctive in highlighting how international law, including the United Nations's Universal Periodic Review and its Convention on the Rights of the Child, could be mobilized to pressure US policymakers to reform policies that have led to cruel consequences for detained children and their families.

17.
International Plasma Market Profits from US and Mexico's Poorest

Stefanie Dodt, Jan Lukas Strozyk, and Dara Lind, "Pharmaceutical Companies are Luring Mexicans across the U.S. Border to Donate Blood Plasma," ProPublica (in conjunction with ARD German TV), October 4, 2019, https://www.propublica.org/article/pharmaceutical-companies-are-luring-mexicans-across-the-u.s.-border-to-donate-blood-plasma.

Lauren Villagran and Stefanie Dodt, "Blood for Money," Searchlight New Mexico (in conjunction with ARD German TV), October 22, 2019, https://web.archive.org/web/20200222024850/https://www.searchlightnm.org/blood-for-money.

Alan MacLeod, "Harvesting the Blood of America's Poor: The Latest Stage of Capitalism," MintPress News, December 3, 2019, https://www.mintpressnews.com/harvesting-blood-americas-poor-late-stage-capitalism/263175/.

Abby Zimet, "In Late-Stage Zombie Capitalism, the Poor are Selling Their Blood," Common Dreams, December 9, 2019, https://www.commondreams.org/further/2019/12/09/late-stage-zombie-capitalism-poor-are-selling-their-blood.

Student Researchers: Tuuli Rantasalo (University of Regina), Meagan Cummins (University of Vermont), and Allegra Wu (University of Vermont)

Faculty Evaluators: Suliman Adam (University of Regina) and Rob Williams (University of Vermont)

US hospitals are currently desperate for blood donors: more than 4000 blood drives were canceled because of the coronavirus pandemic, according to a March 2020 letter co-signed by the AABB, America's Blood Centers, and the American Red Cross.[109] The situation, which resulted in the loss of 130,000 anticipated donations, is unprecedented, according to Claudia Cohn, AABB's chief medical officer and director of the blood bank at the University of Minnesota Medical Center.[110]

Meanwhile, international corporations that operate

donation centers in the United States are buying the blood of poor people from Mexico and the United States and selling the plasma overseas.

Mexican citizens cross the border into the United States to donate their blood plasma at various donation sites established by Big Pharma, according to an October 2019 report from ProPublica. The donation centers are mainly owned by Grifols, a Spanish company that operates seventeen donation centers along the US–Mexico border; CSL, an Australian company; BPL, "an emerging player" headquartered in the United Kingdom; and GCAM Inc., a US firm with four centers along the borderlands, ProPublica reported.

"Donate" is the term these companies prefer to use, but Mexicans are selling their plasma for cash rewards, including bonuses for referring new donors. The companies attract Mexican citizens to the United States because plasma donation is illegal in Mexico, and firms know that prospective donors are likely in desperate need of extra income. "The donors, including some who say the payments are their only income, may take home up to $400 a month," ProPublica reported, an amount that exceeds monthly salaries in border-based assembly plants and many middle-class jobs in Mexico.

Donating blood plasma repeatedly can be detrimental to donors' health. Excessive donation can weaken the immune system, making donors more susceptible to diseases and infections. The United States provides few legal protections for donors. According to ProPublica, "Unlike other nations that limit or forbid paid plasma donations at a high frequency out of concern for donor health and quality control, the U.S. allows companies to pay donors and has comparatively loose standards for monitoring their health." The United States is the largest supplier of blood plasma in a $21 billion global market, according to ProPublica's report.

A 2018 study of US plasma donation centers, conducted by researchers at Case Western Reserve University and MetroHealth Medical Center, found that 57 percent of plasma donors in the study made more than a third of their monthly income (up to $250–300) by donating plasma, and 70 percent of these donors experienced side effects from donation, including weakness, bruising, dehydration, and fainting.[III]

Alan MacLeod of MintPress News identified paid blood donations as indicative of capitalism's latest stage: "In a very real sense," he wrote, "corporations are harvesting the blood of the poor, literally sucking the life out of them." With sales of $28.6 billion in 2017, exports from the United States accounted for 70 percent of the plasma available on the international market, MacLeod reported. From 2016 to 2017, blood exports increased by more than 13 percent. While human blood is not yet sold on the futures markets, plasma increasingly is becoming a global commodity, with some of those selling their blood reporting that its value fluctuates—on some days they earn $75 for a donation, while on other days they make just $20.

A 2006 book, Catherine Waldby and Robert Mitchell's *Tissue Economies*, anticipated this phenomenon, but it has continued to develop outside the scope of establishment news coverage, with a few exceptions.[112] *The El Paso Times*, a subsidiary of *USA Today*, republished a version of Villagran and Dodt's "Blood for Money" report for Searchlight New Mexico.[113] In February 2019 the *New York Times* reported on the "booming" plasma donation business in the United States, noting that, in 2016, blood products accounted for 1.9 percent of all American exports.[114] *The Times*'s report drew on the Case Western Reserve/MetroHealth Medical Center study and addressed the exploitative nature of for-profit plasma donations in the United States, where the plasma for which donors are paid $30 will be worth $300 on the global market. In addition to the sources cited here, independent coverage of the topic has included reports by *The Atlantic*, Axios, and *Latino USA*, a radio program distributed by NPR.[115]

18.
Trump Labor Board Assaults Workers' Rights

Jessica Corbett, "Progressives Blast New NLRB Union Elections Rule That 'Betrays the Workers It is Meant to Protect,'" Common Dreams, December 13, 2019, https://www.commondreams.org/news/2019/12/13/progressives-blast-new-nlrb-union-elections-rule-betrays-workers-it-meant-protect.

William Lewis, "Trump Labor Board Escalates War on Workers' Rights," Truthout, December 21, 2019, https://truthout.org/articles/trump-labor-board-escalates-war-on-workers-rights/.

Lynn Rhinehart, "Under Trump the NLRB Has Gone Completely Rogue," *The Nation*, April 7, 2020, https://www.thenation.com/article/politics/nlrb-workers-rights-trump/.

Student Researcher: Cem Ismail Addemir (North Central College)

Faculty Evaluator: Steve Macek (North Central College)

On December 13, 2019, the Trump administration's National Labor Relations Board (NLRB)—the federal agency charged with enforcing labor law and overseeing union certification elections—escalated its assault against workers' rights by abruptly changing the rules of union elections, without notice or public comment. According to a December 21, 2019, article by William Lewis in Truthout, "Starting in six months, when workers petition for an election, they must wait at least 14 business days until a pre-election hearing."

The NLRB was created by the Wagner Act of 1935 and is charged with protecting workers' rights to unionize and collectively bargain with employers. It consists of up to five politically appointed board members. At the moment, there are only three members of the board—all pro-business Republican lawyers.[116]

Under the new NLRB rules, not only must workers who have asked for a certification election wait fourteen days for a hearing, but the board also has the power to

---

"These changes put unions at a major disadvantage, since employers now have more time to inundate workers with anti-union propaganda in the lead-up to an election."

---

postpone pre-election hearings any time they find "good cause." After a two-week waiting period for a hearing, the scope of the bargaining unit and the eligibility of individual employees to vote in a certification election is subject to litigation. These changes put unions at a major disadvantage, since employers now have more time to inundate workers with anti-union propaganda in the lead-up to an election.

As Lewis noted, if a union looks like it might manage to win a certification vote, "the unelected NLRB now has the ability to suspend the election to resolve any ongoing disputes over the bargaining unit." Moreover, recent changes to NLRB rules make it easier to decertify legally recognized collective bargaining units.

Though these NLRB rule changes erect yet more "legal hurdles" to workers seeking to form a union, Lewis wrote that businesses seeking to prevent their workers from unionizing "can also simply break the law." He cited a 2019 Economic Policy Institute study that found more than 40 percent of employers in union certification elections resort to "unfair labor practices aimed at undermining electoral procedures and retaliating against pro-union workers."[117]

There has been no corporate news coverage of the changes to the NLRB regulations governing union elections. Aside from articles in independent media outlets Truthout and Common Dreams, the only coverage of the NLRB's rule changes has come from two legal news sites, Bloomberg Law and the National Law Review, that reported in detail on the NLRB's actions and included additional information about how the new rules overturn Obama-era regulations designed to streamline union election procedures.[118]

19.
Antibiotic Abuse: Pharmaceutical Profiteering Accelerates Superbugs

Madlen Davies, Rahul Meesaraganda, and Ben Stockton, "Drug Company Reps Give Quack Doctors Fridges and Televisions to Sell Antibiotics," Bureau of Investigative Journalism, August 19, 2019, https://www.thebureauinvestigates.com/stories/2019-08-19/drug-company-reps-give-quack-doctors-fridges-and-televisions-to-sell-antibiotics.

Student Researcher: Allison Rott (North Central College)

Faculty Evaluator: Steve Macek (North Central College)

Pharmaceutical giants Abbott and Sun Pharma are providing dangerous amounts of antibiotics to unlicensed doctors in India and incentivizing them to overprescribe. In August 2019 the Bureau of Investigative Journalism (BIJ) reported that these unethical business practices are leading to a rise in superbugs, or bacterial infections that are resistant to antibiotic treatment. Bacteria naturally evolve a resistance to antibiotics over time, but the widespread and inappropriate use of antibiotics accelerates this process. Superbugs are killing at least 58,000 babies each year and rendering a growing number of patients untreatable with all available drugs.

India's unlicensed medical practitioners, known as "quack" doctors, are being courted by Abbott and Sun Pharma, billion-dollar companies that do business in more than one hundred countries, including the United States. The incentives these companies provide to quack doctors to sell antibiotics have included free medical equipment, gift cards, televisions, travel, and cash, earning some doctors nearly a quarter of their salary. "Sales representatives would also offer extra pills or money as an incentive to buy more antibiotics, encouraging potentially dangerous overprescription," a Sun Pharma sales representative revealed to an undercover BIJ reporter.

India offers free healthcare to its poor citizens, but its healthcare system has an estimated shortage of 600,000 doctors and millions of trained nurses. India's 2.5 million quack doctors vastly outnumber its one million certified doctors. As a result, patients without access to better care often turn to quack doctors for treatment, and many are unaware that their local medical "professionals" have no formal training and are being bribed to sell unnecessary antibiotics.

In September 2019, the BIJ reported on similar problems with broken healthcare systems, medical corruption, and dangerous superbugs in Cambodia.[119] Their account describes how patients often request antibiotics for common colds, to pour onto wounds, and to feed to animals. Illegally practicing doctors and pharmacists in Cambodia admitted that they would often prescribe based on customer requests rather than appropriate medical guidelines. As the BIJ noted, "This kind of misuse speeds up the creation of drug resistant bacteria, or superbugs, which are predicted to kill 10 million people by 2050 if no action is taken."

Although India is generally acknowledged as the epicenter of this growing global threat, there has been little coverage on the shady business practices in India by companies like Abbott and Sun Pharma. In 2017, HuffPost discussed the findings of a 2016 PLOS Medicine study on antibiotic resistance in India, but only briefly mentioned the role of pharmaceutical companies and their sales representatives, failing to identify them as a driving force in the growing problem.[120] A 2019 *Telegraph* article identified the role of doctor shortages in the rise of antibiotic resistance, but did not discuss pharmaceutical companies as being part of the problem.[121]

The only substantial corporate reporting on the unethical sale of antibiotics came from a six-month investigation by the *New York Times* in 2016 that found pharmaceutical representatives from Abbott pressuring their India-based employees to sell to quack doctors, plainly in violation of Indian law and the company's own ethical guidelines.[122] However, the article did not make any connection between these practices and the rise of superbugs in India.

Although superbugs have attracted some attention, their cause and importance remain poorly understood by the public. The Independent and BuzzFlash republished the Bureau of Investigative Journalism's report; otherwise, the role of pharmaceutical companies in the rise of dangerous superbugs has been drastically underreported.[123]

20.
A Comprehensive Framework for Transforming the Criminal-Legal System

Jessica Corbett, "'Vision for Justice': 117 Rights Groups Offer Roadmap to Transform US Criminal-Legal System," Common Dreams, September 5, 2019, https://www.commondreams.org/news/2019/09/05/vision-justice-117-rights-groups-offer-roadmap-transform-us-criminal-legal-system.

Victoria Law, "Arrest, Release, Repeat: New Report Exposes Vicious Cycle of Imprisonment," Truthout, August 27, 2019, https://truthout.org/articles/arrest-release-repeat-new-report-exposes-vicious-cycle-of-imprisonment/.

Student Researchers: Xavier Rosenberg (San Francisco State University) and Carina Ramirez (Sonoma State University)

Faculty Evaluators: Kenn Burrows (San Francisco State University) and Peter Phillips (Sonoma State University)

Calling for policy solutions to dismantle the US system of criminal punishment and the inequalities and white supremacy that this system promotes and perpetuates, Alec Karakatsanis, the executive director of Civil Rights Corps, and 116 other human and civil rights groups released a comprehensive fourteen-point plan to "transform the existing system into one of respect and justice," Jessica Corbett reported for Common Dreams in September 2019.

The groups' "Vision for Justice" plan advocates an expanded view of public safety, prioritizing investments in education, housing, employment, healthcare, and other public programs, guided by three core themes: ensuring equity and accountability in the criminal-legal system, building a restorative system of justice, and rebuilding communities.[124] The plan's fourteen specific recommendations—such as creating a new framework for pretrial justice, and decriminalizing poverty—are rooted in human rights and the practice of restorative justice, Corbett reported.

A study by the Prison Policy Initiative (PPI), released in August 2019, underscored the need for comprehensive criminal justice reform. The study, titled "Arrest, Release, Repeat: How Police and Jails are Misused to Respond to Social Problems," showed that people imprisoned as repeat offenders are likely to be poor, unemployed, or homeless, Victoria Law reported for Truthout. Although police and jails ought to promote public safety, law enforcement is more and more frequently "called upon to respond punitively to medical and economic problems unrelated to public safety issues," according to the PPI study.[125] Consequently, people in need of medical care and social services "cycle in and out of jail without ever receiving the help they need." The study's authors found that repeated arrests are "related to race and poverty, as well as high rates of mental illness and substance use disorders."

According to the study, in 2017 at least 4.9 million individuals were arrested and booked, with the vast majority charged with nonviolent crimes. To better address the conditions that lead marginalized individuals to have contact with the police in the first place, the study's authors recommended "public investments in employment assistance, education and vocational training, and financial assistance."

As of May 2020, neither the "Vision for Justice" policy platform of the coalition of 117 rights groups nor the Prison Policy Initiative's report on how police and jails are misused to respond to social problems appear to have received any coverage by the establishment press.

21.
The Scourge of Human Trafficking in Yemen

Ahmed Abdulkareem, "Human Trafficking is Booming in Yemen as the War Enters Its Fifth Year," MintPress News, September 13, 2019, https://www.mintpressnews.com/human-trafficking-booming-yemen-war/261818/.

Student Researcher: Carlos Alfonso Gutierrez (Sonoma State University)

Faculty Evaluator: Amal Munayer (Sonoma State University)

Owing to the war launched in 2015 by a US-backed coalition of Arab countries, including Saudi Arabia, Yemen now suffers from "a complete absence" of law and order, which has given rise to what Ahmed Abdulkareem described for MintPress News as "a black *Suq* (market) of human trafficking on a scale never before seen in Yemen." Abdulkareem's report is partly based on the accounts of seventeen Yemeni victims of human trafficking who agreed to speak to MintPress News about their ordeals.

Due to lack of educational opportunities and economic collapse, Yemeni people are literally sacrificing their bodies to provide for their families. Between 2015 and 2017, more than ten thousand cases of organ sales have been documented by the Yemen Organization for Combating Human Trafficking, a Sana'a-based NGO. Actual figures are almost certainly higher, because many cases go unreported owing to the practice being illegal, religious concerns, and the stigma of the practice in a conservative society.

In one interview, a 35-year-old man named Tawfiq described selling one of his kidneys to sustain his family. He was relatively fortunate, because many Yemenis die in the process due to illegal, unprofessional procedures. Another Yemeni, named Aisha, who was forced to sell one of her kidneys, told MintPress News that she was paid $5000, though her kidney was sold for $30,000 on the black market.

A Yemeni named Maha told MintPress News that Yemeni brokers help secure passports by contacting staff members from the Yemeni Consulate in Saudi Arabia, who work together with a dealer from the organ black market. They produce a formal medical report to make it appear that the organ is from a legal donor. This clears the way for the sale of kidneys and other organs to neighboring countries.

A Yemeni family, who asked to remain anonymous, told MintPress News how their son was kidnapped. After the body was found, an autopsy showed that the boy's heart had been removed, presumably to be sold on the black market.

Trafficking involves not only human organs but also sexual exploitation. As Abdulkareem reported, trafficked Yemeni women are subjected to rape, violence, extreme cruelty, and other forms of coercion. Female trafficking victims who spoke to MintPress News reported being forced into prostitution networks in Saudi Arabia and the United Arab Emirates. From a rehabilitation center in Sana'a, one trafficking victim said that she was now afraid to return home for fear of being killed for violating her family's honor.

As Abdulkareem reported, the blockade levied against Yemen by the Saudi Coalition since 2015 has helped human trafficking flourish. Under blockade, Yemenis are no longer able to flee violence there or able to travel to neighboring wealthy Gulf countries for work. Furthermore, although Yemen's laws prohibit trafficking and those who are found guilty are sentenced to ten years in prison, these laws go unenforced, in part because government officials themselves appear to be directly involved in the trafficking and illegal organ sales.

Although US corporate news media have reported on forced labor, sexual exploitation, and the organ trade elsewhere in the Middle East, they appear to have devoted no specific coverage to the unprecedented scale of human trafficking taking place in Yemen.

22.
An Emergency Wealth Tax to Confront Coronavirus Pandemic

Larry Elliott, "Wealth Tax Rise Could Raise £174bn to Tackle COVID-19, Expert Says," *The Guardian*, April 22, 2020, https://www.theguardian.com/politics/2020/apr/22/wealth-tax-rise-could-raise-174bn-tackle-covid-19-expert-says.

John R. Talbott, "To Confront Coronavirus, We Need an Emergency Wealth Tax," Truthout, March 25, 2020, https://truthout.org/articles/to-confront-coronavirus-we-need-an-emergency-wealth-tax.

Student Researcher: Weston Pollock (San Francisco State University)

Faculty Evaluator: Kenn Burrows (San Francisco State University)

From March 18 to May 14, 2020, more than 36 million US workers lost their jobs, while the wealth of US billionaires increased by more than $368 billion, an increase of

12.5 percent.[126] The net worth of eight of these billionaires has increased by more than a billion dollars each.[127] An Institute for Policy Studies report, "Billionaire Bonanza 2020," recommended the establishment of a pandemic profiteering oversight committee, passage of a corporate transparency act to discourage wealth hiding, an emergency 10 percent millionaire income tax, and a wealth tax.[128] Acknowledging that enacting a new tax regime on assets would be "challenging in the short term," the report proposed an emergency 10 percent surtax on taxpayers with incomes of more than $2 million—that is, the richest 0.2 percent of Americans—which would apply not only to income from wages and salaries but also from investment returns. The proposed surtax would raise $635 billion over ten years, the Institute for Policy Studies estimated.

The UK government could raise "up to £174bn [roughly $213 billion] a year to help cope with the Covid-19 crisis if it taxed wealth at the same rate as income," the *Guardian* reported in April 2020. Richard Murphy, a professor of political economy at City, University of London, determined that between 2011 and 2018, the United Kingdom taxed income at an average of just 29.4 percent, while wealth—accrued through increased housing prices and personal pensions—had been taxed at just 3.4 percent, making UK taxes highly regressive: When income and wealth are combined, the effective tax rate for the wealthiest 10 percent of the population, the *Guardian* reported, was 18 percent, much less than the 42 percent effective tax rate for the poorest 10 percent.

Murphy told the *Guardian* he was not campaigning for a wealth tax as such, but that the UK government could begin to cover some of the coronavirus crisis bill by picking "low-hanging fruit," such as equalizing the tax rates on income and capital gains, reducing the annual capital gains tax allowance, and abolishing higher-rate tax reliefs for pension contributions.

In the United States, John R. Talbott reported for Truthout that at least one prominent Wall Street figure, Peter Fahey, a retired Goldman Sachs partner, supports a wealth tax to address the pandemic's toll on the economy. Fahey called on "a core group of thoughtful, patriotic billionaires to step forward" to subject themselves to "the equivalent of a substantial wealth tax to address the Federal budget crisis that will emerge from the COVID-19 crisis." Talbott himself advocated a "one-time 3 percent wealth tax on the top 10 percent of the wealthiest people in the world" to provide nine trillion dollars in global emergency relief funds.

Wealth tax proposals have received mixed news coverage in the corporate media. Before the pandemic, establishment news outlets, including the *New York Times* and *Washington Post*, reported on proposals made by Bernie Sanders and Elizabeth Warren in the context of the 2020 Democratic primary elections.[129] As the COVID-19 crisis has developed, additional outlets, including HuffPost, Bloomberg, ABC News, and the *New York Times* have also covered wealth tax proposals made in response to the pandemic. The pandemic is "the perfect opportunity for billionaires to justify their existence," HuffPost reported, but two months into the coronavirus outbreak "America is still waiting for billionaire philanthropists to deliver."[130] Bloomberg published an opinion piece by a former member of the *Financial Times*'s editorial board, opposing a wealth tax.[131] ABC News broadcast a report on the topic, featuring French economist Thomas Piketty, author of the book *Capital in the Twenty-First Century*. After Piketty responded to questions about how much tax he had paid on royalties from his surprise bestseller, he told ABC that the coronavirus crisis "illustrates a virulent inequality" that could lead to the kind of wealth taxes he has advocated.[132] In search of journalistic balance, ABC News also quoted from a Fox Business Network interview in which Larry Kudlow, President Trump's top economic advisor, asked, "Why do we have to raise taxes? ... Let's let people keep their own money." In April 2020 the *New York Times* published an editorial by Daniel Markovits, a professor at Yale Law School, advocating a 5 percent tax on the richest 5 percent of households as a means to raise up to $2 trillion in pandemic relief funds.[133]

23.
"Global Gag Rule" Continues to Compromise Women's Health around World

Monica Kerrigan and Nelly Munyasia, "Three Years Later, Trump's 'Global Gag Rule' Continues to Devastate Global Health," Rewire.News, January 23, 2020, https://rewire.news/article/2020/01/23/three-years-later-trumps-global-gag-rule-continues-to-devastate-global-health/.

Karen J. Coates, "The Global Gag Rule Puts a Choke Hold on Contraception," *Sierra*, November–December 2019, https://www.sierraclub.org/sierra/2019-6-november-december/protect/global-gag-rule-puts-choke-hold-contraception [first published online October 30, 2019].

Student Researcher: Madison Miller (North Central College)

Faculty Evaluator: Steve Macek (North Central College)

The United States's global gag rule continues to put at risk the sexual health of women in developing countries that rely on US aid. This federal rule—formally known as the "Mexico City Policy"—blocks access to the $9 billion of US federal funding for NGOs that provide abortion counseling, referrals, or any kind of abortion services throughout the world. In the first days of the new presidential term in January 2017, the Trump-Pence administration reinstated and drastically expanded the global gag rule. Three years after the implementation of the new guidelines, women continue to be harmed, Rewire.News and other independent news outlets reported.

The global gag rule was first implemented by the Reagan administration in 1984, and has continuously been changed, repealed, and reinstated through partisan presidencies. The Trump administration has advanced the strictest policies yet, expanding its scope to include other forms of assistance from the State Department, USAID, Department of Health and Human Services, and Department of Defense. The federal rule forces organizations to choose between receiving global health assistance from the United States and providing comprehensive reproductive care. The current enforcement of the policy, according to the Rewire.News report, denies funding for "HIV/AIDS prevention and treatment, nutrition, maternal health, family planning, and malaria."

According to the Sierra Club, British-based NGO Marie Stopes International, which works in 37 countries to provide contraception and safe abortions, suffered a huge funding gap for continuing to provide abortion services. Karen J. Coates reported that this cut in finances will lead to an estimated "1.8 million unintended pregnancies, 600,000 unsafe abortions, and 4,600 avoidable maternal deaths." In addition, the current terms of the gag rule are so broad that, along with defunding organizations that provide contraceptive and abortion services, many international health organizations that do not specialize in abortion or family planning are being targeted. As Coates reported, in March 2019 "Secretary of State Mike Pompeo further interpreted the rule to include subcontractors and partner organizations working with any group receiving US health aid."

Despite the stated intentions of the Republican politicians who have supported the policy, the net effect of the global gag rule in its many incarnations from 1984 to now has, ironically, been to increase abortions and suffering. As Coates noted, "One study, published in the *Lancet*, followed three-quarters of a million women in 26 countries over 20 years and found that during previous impositions of the rule, abortions rose by 40 percent in the most affected regions."[134]

In early 2019 US lawmakers introduced the Global Health, Empowerment, and Rights Act. If this bill is passed, it would "permanently repeal the global gag rule and prevent future administrations from easily reimposing it via executive order." To date, the act has yet to make it to a congressional vote.

The global gag rule has received very limited corporate media coverage. *The New York Times* has published a pair of articles and a Q. and A., along with a plethora of opinion pieces from 2001 to 2019 on the policy.[135] The articles, however, cover the politics of the situation without helping readers to understand the policy's impacts on global health organizations, and by extension, women throughout the world. *The Washington Post* covered the story in 2017 but lacked substantial detail concerning the impact the policy would have on groups like Marie Stopes

International.[136] The only substantial coverage of this issue apart from the Rewire.News and *Sierra* reports has come from other independent sources, such as KPFA and The Independent.[137]

24.
Silenced in Savannah: Journalist Abby Martin Challenges Georgia's BDS "Gag Law"

"Abby Martin Banned from Speaking at US University for Refusing to Sign Pro-Israel Pledge," teleSUR English, January 17, 2020, https://www.telesurenglish.net/news/Abby-Martin-Banned-From-Speaking-at-US-University--20200117-0007.html.

"Abby Martin Sues Georgia State Over Law Forcing Loyalty to Israel," teleSUR English, February 10, 2020, https://www.telesurenglish.net/news/Abby-Martin-Sues-Georgia-State-Over-Law-Forcing-Loyalty-to-Israel--20200210-0019.html.

Alan MacLeod, "Journalist Abby Martin Sues State of Georgia Over Law Requiring Pledge of Allegiance to Israel," MintPress News, February 10, 2020, https://www.mintpressnews.com/abby-martin-lawsuit-state-georgia-over-bds-law/264798/.

Sheldon Richman, "Anti-BDS Laws Violate Our Freedom," *CounterPunch*, February 17, 2020, https://www.counterpunch.org/2020/02/17/anti-bds-laws-violate-our-freedom/.

Student Researchers: Kathleen Doyle (University of Vermont) and Troy Patton (Diablo Valley College)

Faculty Evaluators: Rob Williams (University of Vermont) and Mickey Huff (Diablo Valley College)

Journalist and filmmaker Abby Martin, a supporter of the Boycott, Divestment and Sanctions (BDS) movement that aims to end support for Israel's oppression of Palestinians, was scheduled to give a keynote speech to the annual International Critical Media Literacy Conference that was to be held at Georgia Southern University on February 28 and 29, 2020. Her talk was canceled because she refused to sign a contract stating she would not support a boycott of Israel. Georgia, along with 27 other states, has enacted anti-boycott laws that prohibit state offices or agencies from doing business with any companies or individuals that boycott Israel, as teleSUR English reported. Eventually the conference at which Martin was to speak was called off entirely after numerous colleagues supported Martin in her refusal to sign the contractual pledge.

BDS is a global movement driven by citizen activists. It works to peacefully pressure corporations, universities, and cultural organizations to stop doing business with the state of Israel, with the goal of pressuring Israel to obey international law and respect the human rights of Palestinians.

Georgia's anti-boycott legislation was passed by the state's Republican-dominated legislature in 2016 in response to the growing influence of the BDS movement on college campuses. It requires anyone who enters into a contract with the state for more than $1000 worth of work to sign an oath swearing they will not boycott Israel.

BDS advocates argue that anti-boycott legislation, such as the laws adopted by Georgia and other states, violate the First Amendment of the US Constitution. On February 10, 2020, Martin filed a federal lawsuit against Georgia's university system, claiming that the cancelation of her speech violated her constitutionally protected right to free speech. Martin tweeted that "[w]e must stand firmly opposed to these efforts and not cower in fear to these blatant violations of free speech."

Martin's legal action comes on the heels of an executive order signed by President Donald Trump in December 2019 that permits the US government to define Judaism as both a religion and a nationality under federal law. The stated aim of the order was to more effectively allow the government to combat "anti-Semitism on college campuses." In reality, by connecting Jewish religious identity with Israeli national identity, the new policy means any criticism of Israel's government and their actions could be construed as an attack on the Jewish faith and labeled as "anti-Semitic." The new classification means schools that receive federal funding could, by allowing any BDS activism or even discussion on campus, run afoul of the Civil Rights Act of 1964 which forbids those schools from discriminating on the basis of religion or national origin.

This story has received very little corporate coverage. Outside of reports from the Associated Press and Yahoo! Finance (which ran a story from PR Newswire on the topic), what traction the story has gotten has been limited to either independent news sources or news sources that specialize in Israeli/American affairs.[138]

25.
Studies Document Links between Education, Incarceration, and Recidivism

Shani Saxon, "Study Links High-Suspension Schools with Incarceration Later in Life," ColorLines, September 23, 2019, https://www.colorlines.com/articles/study-links-high-sus-pension-schools-incarceration-later-life.

Emily Boudreau, "School Discipline Linked to Later Consequences," Usable Knowledge (Harvard Graduate School of Education), September 16, 2019, https://www.gse.harvard.edu/news/uk/19/09/school-discipline-linked-later-consequences.

Leighanna Shirey, "New Study Proves Vast Benefits of Higher Education for Inmates," Citizen Truth, June 13, 2019, https://citizentruth.org/new-study-proves-vast-benefits-of-higher-education-for-inmates/.

Student Researchers: Jacqueline Archie, Marco Corea, Gabriella Grondalski, Rowan Hamilton, Rebecca Herbert, Kiara Killelea, Ciara Lockwood, Molly McKeogh, Liam O'Sullivan, Alexandra Shore, Eleanor Sprick, Madeline Terrio, Alexander Tran, and Kirstyn Velazquez (University of Massachusetts Amherst)

Faculty Advisor: Allison Butler (University of Massachusetts Amherst)

Two research studies document links between education, incarceration, and recidivism, as covered in articles published by ColorLines, Usable Knowledge, and Citizen Truth.

In September 2019, ColorLines reported that attending a school with a high suspension rate is associated with an increased likelihood of being arrested and a decreased likelihood of enrolling in a four-year college. The ColorLines article reported findings from a study titled "The School to Prison Pipeline: Long-Run Impacts of School Suspensions on Adult Crime" issued by the nonprofit National Bureau of Economic Research.[139] As Emily Boudreau reported for Harvard University's Usable Knowledge, the study provides "some of the first causal evidence that strict schools do indeed contribute to the so-called school-to-prison pipeline."

The study focused primarily on North Carolina's Charlotte-Mecklenburg school district, where approximately 23 percent of middle school students, the majority of whom are male students of color, are suspended annually. Researchers examined school administrative records, data on arrests and incarcerations, and college attendance records to assess how the district's suspension policy and other factors affected later life outcomes. Andrew Bacher-Hicks, the study's lead author, told Usable Knowledge that the study found "large negative impacts on later-life outcomes" for all students—not just those who were suspended—related to attending a school with a high suspension rate. As Emily Boudreau reported, the study's authors recommended that school administrators and teachers "should be cautious of relying heavily on exclusionary practices" and that they should consider alternatives to suspensions, including positive reinforcement, and restorative processes for students returning to the classroom following any disciplinary action.

A RAND Corporation study emphasized the importance of higher education for prison inmates, as Leighanna Shirey reported for Citizen Truth in June 2019. Education serves as a form of rehabilitation, and access to higher education allows incarcerated individuals to develop new skills, leading to reduced recidivism, the RAND study documented.[140]

As Lois Davis, a senior policy researcher at RAND and leader of the study, told Citizen Truth, the study "dispelled the myths about whether or not education helps inmates when they get out. Education is, by far, such a clear winner." She also noted that all of society benefits when incarcerated people can receive an education: "[W]hat do you want for your community?" she asked. "If you don't rehabilitate [prison inmates], how are they going to successfully rejoin society?"

The RAND study corroborated previous research on the value of post-secondary education programs for incarcerated people. For example, the Vera Institute of Justice has found that "education is key to improving many long-term outcomes for incarcerated people, their families, and their communities—including reducing recidivism and increasing employability and earnings after release."[141]

The school-to-prison pipeline has made national headlines in recent years, but establishment media have failed to cover the National Bureau of Economic Research study as important evidence that strict schools contribute to this pattern. In September 2019 the *Los Angeles Times* reported that schools in California have expanded their ban on "willful defiance suspensions" so that elementary and middle school students cannot be suspended for defying authority, citing the counterproductivity of such suspensions and how they are unfairly applied to Black students.[142] An October 2019 article in *Forbes* discussed the school-to-prison pipeline and how students of color face harsher punishments than their white peers, noting, "The more time that Black and Brown children spend outside of the classroom, the more likely they are to be introduced to the criminal justice system."[143] However, neither article addressed the causal evidence documented in the study covered by ColorLines and Usable Knowledge.

Major news outlets, including the *New York Times* and NPR, fail to report on the positive societal effects of higher education in prisons. Instead, their orientation toward education in prisons is primarily concerned with the economics of educational programs and is centered on congressional politics. For example, in February 2018 the *New York Times* reported that Senate leaders might reinstate Pell grants for incarcerated students, "a move that would restore a federal lifeline to the nation's cash-strapped prison education system."[144] More recently, in April 2019 NPR reported on how Congress was again considering legislation to make Pell grants available to incarcerated people.[145] While most US prisoners are still barred from receiving Pell grants, they have been made available to a limited number of incarcerated students through the "Second Chance Pell Pilot Program"; an April 2020 *Washington Post* report on an expansion of the program, which Education Secretary Betsy DeVos refers to as an "experiment," did make a passing mention of the results of the RAND study.[146]

Notes

1. Herbert J. Gans, *Deciding What's News: A Study of* CBS Evening News, NBC Nightly News, Newsweek, *and* Time, *25th Anniversary Edition* (Evanston, IL: Northwestern University Press, 2004 [1979]), 81.

2. Based on extensive fieldwork at CBS, NBC, *Newsweek*, and *Time*, Gans identified incentives, power, the ability to supply suitable information, and geographic and social proximity to journalists as the four main factors that shape story *availability* (pp. 117–28); and he found that story selectors took into consideration story importance, interest, novelty, quality, and balance—as well as commercial and audience consider-ations—in determining story *suitability* (pp. 146–76, 214–48). In a 2004 preface to the 25th anniversary edition of *Deciding What's News*, Gans observed that, despite "transformations of the national news media as a whole," the news organizations that he originally studied "have remained virtually unchanged" (xvi).

3. Ibid., 82.

4. As a daily activity, news work "mandates an emphasis on events, not issues," Tuchman wrote. Thus, for example, "the idea and so the issue of institutionalized racism entails a description of social processes involving the interrelationship of a host of institutions and social problems; it eschews an examination of the prejudices of specific individuals. But newswork emphasizes the primacy of the individual: the individual as source, as legitimated representative, as incumbent, as power broker." This is one of the ways that news for Tuchman is "ideological" in how it "limits access" to ideas and "transforms dissent." Gaye Tuchman, *Making News: A Study in the Construction of Reality* (New York: Free Press, 1978), 134, 177.

5. For example, Gans described "Responsible Capitalism" as one of the enduring values of the news organizations he studied (*Deciding What's News*, 46–48); and, as Tuchman noted, "references in the news to the corporate sector of the economy as 'big business,' rather than 'corporate capitalism' or 'monopoly capitalism,' reinforce corporate power. As a met-aphor, 'big business' invokes images of the competitive marketplace of an earlier era, not the contemporary economic situation" (*Making News*, 164).

6. On "built-in anticipatory avoidance," see Gans, *Deciding What's News*, 275–76.

7. See Gabrielle Kreidie and Lisa Lynch, "Censorship of Al Jazeera Doc-umentary Exposes Influence of Pro-Israel Lobby," story #19 in *Censored 2020: Through the Looking Glass*, eds. Andy Lee Roth and Mickey Huff with Project Censored (New York: Seven Stories Press, 2019), 65–67, https://www.projectcensored.org/19-censorship-of-al-jazeera-documen-tary-exposes-influence-of-pro-israel-lobby/.

8. Tuchman, *Making News*, 164.

9. Ibid., 179, 180.

10. For information on how to nominate a story, see "How to Support Project Censored" at the back of this volume.

11. Validated Independent News stories are archived on the Project Censored website at https://www.projectcensored.org/category/validat-ed-independent-news.

12. For a complete list of the Project's judges and their brief biographies, see the acknowledgments at the back of this volume.

13. Here and following, our use of the terms "women and girls" should be read as including those who identify as Two-Spirit, lesbian, gay, bisexual, transgender, queer, questioning, intersex, or asexual.

14. Nick Martin, "The Cyclical Crisis of Missing and Murdered Indigenous Women," *New Republic*, January 22, 2020, https://newrepublic.com/article/156263/cyclical-crisis-missing-murdered-indigenous-women.

15. "Missing and Murdered Indigenous Women & Girls," Urban Indian Health Institute (Seattle Indian Health Board), November 2018, https://www.uihi.org/wp-content/uploads/2018/11/Missing-and-Murdered-Indigenous-Women-and-Girls-Report.pdf, 2.

16. "Overall, more than 1.5 million American Indian and Alaska Native women have experienced violence in their lifetime." André B. Rosay, "Violence Against American Indian and Alaska Native Women and Men: 2010 Findings from the National Intimate Partner and Sexual Violence Survey," National Institute of Justice, U.S. Department of Justice, May 2016, https://www.ncjrs.gov/pdffiles1/nij/249736.pdf, 2, 11.

17. See, for example, Faith Spotted Eagle & the Kunsi Circle of Brave Heart Society, Annita Lucchesi, Alex Romero Frederick, and Carla Rae Marshall, "Zuya Winyan Wicayuonihan—Honoring Warrior Women: A Study on Missing & Murdered Indigenous Women and Girls in States Impacted by the Keystone XL Pipeline," Sovereign Bodies Institute and Brave Heart Society, undated, https://www.sovereign-bodies.org/reports [accessed May 8, 2020], 15–20. On settler colonialism, see Roxane Dunbar-Ortiz, *An Indigenous Peoples' History of the United States* (Boston: Beacon Press, 2014), 2: "The history of the United States is a history of settler colonialism."

18. See also Garet Bleir and Anya Zoledziowski, "Cases of Missing and Murdered Native American Women Challenge Police, Courts," News 21 (Hate in America series), August 15, 2018, https://hateinamerica.news21.com/cases-of-missing-murdered-native-american-women-challenge-police-courts/.

19. "U.S. Department of Justice Declinations of Indian Country Criminal Matters," United States Government Accountability Office, December 13, 2010, https://www.gao.gov/new.items/d11167r.pdf, 24.

20. Faith Spotted Eagle & the Kunsi Circle of Brave Heart Society, Lucchesi, Romero Frederick, and Marshall, "Zuya Winyan Wicayuonihan," 16.

21. "Missing and Murdered Indigenous Women & Girls," Urban Indian Health Institute, 3.

22. Ibid., 1.

23. Donald J. Trump, "Executive Order on Establishing the Task Force on Missing and Murdered American Indians and Alaska Natives," White House, November 26, 2019, https://www.whitehouse.gov/presidential-actions/executive-order-establishing-task-force-missing-murdered-american-indians-alaska-natives/.

24. Martin, "The Cyclical Crisis."

25. Cecily Hilleary, "Native American Views Mixed on Trump Task Force for Missing, Murdered," Voice of America (VOA), December 2, 2019,

https://www.voanews.com/usa/native-american-views-mixed-trump-task-force-missing-murdered.

26. Ibid.

27. Jack Healy's reporting for the *New York Times* has been especially powerful. See, e.g., Jack Healy, "In Indian Country, a Crisis of Missing Women. And a New One When They're Found," *New York Times*, December 25, 2019, https://www.nytimes.com/2019/12/25/us/native-women-girls-missing.html; and Jack Healy, "Rural Montana Had Already Lost Too Many Native Women. Then Selena Disappeared," *New York Times*, January 20, 2020, updated January 22, 2020, https://www.nytimes.com/2020/01/20/us/selena-not-afraid-missing-montana.html. From the *Seattle Times*, see Bettina Hansen and Lauren Frohne's "Not Invisible: Confronting a Crisis of Violence against Native Women," https://projects.seattletimes.com/2019/mmiw/, an ongoing video series, begun August 11, 2019, that documents efforts by activists, communities, lawmakers, and law enforcement to raise awareness and work for change.

28. "Reclaiming Power and Place: The Final Report of the National Inquiry into Missing and Murdered Indigenous Women and Girls," National Inquiry into Missing and Murdered Indigenous Women and Girls, June 3, 2019, https://www.mmiwg-ffada.ca/final-report/.

29. *The Washington Post* reported the "explosive conclusion" of the national inquiry: "Canada's indigenous women and girls are 'under siege,' and their deaths and disappearances amount to 'a race-based genocide.'" Amanda Coletta, "Canadian Government Inquiry Assails 'Genocide' of Indigenous Women, Girls," *Washington Post*, June 3, 2019, https://www.washingtonpost.com/world/the_americas/canadian-government-inquiry-indigenous-women-have-been-victims-of-race-based-genocide/2019/06/02/3d46f670-8329-11e9-b585-e36b16a531aa_story.html. As *Time* magazine reported, "The disappearance of indigenous women and girls in Canada was determined to be genocide by a three-year national inquiry." Amy Gunia, "'Genocide' was Committed against Canada's Indigenous Women, an Inquiry Found," *Time*, June 3, 2019, https://time.com/5600293/canada-indigenous-women-genocide/.

30. Ari Shapiro, interview with Annita Lucchesi, "How the Treatment of Indigenous Women in the U.S. Compares to Canada," *All Things Considered*, NPR, June 7, 2019, https://www.npr.org/2019/06/07/730758953/how-the-treatment-of-indigenous-women-in-the-u-s-compares-to-canada. The program's host, Ari Shapiro, assessed the situation in the United States as "likely even worse than in Canada."

31. Dan Bilefsky, "'Why are So Many of Our Girls Dying?' Canada Grapples with Violence against Indigenous Women," *New York Times*, May 30, 2019, https://www.nytimes.com/2019/05/30/world/canada/canada-indigenous-violence.html.

32. For example, in June 2019 CBS News reported on the progress of Savanna's Act in the Senate, versions of the Not Invisible Act in the House and Senate, and congressional disputes over reauthorization of the Violence Against Women Act. See Grace Segers, "Congress Tackles Crisis of Missing and Murdered Native American Women," CBS News, June 12, 2019, https://www.cbsnews.com/news/congress-crisis-missing-and-murdered-native-american-women/.

33. The House version included amendments that would provide advocate services in state courts for Native women living in cities, require the Government Accountability Office to report on law enforcement agencies' responses to the crisis, authorize tribal law enforcement to prosecute non-Native perpetrators in cases of domestic violence, expand the 1968 Indian Civil Rights Act's definition of domestic violence to include violence against children and elders, and grant tribal jurisdiction over sexual assault and other crimes. See, for example, Dan Desai Martin, "Mitch McConnell Has Blocked Help for Abuse Victims for More Than 6 Months," American Independent, October 10, 2019, https://americanindependent.com/senate-violence-against-women-act-mitch-mcconnell-john-cornyn-vawa-congress/; and Amy Goodman and Denis Moynihan, "Is Mitch McConnell Trying to Kill the Violence Against Women Act?" Truthdig, October 24, 2019, https://www.truthdig.com/articles/is-mitch-mcconnell-trying-to-kill-the-violence-against-women-act/.

34. Quincy Walters, "Self-Defense Classes Help Indigenous Women Face Kidnapping Threat," All Things Considered, NPR, January 28, 2020, https://www.npr.org/2020/01/28/800559379/self-defense-classes-help-indigenous-women-face-kidnapping-threat; Travis DeShong, "'Our Existences are Political': What It Means That a Gay, Indigenous Couple Won Canada's 'Amazing Race,'" Washington Post, September 19, 2019, https://www.washingtonpost.com/lifestyle/2019/09/19/our-existences-are-political-what-it-means-that-gay-indigenous-couple-won-canadas-amazing-race/; and Ailsa Chang, "A Native American Woman's Search for Truth in 'Yellow Bird,'" All Things Considered, NPR, March 11, 2020, https://www.npr.org/2020/03/11/814603295/a-native-american-womans-search-for-truth-in-yellow-bird.

35. Readers seeking to become more informed are advised to visit the websites of the National Indigenous Women's Resource Center, which maintains an impressive page of resources, at https://www.niwrc.org/resources; the Sovereign Bodies Institute, at https://www.sovereign-bodies.org/; and the Urban Indian Health Institute, at https://www.uihi.org/.

36. See, for example, Sam Levin and Patrick Greenfield, "Monsanto Ordered to Pay $289m as Jury Rules Weedkiller Caused Man's Cancer," The Guardian, August 11, 2018, https://www.theguardian.com/business/2018/aug/10/monsanto-trial-cancer-dewayne-johnson-ruling. In March 2019, a federal jury found Monsanto liable in a third case, ruling that Roundup was to blame for another California man's cancer and ordering the company to pay $80 million in damages. See Sam Levin, "Monsanto Found Liable for California Man's Cancer and Ordered to Pay $80m in Damages," The Guardian, March 27, 2019, https://www.theguardian.com/business/2019/mar/27/monsanto-trial-verdict-cancer-jury.

37. Nathaniel Weixel, "Monsanto Sought to Discredit Journalists, Critics: Report," The Hill, August 9, 2019, https://thehill.com/policy/healthcare/456874-report-monsanto-sought-to-discredit-journalists-and-critics.

38. Soo Youn, "Monsanto is Contacting the Journalists, Activists It Tracked on 'Watch Lists' in 7 Countries," ABC News, June 18, 2019, https://abcnews.go.com/Business/monsanto-contacting-journalists-activists-tracked-watch-lists-countries/story?id=63784483.

39. Paul D. Thacker, "Monsanto's Spies," HuffPost, September 14, 2019, updated October 29, 2019, https://www.huffpost.com/entry/monsantos-spies_n_5d7ba20de4b03b5fc88233c4.

40. The US military's status as the world's worst polluter was story #2 on *Censored 2011*'s top 25 list; see, "US Department of Defense is the Worst Polluter on the Planet," in *Censored 2011: The Top 25 Censored Stories of 2009–10*, eds. Mickey Huff, Peter Phillips, and Project Censored (New York: Seven Stories Press, 2010), 15–24, https://www.projectcensored.org/2-us-department-of-defense-is-the-worst-polluter-on-the-planet/. For a synopsis and update of Project Censored's original story, see Chapter 2 of this volume.

41. Oliver Belcher, Patrick Bigger, Ben Neimark, and Cara Kennelly, "Hidden Carbon Costs of the 'Everywhere War': Logistics, Geopolitical Ecology, and the Carbon Boot-Print of the US Military," *Transactions of the Institute of British Geographers*, Vol. 45 No. 1 (March 2020), 65–80, https://doi.org/10.1111/tran.12319 [first published online June 19, 2019].

42. Ibid., 72.

43. Ibid., 75.

44. Benjamin Neimark, Oliver Belcher, and Patrick Bigger, "US Military is a Bigger Polluter Than as Many as 140 Countries—Shrinking This War Machine is a Must," Yahoo! News, June 24, 2019, https://news.yahoo.com/us-military-bigger-polluter-many-140153707.html; Benjamin Neimark, Oliver Belcher, and Patrick Bigger, "U.S. Military Produces More Greenhouse Gas Than up to 140 Countries," *Newsweek*, June 25, 2019, https://www.newsweek.com/us-military-greenhouse-gases-140-countries-1445674; James Pero, "The US Military is Among the World's Biggest Contributors to Climate Change and is Responsible for More Emissions Than Some Entire COUNTRIES, Study Says," *Daily Mail*, June 20, 2019, https://www.dailymail.co.uk/sciencetech/article-7163857/New-study-shows-military-bigger-contributor-climate-change-countries.html; and Lancaster University, "US Military Consumes More Hydrocarbons Than Most Countries—Massive Hidden Impact on Climate," ScienceDaily, June 20, 2019, https://www.sciencedaily.com/releases/2019/06/190620100005.htm.

45. Benjamin Neimark, Oliver Belcher, and Patrick Bigger, "Why We Can't Ignore U.S. Military Emissions," *YES! Magazine*, July 6, 2019, https://www.yesmagazine.org/environment/2019/07/06/climate-change-military-pollution/; Benjamin Neimark, Oliver Belcher, and Patrick Bigger, "US Military Pollution," The Ecologist, June 27, 2019, https://theecologist.org/2019/jun/27/us-military-pollution; and Benjamin Neimark, Oliver Belcher, and Patrick Bigger, "The US Military is a Bigger Polluter Than More Than 100 Countries Combined," Quartz, June 28, 2019, https://qz.com/1655268/us-military-is-a-bigger-polluter-than-140-countries-combined/.

46. "The JUST Capital Rankings on Corporate Tax Reform," JUST Capital, February 28, 2018, https://justcapital.com/news/the-just-capital-rankings-on-corporate-tax-reform/.

47. "Energy and the Environment Explained: Where Greenhouse Gases Come From," U.S. Energy Information Administration, June 19, 2019, https://www.eia.gov/energyexplained/energy-and-the-environment/where-greenhouse-gases-come-from.php.

48. Clare Charlesworth and Rob Williams, "Shell Understood Climate Change as Early as 1991—and Ignored It," in *Censored 2018: Press Freedoms in a "Post-Truth" World*, eds. Andy Lee Roth and Mickey Huff with Project Censored (New York: Seven Stories Press, 2017), 77–79, https://www.projectcensored.org/15-shell-understood-climate-change-early-1991-ignored/.

49. Irina Ivanova, "Bonuses from 2017 Tax Cuts Amounted to $28 per Worker, Congressional Researchers Say," CBS News, May 29, 2019, https://www.cbsnews.com/news/tax-cuts-and-jobs-act-bonuses-from-2017-tax-cuts-amounted-to-28-per-worker-congressional-office-says/.

50. See, for example, Max Fisher and Emma Bubola, "As Coronavirus Deepens Inequality, Inequality Worsens Its Spread," *New York Times*, March 15, 2020, updated March 16, 2020, https://www.nytimes.com/2020/03/15/world/europe/coronavirus-inequality.html; and Linda Villarosa, "'A Terrible Price': The Deadly Racial Disparities of Covid-19 in America," *New York Times*, April 29, 2020, updated May 20, 2020, https://www.nytimes.com/2020/04/29/magazine/racial-disparities-covid-19.html.

51. "Retirement Security: Income and Wealth Disparities Continue through Old Age," United States Government Accountability Office, August 2019, https://www.gao.gov/assets/710/700836.pdf.

52. "Summary File Data," American Community Survey, United States Census Bureau, 2018, https://www.census.gov/programs-surveys/acs/data/summary-file.html.

53. "Life Expectancy," Chicago Health Atlas, 2017 data, https://www.chicagohealthatlas.org/indicators/life-expectancy.

54. Brittney S. Lange-Maia, Fernando De Maio, Elizabeth F. Avery, Elizabeth B. Lynch, Emily M. Laflamme, David A. Ansell, and Raj C. Shah, "Association of Community-Level Inequities and Premature Mortality: Chicago, 2011–2015," *Journal of Epidemiology & Community Health*, Vol. 72 No. 12 (December 2018), 1099–1103, https://jech.bmj.com/content/72/12/1099 [first published online August 31, 2018].

55. "Safety and Health at the Heart of the Future of Work: Building on 100 Years of Experience," International Labour Organization, 2019, https://www.ilo.org/wcmsp5/groups/public/---ed_protect/---protrav/---safework/documents/publication/wcms_686761o.pdf, 3.

56. Ibid., 49.

57. Ryan Smith, a freelance reporter who worked for Journatic, coined the term "pink slime journalism." In 2012, Smith stated, "People didn't think much about the beef they were eating until someone exposed the practice of putting so-called 'pink slime' into ground beef.... [C]ompanies like Journatic are providing the public 'pink slime' journalism." See Anna Tarkov, "Journatic Worker Takes 'This American Life' inside Outsourced Journalism," Poynter, June 30, 2012, https://www.poynter.org/reporting-editing/2012/journatic-staffer-takes-this-american-life-inside-outsourced-journalism/.

58. Joe Mahr, "Conservative Illinois Publications Blur Lines between Journalism, Politics," *Chicago Tribune*, April 6, 2018, https://www.chicagotribune.com/news/ct-met-illinois-conservative-news-20180327-story.html.

59. See Anne Nelson, *Shadow Network: Media, Money, and the Secret Hub of the Radical Right* (New York: Bloomsbury Publishing, 2019); Katherine Stewart, *The Power Worshippers: Inside the Dangerous Rise of Religious*

Nationalism (New York: Bloomsbury Publishing, 2020); and Andrew L. Whitehead and Samuel L. Perry, *Taking America Back for God: Christian Nationalism in the United States* (New York: Oxford University Press, 2020).

60. Dan Levin, "Mimicking Local News, a Network of Michigan Websites Pushes Politics," *New York Times*, October 21, 2019, https://www.nytimes.com/2019/10/21/us/michigan-metric-media-news.html.

61. Seong-Jae Min and John C. Feaster, "Missing Children in National News Coverage: Racial and Gender Representations of Missing Children Cases," *Communication Research Reports*, Vol. 27 No. 3 (July–September 2010), 207–216, available online at https://www.csus.edu/faculty/m/fred.molitor/docs/news-coverage-of-missing-children.pdf.

62. Jada L. Moss, "The Forgotten Victims of Missing White Woman Syndrome: An Examination of Legal Measures that Contribute to the Lack of Search and Recovery of Missing Black Girls and Women," *William & Mary Journal of Race, Gender, and Social Justice*, Vol. 25 No. 3 (April 2019), 737–62, https://scholarship.law.wm.edu/cgi/viewcontent.cgi?article=1508&context=wmjowl.

63. "Most Suspected Incidents of Human Trafficking Involved Allegations of Prostitution of an Adult or Child," Bureau of Justice Statistics, April 28, 2011, https://www.bjs.gov/content/pub/press/cshti081opr.cfm.

64. Michelle Lillie, "Human Trafficking: Not All Black or White," Human Trafficking Search, 2014, https://humantraffickingsearch.org/human-trafficking-not-all-black-or-white/.

65. Note, for example, what's missing from the title of NBC News's coverage: Chandelis R. Duster, "Congressional Leaders Call for Action on Missing Women and Girls," NBC News, April 27, 2017, https://www.nbcnews.com/news/nbcblk/congressional-leaders-call-action-missing-women-girls-n751721.

66. Jasmine Brown and Steve Osunsami, "Families of Missing Black Americans Fight for Media, Police to Focus on Their Loved Ones' Cases," ABC News, July 23, 2019, https://abcnews.go.com/US/families-missing-black-americans-fight-media-police-focus/story?id=64509892.

67. Harmeet Kaur, "Black Kids Go Missing at a Higher Rate Than White Kids. Here's Why We Don't Hear about Them," CNN, November 3, 2019, https://www.cnn.com/2019/11/03/us/missing-children-of-color-trnd/index.html.

68. Eric Heinz, "LA City Council President to Propose City's First Public Bank," *Los Angeles Daily News*, October 7, 2019, https://www.dailynews.com/2019/10/07/la-city-council-president-to-propose-citys-first-public-bank; and Christine Kilpatrick, "San Francisco Sets Timeline for Launching Public Bank—the First in California," *San Francisco Business Times*, November 13, 2019, https://www.bizjournals.com/sanfrancisco/news/2019/11/13/san-francisco-sets-timeline-for-launching-public.html.

69. David Levinsky, "Murphy Creates Task Force to Research Launch of NJ Public Bank," *Burlington County Times*, November 13, 2019, https://www.burlingtoncountytimes.com/news/20191113/murphy-creates-task-force-to-research-launch-of-nj-public-bank.

70. Sebastian Leder Macek, "White Paper: Public Banking in the Northeast and Midwest States," Northeast-Midwest Institute, September 2019,

https://www.nemw.org/wp-content/uploads/2019/09/Public-Banking-White-Paper.pdf.

71. Timothy Knowles and Ameya Pawar, "Missing So Far from the Prescription for a Coronavirus Economic Recovery: Public Banks," MarketWatch, April 14, 2020, https://www.marketwatch.com/story/missing-ingredient-so-far-in-coronavirus-economic-recovery-plans-public-banks-2020-04-13.

72. Ibid.

73. Isaiah Poole and Rick Girling, "Public Banking Would Help Speed the Economic Recovery from COVID-19," The Hill, April 17, 2020, https://thehill.com/opinion/finance/493314-public-banking-would-help-speed-the-economic-recovery-from-covid-19.

74. 442 nuclear power plants operating in 2019: "Nuclear Power in the World Today," World Nuclear Association, March 2020, https://www.world-nuclear.org/information-library/current-and-future-generation/nuclear-power-in-the-world-today.aspx.

75. John Vidal, "What are Coastal Nuclear Power Plants Doing to Address Climate Threats?" Ensia, August 8, 2018, https://ensia.com/features/coastal-nuclear/.

76. "Greenland Ice Sheet Shrinks by Record in 2019," Al Jazeera, April 16, 2020, https://www.aljazeera.com/news/2020/04/greenland-ice-sheet-shrinks-record-2019-200417033026664.html; and Adam Vaughan, "Sea Level Rise Could Hit 2 Metres by 2100—Much Worse Than Feared," *New Scientist*, May 20, 2019, https://www.newscientist.com/article/2203700-sea-level-rise-could-hit-2-metres-by-2100-much-worse-than-feared/.

77. John M. Broder, "Climate Change Will Cause More Energy Breakdowns, U.S. Warns," *New York Times*, July 11, 2013, https://www.nytimes.com/2013/07/11/us/climate-change-will-cause-more-energy-breakdowns-us-warns.html.

78. Alan Neuhauser, "Nuclear Power, Once Seen as Impervious to Climate Change, Threatened by Heat Waves," *U.S. News & World Report*, July 1, 2019, https://www.usnews.com/news/national-news/articles/2019-07-01/nuclear-power-once-seen-as-impervious-to-climate-change-threatened-by-heat-waves.

79. "The single biggest tranche of money in the package is . . . aimed at industry rescues, but with no guardrails to ensure that public money is directed toward saving the jobs, wages, and benefits of typical workers rather than the wealth of shareholders, creditors, and corporate executives." Josh Bivens and Heidi Shierholz, "Despite Some Good Provisions, the CARES Act Has Glaring Flaws and Falls Short of Fully Protecting Workers during the Coronavirus Crisis," Economic Policy Institute, March 25, 2020, https://www.epi.org/blog/despite-some-good-provisions-the-cares-act-has-glaring-flaws-and-falls-short-of-fully-protecting-workers-during-the-coronavirus-crisis/.

80. Sonali Kohli and Howard Blume, "L.A. Unified Plans for Teaching by Television after Canceling All Large Gatherings," *Los Angeles Times*, March 12, 2020, https://www.latimes.com/california/story/2020-03-11/lausd-events-cancelled-coronavirus.

81. On proposals by Craig Aaron and others to prevent the pandemic's worst impacts on journalism, Sullivan opined, "I don't know whether any of the proposals for doing that would be successful. But at a time when good reporting has seldom been more vital and more threatened, I do know that we need to try our damnedest." Margaret Sullivan, "Local Journalism Needs a Coronavirus Stimulus Plan, Too," *Washington Post*, March 26, 2020, https://www.washingtonpost.com/lifestyle/media/local-journalism-needs-a-coronavirus-stimulus-plan-too/2020/03/25/08358062-6ec6-11ea-b148-e4ce3fbd85b5_story.html.

82. Victor Pickard, "The Answer to the Media Industry's Woes? Publicly Owned Newspapers," *Washington Post*, May 18, 2020, https://www.washingtonpost.com/outlook/2020/05/18/answer-media-industrys-woes-publicly-owned-newspapers/.

83. For prior Project Censored coverage of this topic, see Melissa Reed and Susan Rahman, "FBI Surveilled Peaceful Climate Change Protestors," in *Censored 2020: Through the Looking Glass*, eds. Andy Lee Roth and Mickey Huff with Project Censored (New York: Seven Stories Press, 2019), 55–58, https://www.projectcensored.org/14-fbi-surveilled-peaceful-climate-change-protesters/; and Sverre Tysl and Scott Suneson, "Terror Act Against Animal Activists," in *Censored 2008: The Top 25 Censored Stories of 2006–07*, eds. Peter Phillips and Andy Lee Roth with Project Censored (New York: Seven Stories Press, 2007), 109–114, https://www.projectcensored.org/20-terror-act-against-animal-activists/.

84. Rachel Delia Benaim, "Three States Pass Laws Criminalizing Fossil Fuel Protests Amid Coronavirus Chaos," Weather.com, April 2, 2020, https://weather.com/science/environment/news/2020-04-02-three-states-pass-laws-criminalizing-fossil-fuel-protests.

85. Alexander C. Kaufman, "States Quietly Pass Laws Criminalizing Fossil Fuel Protests Amid Coronavirus Chaos," HuffPost, March 27, 2020, updated March 31, 2020, https://www.huffpost.com/entry/pipeline-protest-laws-coronavirus_n_5e7e7570c5b6256a7a2aab41; Tal Axelrod, "Three States Push Criminal Penalties for Fossil Fuel Protests Amid Coronavirus," The Hill, March 27, 2020, https://thehill.com/policy/energy-environment/489960-three-states-push-criminal-penalties-for-fossil-fuel-protests-amid; and ibid.

86. Elizabeth Dwoskin, "Facebook Says Private Groups are Its Future. Some are Hubs for Misinformation and Hate," *Washington Post*, July 5, 2019, https://www.washingtonpost.com/technology/2019/07/05/facebook-says-private-groups-are-its-future-some-are-hubs-misinformation-hate/.

87. Alicia Victoria Lozano, "13 Philadelphia Officers to be Fired Over Racist, Violent Facebook Posts," NBC10 Philadelphia, July 18, 2019, updated July 19, 2019, https://www.nbcphiladelphia.com/news/national-international/philadelphia-police-officers-facebook-posts/170494/.

88. "11,467 people on parole in Colorado will now be able to vote." Jesse Paul, "11,467 Colorado Parolees Can Now Vote after New Law Goes into Effect," Colorado Sun, July 1, 2019, https://coloradosun.com/2019/07/01/parole-felon-voting-colorado-laws/.

89. For analysis of these claims, see Stephanie Saul and Reid J. Epstein, "Falsehoods and Facts on Voting by Mail," *New York Times*, April 9, 2020, Section A, 20, updated and retitled "Trump is Pushing a False Argument

on Vote-by-Mail Fraud. Here are the Facts," June 2, 2020, https://www.nytimes.com/article/mail-in-voting-explained.html.

90. Michael Wines, "Voting by Mail Could be What States Need. But Can They Pull It Off?" *New York Times*, April 11, 2020, https://www.nytimes.com/2020/04/11/us/coronavirus-voting-by-mail-elections.html.

91. John Hickenlooper, "We've been Voting at Home for Six Years in Colorado. It's Time to Do It Nationally," *Washington Post*, April 8, 2020, https://www.washingtonpost.com/opinions/2020/04/08/my-state-has-proved-vote-at-home-works-we-need-do-it-nationally/.

92. Dana Brown, "Medicine for All: The Case for a Public Option in the Pharmaceutical Industry," Democracy Collaborative, September 2019, https://thenextsystem.org/sites/default/files/2019-09/Medicine-forAll_WEB.pdf, 5. In a July 1, 2019, Truthout article, "Replace Patent Monopolies with Direct Public Funding for Drug Research," Dean Baker wrote that Americans "will spend roughly $460 billion this year on drugs that would likely sell for less than $80 billion in a true free market." (https://truthout.org/articles/replace-patent-monopolies-with-direct-public-funding-for-drug-research/).

93. Brown, "Medicine for All," 37–38.

94. Ekaterina Galkina Cleary, Jennifer M. Beierlein, Navleen Surjit Khanuja, Laura M. McNamee, and Fred D. Ledley, "Contribution of NIH Funding to New Drug Approvals 2010–2016," *PNAS*, Vol. 115 No. 10 (March 6, 2018), 2329–34, https://www.pnas.org/content/115/10/2329 [first published online February 12, 2018].

95. On Big Pharma's "documented history" of dangerous and illegal misbranding, and its multi-billion dollar expenditures to influence doctors' prescribing decisions, also see Brown, "Medicine for All," 19.

96. Brown, "Medicine for All," 23.

97. A September 2019 *New Republic* article noted that the public is "mad as hell about drug prices" and cited the results of March 2019 Kaiser Family Foundation poll, which found that 79 percent of respondents believed drug prices were unreasonable, 80 percent attributed that partly to drug company profits, and 89 percent—including 85 percent of Republicans—favored making it easier for generics to come to market. See Libby Watson, "Democrats' Drug Price Bill May be Dead on Arrival," *New Republic*, September 20, 2019, https://newrepublic.com/article/155140/democrats-drug-price-bill-may-dead-arrival.

98. Thia James, "State of Emergency Declared on Makwa Sahgaiehcan First Nation after Suicides, Attempts," *Saskatoon StarPhoenix*, November 23, 2019, https://thestarphoenix.com/news/local-news/state-of-emergency-declared-on-makwa-sahgaiehcan-first-nation-after-suicides-attempts/; and Chelsea Laskowski, "'We are Hurting': As Sask. First Nations Grapple with Suicides, Feds Announce $2.5m in Prevention Funding," CBC News, December 19, 2019, https://www.cbc.ca/news/canada/saskatoon/suicide-prevention-crisis-ochapowace-1.5403081.

99. As one of Heinen's sources—Bree Swanson, a social services administrator—explained, the Northwest Arctic tribal health region was the worst region for Indigenous suicide in Alaska from 2012 to 2015. Swanson identified generational trauma as one risk factor. Noting that colonization in the mainland United States was "hundreds of years old," Swanson said

it is "more recent" in Alaska. "We're talking grandparent generation," Swanson told *New Statesman*.

100. For another instance of the power with which in-depth investigative journalism can convey the challenges faced by determined Indigenous families and communities confronting violence, see Eilís Quinn, "Death in the Arctic," Eye on the Arctic, December 14, 2018, https://www.rcinet.ca/eye-on-the-arctic-special-reports/death-nunavik-quebec-arctic-canada/#home. Quinn reported the story of the violent death Robert Adams, a nineteen-year-old Inuk from Northern Quebec, and his father's struggle for access to mental health services, coroner's services, and the Inuit justice system. In January 2020, "Death in the Arctic" won the silver medal at the Canadian Online Publishing Awards. "Eye on the Arctic report *Death in the Arctic* Wins Prize at Canadian Online Publishing Awards," Eye on the Arctic, January 13, 2020, https://www.rcinet.ca/eye-on-the-arctic/2020/01/13/eye-on-the-arctic-report-death-in-the-arctic-wins-prize-at-canadian-online-publishing-awards-copa-justice-journalism-nunavik/.

101. "Suicide Emergency Prompts Fort Belknap Community Response," *U.S. News & World Report* (via Associated Press), August 2, 2019, https://www.usnews.com/news/best-states/montana/articles/2019-08-02/suicide-emergency-prompts-fort-belknap-community-response.

102. Alia E. Dastagir, "She Worked in Suicide Prevention. Then One Day She Had to Save Herself," *USA Today*, June 21, 2019, https://www.usatoday.com/in-depth/news/investigations/surviving-suicide/2018/11/28/native-american-suicides-coping-historical-trauma-suicide-prevention/972282002/.

103. Abe Streep, "What the Arlee Warriors were Playing for," *New York Times*, April 4, 2018, https://www.nytimes.com/2018/04/04/magazine/arlee-warriors-montana-basketball-flathead-indian-reservation.html.

104. "Basic Facts about the UPR," United Nations Human Rights Council, undated, https://www.ohchr.org/en/hrbodies/upr/pages/basicfacts.aspx [accessed May 18, 2020].

105. Ibid.

106. In their August 2019 *American Prospect* article, Bochenek and Binford reported that the United States was due for Universal Periodic Review in May 2020. As of that date, however, the Universal Periodic Review website states that the United States will undergo review in November 2020. See "Timeline for UPR Engagement in the Current Cycle: United States," UPR Info, undated, https://www.upr-info.org/en/review/United-States [accessed May 18, 2020].

107. As of May 2020, the ACLU's Human Rights Program, Planned Parenthood, and the US Human Rights Network had submitted statements. See "Civil Society and Other Submissions: Timeline for UPR Engagement in the Current Cycle: United States," UPR Info, undated, https://www.upr-info.org/en/review/United-States/Session-36---May-2020/Civil-society-and-other-submissions [accessed May 18, 2020].

108. Louis Casiano, "Homeland Security Watchdog Reports Overcrowding and Migrants Pleading for Help during Detention-Facility Tour," Fox News, July 2, 2019, https://www.foxnews.com/

politics/homeland-security-watchdog-reports-overcrowding-and-mi-grants-pleading-for-help-during-detention-facility-tour.

109. AABB, America's Blood Centers, and American Red Cross, Joint Letter to Commissioner of Food and Drugs Stephen M. Hahn (U.S. Food and Drug Administration), AABB (formerly American Association of Blood Banks), March 20, 2020, http://www.aabb.org/advocacy/correspondence/Documents/Joint-Letter-to-FDA-on-Blood-Supply-Chain.pdf.

110. Hannah Miller, "Blood Donations Needed during Coronavirus Pandemic," CNBC, March 23, 2020, https://www.cnbc.com/2020/03/23/blood-donations-needed-during-coronavirus-pandemic.html.

111. Heather Olsen, David Margolius, Anupuma Cemballi, Kristin Berg, Sarah Shick, and Adam Perzynski, "Bearing Many Burdens: Source Plasma Donation in the U.S.," Patient Centered Media Lab at the Center for Health Care Research and Policy, Case Western Reserve University and MetroHealth Medical Center, August 1, 2018, http://chrp.org/wp-content/uploads/2019/01/PDC-presentation-web-version.pdf.

112. Catherine Waldby and Robert Mitchell, *Tissue Economies: Blood, Organs, and Cell Lines in Late Capitalism* (Durham, NC: Duke University Press, 2006).

113. Lauren Villagran and Stefanie Dodt, "Luring Donors from Mexico, El Paso Offers Rich Market for Plasma Collection," *El Paso Times*, October 11, 2019, https://www.elpasotimes.com/story/news/2019/10/11/mexicans-donate-blood-plasma-border-immigration/3944750002/.

114. Zoe Greenberg, "What is the Blood of a Poor Person Worth?" *New York Times*, February 1, 2019, https://www.nytimes.com/2019/02/01/sunday-review/blood-plasma-industry.html.

115. H. Luke Shaefer and Analidis Ochoa, "How Blood-Plasma Companies Target the Poorest Americans," *The Atlantic*, March 15, 2018, https://www.theatlantic.com/business/archive/2018/03/plasma-donations/555599/; Caitlin Owens, "U.S. Drug Companies Lure Mexican Blood Plasma Donors," Axios, October 7, 2019, https://www.axios.com/us-mexico-blood-plasma-donations-62248f51-6338-4b24-bf3c-e1c67c43f3d7.html; and Latin America News Dispatch, "Report Alleges US Pharma Companies Lure Mexicans across Border to Donate Plasma," *Latino USA* (distributed by NPR), October 9, 2019, https://www.latinousa.org/2019/10/09/uspharma/.

116. "Members of the NLRB Since 1935," National Labor Relations Board, undated, https://www.nlrb.gov/about-nlrb/who-we-are/the-board/members-of-the-nlrb-since-1935 [accessed May 22, 2020].

117. Celine McNicholas, Margaret Poydock, Julia Wolfe, Ben Zipperer, Gordon Lafer, and Lola Loustaunau, "Unlawful: U.S. Employers are Charged with Violating Federal Law in 41.5% of All Union Election Campaigns," Economic Policy Institute, December 11, 2019, https://www.epi.org/publication/unlawful-employer-opposition-to-union-election-campaigns/.

118. Robert Iafolla, "Union Elections Slower, More Complex under NLRB Changes," Bloomberg Law, December 13, 2019, https://news.bloomberglaw.com/daily-labor-report/union-elections-slower-more-complex-under-nlrb-changes; and Anthony K. Glenn, "Labor Board Dials Back Ambush Election Rules," National Law Review, December 13,

2019, https://www.natlawreview.com/article/labor-board-dials-back-am-bush-election-rules.

119. Madlen Davies and Ben Stockton, "'Invisible' Pharmacists Selling Knock-Off Drugs: The Rise of Antibiotic Resistance in Cambodia," Bureau of Investigative Journalism, September 20, 2019, https://www.thebureauinvestigates.com/stories/2019-09-20/cambodia.

120. Susmita Baral, "Here's What's Causing India's 'Superbug' Problem," HuffPost, July 6, 2017, https://www.huffpost.com/entry/india-super-bug_n_5949b329e4b0db570d3778cc.

121. Joe Wallen, "India Doctor Shortage Drives Rise in Superbugs, Report Warns," *Telegraph*, April 23, 2019, https://www.telegraph.co.uk/global-health/science-and-disease/india-doctor-shortage-drives-rise-su-perbugs-report-warns/.

122. Geeta Anand and Frederik Joelving, "Driven to Suicide by an 'Inhuman and Unnatural' Pressure to Sell," *New York Times*, August 11, 2016, https://www.nytimes.com/2016/08/11/business/international/abbott-india-sui-cide-inhuman-drug-sales-tactics.html.

123. Madlen Davies, Ben Stockton, and Rahul Meesaraganda, "Drug Company Representatives are Giving 'Quack' Doctors Fridges and Televisions to Sell Antibiotics," The Independent, August 19, 2019, https://www.independent.co.uk/news/world/asia/drug-company-india-antibi-otics-superbug-money-a9069896.html; and Madlen Davies, Rahul Meesaraganda, and Ben Stockton, "Drug Company Reps Give Quack Doctors Fridges and Televisions to Sell Antibiotics," BuzzFlash, August 21, 2019, https://buzzflash.com/articles/drug-company-reps-give-quack-doctors-fridges-and-televisions-to-sell-antibiotics.

124. "Vision for Justice 2020 and Beyond: A New Paradigm for Public Safety," The Leadership Conference and Civil Rights Corps, September 2019, http://civilrightsdocs.info/pdf/reports/Vision-For-Justice-2020-SHORT.pdf.

125. Alexi Jones and Wendy Sawyer, "Arrest, Release, Repeat: How Police and Jails are Misused to Respond to Social Problems," Prison Policy Initiative, August 2019, https://www.prisonpolicy.org/reports/repeatarrests.html.

126. "Billionaire Bonanza 2020 Updates: Pandemic Profiteering," Inequality.org (Institute for Policy Studies), May 14, 2020, https://inequality.org/billionaire-bonanza-2020-updates/. This is one of several updates to the original report by Chuck Collins, Omar Ocampo, and Sophia Paslaski, "Billionaire Bonanza 2020: Wealth Windfalls, Tumbling Taxes, and Pandemic Profiteers," Institute for Policy Studies, April 23, 2020, https://ips-dc.org/billionaire-bonanza-2020/.

127. Collins, Ocampo, and Paslaski, "Billionaire Bonanza 2020: Wealth Windfalls, Tumbling Taxes, and Pandemic Profiteers." These eight billionaires, identified by Inequality.org as "pandemic profiteers," are Jeff Bezos (Amazon), MacKenzie Bezos (Amazon), Eric Yuan (Zoom), Steve Ballmer (Microsoft), John Albert Sobrato (Silicon Valley real estate), Elon Musk (Tesla and SpaceX), Joshua Harris (Apollo Global Management), and Rocco Commisso (Mediacom).

128. Collins, Ocampo, and Paslaski, "Billionaire Bonanza 2020: Wealth Windfalls, Tumbling Taxes, and Pandemic Profiteers."

129. For example, Alan Rappeport and Thomas Kaplan, "Democrats' Plans to Tax Wealth Would Reshape U.S. Economy," *New York Times*, October 1, 2019, updated October 2, 2019, https://www.nytimes.com/2019/10/01/us/politics/sanders-warren-wealth-tax.html; and Christopher Ingraham, "Over 60 Percent of Voters—Including Half of Republicans—Support Elizabeth Warren's Wealth Tax," *Washington Post*, February 5, 2019, https://www.washingtonpost.com/us-policy/2019/02/05/over-percent-voters-including-half-republicans-support-elizabeth-warrens-wealth-tax/.

130. Michael Hobbes, "COVID-19 is the Best Argument Yet for a Wealth Tax," HuffPost, March 26, 2020, updated April 1, 2020, https://www.huffpost.com/entry/coronavirus-wealth-tax-billionaires_n_5e7ccocfc-5b6256a7a260ebb.

131. Ferdinando Giugliano, "A Wealth Tax Isn't the Right Way to Pay for the Pandemic," Bloomberg, April 21, 2020, https://www.bloomberg.com/opinion/articles/2020-04-21/coronavirus-a-wealth-tax-isn-t-the-right-way-to-pay-for-pandemic.

132. Josh Boak, "COVID-19 Reinforces an Economist's Warnings about Inequality," ABC News, April 25, 2020, https://abcnews.go.com/Business/wireStory/covid-19-reinforces-economists-warnings-inequality-70348292.

133. Daniel Markovits, "A Wealth Tax is the Logical Way to Support Coronavirus Relief," *New York Times*, April 21, 2020, https://www.nytimes.com/2020/04/21/opinion/coronavirus-wealth-tax.html.

134. Nina Brooks, Eran Bendavid, and Grant Miller, "USA Aid Policy and Induced Abortion in Sub-Saharan Africa: An Analysis of the Mexico City Policy," *The Lancet*, Vol. 7 No. 8 (August 1, 2019), https://www.thelancet.com/journals/langlo/article/PIIS2214-109X(19)30267-0/fulltext [first published online June 27, 2019].

135. Edward Wong, "U.S. Expands Anti-Abortion Policies with New Overseas Funding Rules," *New York Times*, March 26, 2019, https://www.nytimes.com/2019/03/26/us/politics/state-department-abortion-funding.html; Somini Sengupta, "Trump Revives Ban on Foreign Aid to Groups That Give Abortion Counseling," *New York Times*, January 23, 2017, https://www.nytimes.com/2017/01/23/world/trump-ban-foreign-aid-abortions.html; and Hanna Ingber, "Q. and A.: How Trump's Revival of an Abortion Ban will Affect Women in Kenya," *New York Times*, January 26, 2017, https://www.nytimes.com/2017/01/26/world/africa/trump-abortion-ban.html.

136. Editorial Board, "The 'Global Gag Rule' on Abortion Just Got Much Bigger—and Much Worse," *Washington Post*, May 16, 2017, https://www.washingtonpost.com/opinions/the-global-gag-rule-on-abortion-just-got-much-bigger--and-much-worse/2017/05/16/2406671e-39a6-11e7-8854-21f359183e8c_story.html.

137. Jeannine Etter, interview with Anu Kumar, "The Anti-Abortion 'Global Gag Rule' Turns 36 Years Old; Plus, Organizers Plan No War with Iran March in SF for Saturday," *UpFront*, KPFA, January 24, 2020, https://kpfa.org/episode/upfront-january-24-2020/ [interview begins at 34 min.]; and Maya Oppenheim, "Trump's 'Global Gag Rule' Killing Women by Depriving Them of Crucial Abortion Advice, Report Finds," The

Independent, June 6, 2019, https://www.independent.co.uk/news/world/americas/trump-global-gag-rule-abortion-mexico-city-policy-women-health-coalition-a8943901.html.

138. Jeff Martin, "Filmmaker Who Wouldn't Sign Georgia's Israel Oath Sues State," Associated Press, February 12, 2020, https://apnews.com/796ae-3c36b7f58594207308855b7bfde; and "CAIR-GA: Civil Rights Groups to Announce Federal Free Speech Lawsuit Against Georgia's Unconstitutional 'Israel Boycott' Law," Yahoo! Finance (via PR Newswire), February 10, 2020, https://finance.yahoo.com/news/cair-ga-civil-rights-groups-165700544.html.

139. Andrew Bacher-Hicks, Stephen B. Billings, and David J. Deming, "The School to Prison Pipeline: Long-Run Impacts of School Suspensions on Adult Crime," National Bureau of Economic Research, Working Paper No. 26257, September 2019, https://www.nber.org/papers/w26257.

140. Robert Bozick, Jennifer L. Steele, Lois M. Davis, and Susan Turner, "Does Providing Inmates with Education Improve Postrelease Outcomes? A Meta-Analysis of Correctional Education Programs in the United States," *Journal of Experimental Criminology*, Vol. 14 (2018), 389–428 [first published online May 24, 2018]; posted at RAND.org on July 3, 2018, https://www.rand.org/pubs/external_publications/EP67650.html.

141. Margaret diZerega, "College in Prison: Postsecondary Education Opportunities for Incarcerated People," Vera Institute of Justice, undated, https://www.vera.org/projects/college-in-prison/overview [accessed May 19, 2020].

142. Nina Agrawal, "California Expands Ban on 'Willful Defiance' Suspensions in Schools," *Los Angeles Times*, September 10, 2019, https://www.latimes.com/california/story/2019-09-10/school-suspension-willful-defiance-california.

143. Sade Green, "How the Political Pipeline Disenfranchises Young People of Color," *Forbes*, October 2, 2019, https://www.forbes.com/sites/civicnation/2019/10/02/how-the-political-pipeline-disenfranchises-young-people-of-color/#5177de6d2b2d.

144. Erica L. Green, "Senate Leaders Reconsider Ban on Pell Grants for Prisoners," *New York Times*, February 15, 2018, https://www.nytimes.com/2018/02/15/us/politics/pell-grants-prisoners.html.

145. Elissa Nadworny, "Congress Considers Making College More Accessible to People in Prison," NPR, April 20, 2019, https://www.npr.org/2019/04/20/713874091/congress-considers-making-college-more-accessible-to-people-in-prison.

146. Danielle Douglas-Gabriel, "Education Dept. Expands Pell Grant Initiative for Inmates to Take College Classes," *Washington Post*, April 24, 2020, https://www.washingtonpost.com/education/2020/04/24/education-dept-expands-pell-grant-initiative-inmates-take-college-classes/.

CHAPTER 2

Déjà Vu All Over Again
What Happened to Previous *Censored* Stories

STEVE MACEK and ZACH MCNANNA

Starting in the mid-1990s, Project Censored published an annual Déjà Vu chapter reviewing the fate of under-reported news stories featured in previous years' Top 25 lists. The chapter explored the stories' subsequent developments, investigated whether they had received any corporate or independent news coverage, and gauged the extent to which they had become part of the "broader public discourse." While a few of those stories would end up receiving more corporate media attention, the bulk of the stories continued to be ignored and underreported except by the independent press. The last edition of Project Censored's yearbook to contain a Déjà Vu chapter was *Censored 2017*, the fortieth anniversary edition.

Happily, Déjà Vu is back after a four-year hiatus. This chapter provides updates on five stories from the past decade, including significant developments, substantial changes in the amount of media attention the stories have received, or both. From *Censored 2011*, we look back at story #2, on Pentagon pollution. From *Censored 2018*, we update story #10, on global internet shutdowns; and story #17, on the pioneering climate change lawsuit

Juliana v. US. From *Censored 2019*, we review story #19, on $21 trillion in government accounting errors. Finally, we reflect on story #25 from *Censored 2020*, regarding the serious privacy concerns raised by Google's Screenwise Meter.

These were not the only stories from recent *Censored* volumes we reinvestigated. For instance, we reviewed story #10 from *Censored 2020*, on the Pentagon's use of social media data to predict the outbreak of domestic protests. However, we were unable to find any additional coverage of this terrifying initiative in either the establishment media or the independent press. Similarly, we were unable to find any further reporting by any news organization about *Censored 2020*'s story #17, on the high unemployment rate among former prisoners.

Some of the stories we looked into have recently received considerable coverage from corporate news outlets—notably, the story about the trillions of dollars in governmental accounting errors, and the story about *Juliana v. US*—yet even then, the establishment media's reporting on the stories has far too often left out essential facts or context crucial to meaningful analysis. And, as usual, many of the previous stories we explored have been the subject of important new reporting by independent journalists even as they continue to be overlooked or minimized by the corporate press.

US Department of Defense is the Worst Polluter on the Planet

Sara Flounders, "Add Climate Havoc to War Crimes: Pentagon's Role in Global Catastrophe," International Action Center, December 18, 2009, https://web.archive.org/web/20091226055024/http://www.iacenter.org/o/world/climatesummit_pentagon121809/.

Mickey Z., "Can You Identify the Worst Polluter on the Planet? Here's a Hint: Shock and Awe," Planet Green, August 11, 2009, https://web.archive.org/web/20090812104854/http://planetgreen.discovery.com/tech-transport/identify-worst-polluter-planet.html.

Juan González, interview with Julian Aguon, "Guam Residents Organize Against US Plans for $15B Military Buildup on Pacific Island," Democracy Now!, October 9, 2009, http://www.democracynow.org/2009/10/9/guam_residents_organize_against_us_plans.

Ian MacLeod, "U.S. Navy Plots Arctic Push," Ottawa Citizen, November 28, 2009, https://web.archive.org/web/20100830234614/http://www.ottawacitizen.com/technology/navy+plots+Arctic+push/2278324/story.html.

Nick Turse, "Casualties Continue in Vietnam," In These Times, April 24, 2009, http://www.inthesetimes.com/article/4363/casualties_continue_in_vietnam

Jalal Ghazi, "Cancer—The Deadly Legacy of the Invasion of Iraq," New America Media January 6, 2010, https://web.archive.org/web/20100111052152/http://news.newamericamedia.org/news/view_article.html?article_id=80e260b3839daf2084fdeb0965ad31ab.

Student Researchers: Dimitrina Semova, Joan Pedro, and Luis Luján (Complutense University of Madrid); Ashley Jackson-Lesti, Ryan Stevens, Chris Marten, and Kristy Nelson (Sonoma State University); Christopher Lue (Indian River State College); and Cassie Barthel (St. Cloud State University)

Faculty Evaluators: Ana I. Segovia (Complutense University of Madrid), Julie Flohr and Myrna Goodman (Sonoma State University), Elliot D. Cohen (Indian River State College), and Julie Andrzejewski (St. Cloud State University)

In 2010, several independent news reports revealed that the US military was "the most egregious and widespread" polluter on the planet, and Project Censored identified the story as the second most important and underreported of the year. Sara Flounders of the International Action Center observed at the time that the Pentagon was "the largest institutional user of petroleum products and energy in general," consuming some 320,000 barrels of oil per day according to official records, and a major contributor of the greenhouse gases scientists believe are responsible for climate change. Indeed, according to Steve Kretzmann of Oil Change International, the first five years of the Iraq War generated the equivalent of some 141 million metric tons of carbon dioxide, emitting more than 60 percent of all the countries in the world.[1]

As the *Censored 2011* summary detailed, the US military has consistently been shielded from responsibility for its environmentally destructive activities. During the Kyoto Accords negotiations in December 1997, the United States demanded as a condition for signing that its military operations worldwide be exempt from requirements to reduce or even measure the fossil fuels they consume. In 2001 the Bush administration refused to sign the agreement even with the exemption, and Congress passed a provision ensuring the US military's exemption from any energy use reductions that might ultimately be negotiated. An executive order signed by President Barack Obama in 2009 continued the military's exemption, even as it required other federal agencies to cut their greenhouse gas emissions 20 percent by the year 2020.

Releasing huge amounts of carbon dioxide into the atmosphere is not the only way the Pentagon has contributed to environmental degradation. The American military has also contaminated large swaths of Asia and the Middle East with tens of thousands of pounds of highly toxic depleted uranium, polluted Southeast Asia with poisonous dioxin that is still causing cancers and birth defects four decades after the conclusion of the Vietnam War, and left behind rusting barrels of chemicals, solvents, and millions of rounds of ammunition at bases throughout the world.

As an example of the Pentagon's ongoing pollution of

the planet, Project Censored in 2010 highlighted the way that a proposed $15 billion military buildup in the unincorporated US territory of Guam threatened the island's fragile ecology and fresh water supply, a move with devastating consequences for its Indigenous people, for the coral reefs surrounding the island, and for several endangered species whose habitat would be destroyed.

Update

In an October 10, 2019 article published by Fairness & Accuracy In Reporting (FAIR), Joshua Cho argued that a decade after Project Censored first spotlighted this story, the full facts surrounding the Pentagon's ongoing and rampant pollution of the environment continue to go unreported.[2]

Cho observed that two major studies about US military contributions to global climate change published in 2019 were largely ignored by the corporate press. The first, "Pentagon Fuel Use, Climate Change, and the Cost of War," released by Brown University's Costs of War Project, confirmed that the military has been responsible for the equivalent of some 1.2 billion metric tons of carbon dioxide since 2001, more than any other agency of the federal government.[3] The second, an article published in the *Transactions of the Institute of British Geographers* entitled "Hidden Carbon Costs of the 'Everywhere War': Logistics, Geopolitical Ecology, and the Carbon Boot-Print of the US Military," found that if the US military were a country, its fuel usage would make it the 47th biggest emitter of greenhouse gases in the world, ahead of Sweden and Portugal.[4]

According to Cho's research, none of the explosive revelations contained in these two studies were covered by corporate media like the *New York Times*, *Wall Street Journal*, ABC, CBS, or CNN in the four months from June 1 to October 1, 2019. Independent news outlets such as the *Washington Examiner*, *The Nation*, and The Real News Network covered the Costs of War study and the *Daily Mail* and ScienceDaily covered the findings of the *Transactions of the Institute of British Geographers* article.[5] Since the publication of Cho's FAIR piece, there has been no further coverage of either study in either the establishment or the independent press.

Meanwhile, an important component of the original 2010 Project Censored synopsis of this story—the devastating impact of the military buildup in Guam—has been all but ignored by corporate news organizations. While establishment news outlets have occasionally acknowledged that the coral reefs and other aspects of the flora and fauna of Guam are being degraded, such reports usually fail to identify the US Armed Forces as the primary cause of the ecological destruction. In December 2018, the popular science magazine *National Geographic*, currently co-owned by the National Geographic Society and the Walt Disney Company, did publish an article by Alexandra Ossola on the threat posed to biodiversity by base expansion on the island.[6] Other than that, the only substantive documentation of how the US military's presence in Guam is hurting the local ecosystem—or of how local Indigenous and environmental activists are fighting back—has come from the progressive magazine *The Nation* and the conservationist website Mongabay.[7]

To be fair, even though the corporate media have generally ignored damning stories like the one about the Pentagon's massive carbon bootprint, over the past decade establishment news outlets have occasionally reported on the specific ecological consequences of military activity for communities located near domestic military installations. For instance, on March 14, 2019 the *New York Times* ran a lengthy article detailing the Pentagon's efforts to pressure the Environmental Protection Agency into loosening standards governing acceptable levels of groundwater pollution in a bid to evade cleanup costs at bases in Florida and elsewhere.[8] But such coverage has been the exception rather than the rule. Generally, corporate media deal with this topic episodically at best and fail to provide the public with complete and accurate information about the US military's responsibility for pollution on a global scale.

Censored 2018 #10

2016: A Record Year for Global Internet Shutdowns

Devin Coldewey, "Study Estimates Cost of Last Year's Internet Shutdowns at $2.4 Billion," TechCrunch, October 24, 2016, https://techcrunch.com/2016/10/24/study-suggests-internet-shutdowns-may-cost-countries-billions/.

Kevin Collier, "Governments Loved to Shut Down the Internet in 2016—Here's Where," Vocativ, December 23, 2016, http://www.vocativ.com/386042/internet-access-shut-off-censorship/.

Lyndal Rowlands, "More Than 50 Internet Shutdowns in 2016," Inter Press Service, December 30, 2016, http://www.ipsnews.net/2016/12/more-than-50-internet-shutdowns-in-2016/.

Azad Essa, "What Can the UN Do If Your Country Cuts the Internet?" Al Jazeera, May 8, 2017, http://www.aljazeera.com/indepth/features/2017/05/country-cuts-internet-170504064432840.html.

Student Researcher: Hugo Sousa (Citrus College)

Faculty Evaluator: Andy Lee Roth (Citrus College)

Governments throughout the world shut down internet access more than fifty times in 2016, Lyndal Rowlands reported for the Inter Press Service (IPS) in December of that year. Those shutdowns limited freedom of speech, skewed elections, and damaged economies in the process. "In the worst cases," Rowlands wrote, "internet shutdowns have been associated with human rights violations," as happened in Ethiopia and Uganda.

As Kevin Collier reported for Vocativ, digital rights organization Access Now documented 53 instances in 2016 in which national governments shut down the internet for all or part of a country, "throttled" access speeds to make the internet essentially unusable, or blocked specific websites. These 53 cases represented a sharp uptick from the fifteen shutdowns identified by Access Now the previous year. As Collier noted, Access Now uses a "conservative metric," counting "repeated, similar outages"—like those which occurred during Gabon's widely criticized internet "curfew"—as a single instance.

Many countries intentionally blacked out internet access during elections and to quell protest. Not only did these shutdowns restrict freedom of speech, they also hurt economies throughout the world. TechCrunch, IPS, and other independent news organizations reported that internet shutdowns cost countries $2.4 billion between July 2015 and June 2016. The biggest losses were in India (an estimated $968 million), Saudi Arabia ($465 million), and Morocco ($320 million).

As Deji Olukotun, a senior manager at Access Now, told IPS, one way to stop government shutdowns is for internet service providers to resist government demands. He also called on international organizations—including the International Telecommunications Union, which is the UN agency for information and communication technologies—to issue statements in response to specific incidents.

On July 1, 2016, in a nonbinding resolution signed by more than seventy countries, the UN Human Rights Council lauded the internet's "great potential to accelerate human progress," and condemned "measures to intentionally prevent or disrupt access to or dissemination of information online." The United Nations's special rapporteur on freedom of opinion and expression, David Kaye, told Al Jazeera that advocates of online rights "need to be constantly pushing for laws that protect this space and demand that governments meet their obligations in digital spaces just as in non-digital spaces."

Corporate news coverage of internet shutdowns in 2015–2016 tended to focus on specific countries, especially ones in Africa. Although this coverage made passing reference to Access Now's findings on internet disruptions around the world, it rarely explored the implications of those findings in depth. Corporate media reports about this story tended not to address the larger, global scope of internet shutdowns—and, unlike independent news coverage, these reports often did not discuss how internet providers might resist government demands or mention the actions taken by the United Nations to address this issue.

Update

Since Project Censored originally spotlighted this story, the rate of government interference with internet service throughout the world has accelerated dramatically. A new study by Access Now published in July 2019 documents 196 internet shutdowns in 2018, nearly quadrupling the 53 they reported in 2016.[9] These 196 internet shutdowns occurred in 25 countries, with 134 shutdowns occurring in India alone. In 2019, Access Now documented 213 shutdowns in 33 countries.[10] These blackouts have led to reported commercial losses of $2.5 billion in Iran over the past decade, $3 billion in India between 2012 and 2017, $1.4 billion in Kashmir between August and December of 2019, and many smaller losses, such as an estimated $17 million in Zimbabwe over just a three-day period in January 2019.[11]

The increase in the number and severity of internet shutdowns has brought with it a rise in corporate media coverage. In late 2019 and early 2020, the *New York Times*, *Washington Post*, *Los Angeles Times*, *Chicago Tribune*, and a host of other major establishment news outlets published stories about internet shutdowns.[12] While the issue of government interference with internet access is starting to gain attention, it is worth emphasizing that the delay in coverage allowed hundreds of shutdowns that occurred prior to 2019 to go mostly unreported.

Even more interesting to consider is which countries the corporate press chose to focus on in their reporting about this issue. Despite experiencing relatively few internet shutdowns in 2019, Iran was the subject of a disproportionate number of establishment media reports on the topic, usually in connection with the Iranian government blocking internet service during times of civil unrest and mass protest. A significant number of the corporate media's reports about Iran's suppression of online speech came just weeks before (and after) the US assassination of Iranian General

Qasem Soleimani. On the other hand, US ally India was responsible for hundreds of shutdowns in 2018 and 2019, yet corporate news outlets paid far less attention to shutdowns in India than they did to shutdowns in Iran.[13]

India-based activist group Software Freedom Law Centre has reported an astonishing 180 internet shutdowns since 2012 in the Indian-occupied region of Kashmir, including the longest recorded shutdown in history, beginning August 4, 2019 and ending January 26, 2020.[14] Moreover, the restoration of internet service that was permitted after January 26 was only partial, allowing users in the area to access just 301 government-approved websites and limiting mobile internet speeds.[15] One of the few corporate news dispatches regarding India's digital quarantine of Kashmir was a *Washington Post* article, "India's Internet Shutdown in Kashmir is the Longest Ever in a Democracy," published on December 15, 2019, that surveyed the impact of the blackout on ordinary people in the region.[16] The article described citizens taking daily seventy-mile train journeys to areas with internet access, doctors cut off from their patients, students falling behind in online classes, and online businesses losing customers and revenue as a result of the shutdown.

Modern democratic societies rely on unfettered access to online communication. So, in fact, do news outlets of all kinds, both corporate and independent. While it is heartening that the corporate media have finally awoken to the alarming frequency and scope of government interference with people's use of the internet throughout the world, it is troubling that they have not devoted more attention to US allies like India who are responsible for the bulk of the world's internet shutdowns.

Young Plaintiffs Invoke Constitutional Grounds for Climate Protection

James Conca, "Federal Court Rules on Climate Change in Favor of Today's Children," *Forbes*, April 10, 2016, http://www.forbes.com/sites/jamesconca/2016/04/10/federal-court-rules-on-climate-change-in-favor-of-todays-children/#5e5973246219.

Michelle Nijhuis, "The Teen-Agers Suing Over Climate Change," *New Yorker*, December 6, 2016, http://www.newyorker.com/tech/elements/the-teen-agers-suing-over-climate-change.

Gabriela Steier, "No Ordinary Lawsuit: Juliana v. United States is a Landmark Precedent for Climate Change Legislation," JURIST, January 6, 2017, http://www.jurist.org/forum/2017/01/Gabriela-Steier-juliana-v-united-states.php.

Zahra Hirji, "Children's Climate Lawsuit Against U.S. Adds Trump as Defendant," Inside Climate News, February 9, 2017, https://insideclimatenews.org/news/09022017/climate-change-lawsuit-donald-trump-children.

Ciara O'Rourke, "The 11-Year-Old Suing Trump over Climate Change," *The Atlantic*, February 9, 2017, https://www.theatlantic.com/science/archive/2017/02/trump-climate-lawsuit/516054/.

Student Researchers: Sabrina Salinas and Eric Osterberg (Citrus College)

Faculty Evaluator: Andy Lee Roth (Citrus College)

In September 2015, 21 young environmental activists represented by Eugene, Oregon-based advocacy group Our Children's Trust sued the federal government and President Barack Obama for knowingly endangering their lives by failing to do enough to prevent climate change. According to the suit, now known as *Juliana v. US*, the defendants "deliberately allow[ed] atmospheric CO_2 concentrations to escalate to levels unprecedented in human history," thus violating their constitutional rights. As James Conca noted in his *Forbes* article on the case, the lawsuit's assertion that the federal government has an obligation to protect the "natural systems required for the people's survival" was the first of its kind.

Three fossil fuel trade associations, including the American Petroleum Institute, initially attempted to intervene in the lawsuit, alleging it constituted a "direct, substantial threat to [their] businesses," although by June 2017 they were no longer defendants in the suit.

Following pre-trial hearings, US District Court Judge Thomas Coffin in April 2016 rejected Justice Department motions to have the case dismissed. In doing so, he found that the government is subject to public trust doctrine and a "trustee" of the natural resources people depend on for "life, liberty and the pursuit of happiness."

In November 2016, US District Court Judge Ann Aiken affirmed Coffin's ruling, clearing the way for the case to go to trial. In February 2017, the plaintiffs updated their suit to name President Donald Trump as a defendant in place of Obama. As *Censored 2018* went to press in summer 2017, lawyers for the young environmental activists sought to depose Trump's then–Secretary of State, Rex Tillerson, former CEO of ExxonMobil, and were preparing for a trial projected to begin in the autumn of 2017.

As Project Censored observed in its original write-up, in autumn 2015 corporate news coverage of the pioneering lawsuit was scant, with the lone exception being MSNBC's November 2015 report framing the case as "long on sym-bolism" and "unlikely to win." However, by the spring and summer of 2016, CBS, Fox News, *Forbes*, and *The Atlantic* had also reported about the lawsuit.

Update

Since appearing in *Censored 2018*, *Juliana v. US* gradually received more establishment media attention as the suit slowly made its way through the courts. In the three years since the story of the lawsuit originally broke, the *New*

York Times, *Washington Post*, *Chicago Tribune*, PBS, and CBS have all done updates on the case.[17] Most notably, CBS has run two *60 Minutes* specials detailing the young plaintiffs involved, the case's progress, and the attention it has received in legal and environmental circles.

The trial was originally set to begin in October 2017. However, the Trump administration appealed Judge Aiken's 2016 ruling three times to the Ninth Circuit Court in California, and twice to the US Supreme Court, on the grounds that the lawsuit was "misguided" because there is no constitutional right to "a stable climate," and that the remedies being sought were not viable.[18] In each instance, the government's appeal was denied, meaning that the case was poised to go to trial sometime in 2020 despite numerous attempts to delay the proceedings.

Then, on January 17, 2020, a panel of the Ninth Circuit Court of Appeals on a 2–1 vote threw out the case for lack of standing. In his majority opinion Judge Andrew Hurwitz wrote that the young plaintiffs had "made a compelling case that action is needed," but added that "such relief is beyond our constitutional power."[19] The lawsuit's dismissal was covered by the *New York Times*, *Time*, and several other establishment news organizations.[20]

If the plaintiffs had won their landmark suit, the implications would have been enormous. Our Children's Trust was asking to "get the federal government out of the business of in any way subsidizing fossil fuels and get them into the business of dramatically curtailing greenhouse gases," as professor of environmental law at UCLA Ann Carlson put it. Carlson observed that "there have been court decisions that have asked governments to do very dramatic things. This might be the biggest."[21]

During the protracted legal wrangling over the case, op-eds and commentaries published by numerous media outlets offered diverse perspectives on the validity of the young activists' arguments and the larger philosophical issues *Juliana* raised. The case sparked heated exchanges regarding the rights of citizens to a healthy environment, the rights of children to a viable future, the validity of claims on behalf of future persons, and the responsibilities of corporations and our government to preserve an environment capable of sustaining human civilization.

An *In These Times* piece by progressive journalist Arun Gupta offered a balanced but hopeful account of the case, discussing the constitutional justifications for the arguments made on behalf of the plaintiffs.[22] Gupta noted that, "[w]hile the right to a 'stable climate system' is not enumerated in the Constitution, the Ninth Amendment states that other rights exist even if not listed."

On the other hand, center-right political website The Hill published a commentary by law professor Donald J. Kochan arguing that the demands made by the young environmental activists in their lawsuit are unconstitutional.[23] Kochan claimed that it is not the job of the judicial system to force the legislative branch into action.

Though the coverage by corporate news media and media commentary surrounding *Juliana* did pick up considerably in 2019 and 2020, the attention it received arguably failed to match the magnitude of the case. Given the potential consequences of even a partial victory for the environmental activists in this lawsuit, one would have expected *Juliana v. US* to have dominated the headlines rather than receiving the intermittent coverage it was allotted.

On March 3, 2020, Our Children's Trust petitioned the

Ninth Circuit Court of Appeals to convene a new panel of eleven judges to reconsider the January ruling.[24] Ten *amicus curiae* (friend of the court) briefs have been filed in support of the petition, including one from the National League of Women Voters and one submitted by 24 members of the US Congress.[25] Yet even if the court decides to review and overturn their earlier decision, allowing the lawsuit at long last to go to trial, the corporate media's interest in properly covering the story remains to be seen.

Censored 2019 #16

$21 Trillion in Unaccounted-for Government Spending from 1998 to 2015

Greg Hunter, "Missing $21 Trillion Means Federal Government is Lawless—Dr. Mark Skidmore," USAWatchdog, December 3, 2017, https://usawatchdog.com/missing-21-trillion-means-federal-government-is-lawless-dr-mark-skidmore/.

Andy Henion, "MSU Scholars Find $21 Trillion in Unauthorized Government Spending; Defense Department to Conduct First-Ever Audit," MSU Today, December 11, 2017, https://msutoday.msu.edu/news/2017/msu-scholars-find-21-trillion-in-unauthorized-government-spending-defense-department-to-conduct/.

"$21 Trillion of Unauthorized Spending by US Govt Discovered by Economics Professor," RT, December 16, 2017, https://www.rt.com/usa/413411-trillions-dollars-missing-research/.

Student Researcher: Andrea Fekete (North Central College)

Faculty Evaluator: Steve Macek (North Central College)

The sixteenth story on Project Censored's Top 25 list for 2018–2019 was stunning: according to a study conducted by Michigan State University Professor of Economics Mark Skidmore, two federal agencies—the Department of Defense (DoD) and the Department of Housing and Urban Development (HUD)—had together accumulated as much as $21 trillion in unaccounted-for expenditures.

This news received little corporate media attention when it first broke but has since become the focus of countless establishment newspaper articles and broadcast news packages—yet, as explained below, much of that reporting continues to ignore the main thrust of Skidmore's research.

After overhearing HUD's Assistant Secretary Catherine Austin Fitts reference a report that showed the Army had *$6.5 trillion* in inadequately documented budget adjustments in fiscal year 2015, Skidmore worked with Fitts and two graduate students to comb through reports from the websites of HUD and the DoD in an effort to find additional unaccounted-for spending. In one of these reports, Skidmore discovered an appendix showing a transfer of $800 billion from the US Treasury to the Army (which at the time had an authorized annual budget of only $122 billion). As MSU Today reported, Skidmore's queries to the Office of Inspector General about the discrepancy went unanswered, and at one point the OIG disabled the links to documents he was studying.

Shortly after Skidmore's findings went public, the Pentagon announced it would undergo its first-ever audit.[26] The announced audit was to begin in 2018 and audits were projected to occur annually. RT's story on the audit quoted the Defense Department's Comptroller David L. Norquist explaining that the Pentagon had hired independent account firms to audit its finances because it is important "that the Congress and the American people have confidence in DoD's management of every taxpayer dollar."

At the time of *Censored 2019*'s publication in October 2018, the only corporate media mentions of Skidmore's findings were in two brief *Forbes* articles co-written by

Skidmore himself and two NPR pieces on the decision to audit the Pentagon.[27]

Update

Since *Censored 2019* highlighted Mark Skidmore's research, corporate media outlets have begun to take notice of the Pentagon's alarming accounting issues, thanks in large part to a social media gaffe by celebrity politician Alexandria Ocasio-Cortez (D-NY). In a December 2, 2018 tweet, then Representative-elect Ocasio-Cortez referenced an article posted on *The Nation*'s website explaining Skidmore's findings: "\$21 TRILLION of Pentagon financial transactions 'could not be traced, documented, or explained.' \$21T in Pentagon accounting errors. Medicare for All costs ~ \$32T. That means 66% of Medicare for All could have been funded already by the Pentagon."[28]

What followed was an absolute frenzy of corporate media commentary on Ocasio-Cortez's misinterpretation of Skidmore's research. In the *Nation* article she referenced, author Dave Lindorff explained that Skidmore's discoveries do not imply that \$21 trillion has been spent by the Pentagon or has somehow gone missing; rather, they indicate just how bad the DoD and other federal agencies are at maintaining orderly financial records. Outlets such as the *New York Times*, *New York Post*, *Baltimore Sun*, *Daily Herald*, Associated Press, Fox News, and CNN were quick to point out and dissect Ocasio-Cortez's mistake. *The Washington Post*'s fact-checkers gave her tweet "Four Pinocchios," a rating the paper reserves for brazen lies.[29] But not one of these news organizations followed up with in-depth investigations of the Pentagon's (or HUD's) accounting errors.

One fact that Lindorff's article revealed, which has gone relatively unnoticed due to the corporate media's focus on Ocasio-Cortez's error, is that the Pentagon flunked its first-ever comprehensive audit. Ernst & Young along with other private accounting firms concluded that the Department of Defense's financial records were "riddled with so many bookkeeping deficiencies, irregularities, and errors that a reliable audit was simply impossible."[30] While Reuters and a few other corporate news organizations did report the story, the coverage that the failed audit received pales in comparison to the attention received by AOC's social media misstatements.[31]

In many ways, corporate media treatment of this story since October 2018 is a perfect example of what Project Censored calls "News Abuse," reporting that minimizes a story's true importance or that frames it in a propagandistic manner, thereby "abusing" the public trust. (See Chapter 4 of this volume for more on News Abuse.)

Moreover, none of the corporate media who excoriated AOC for her mistake have reported on the fact that the federal government recently adopted new regulations designed to prevent journalists and ordinary citizens from accessing exactly the sort of data Skidmore used to expose the Pentagon's massive accounting errors.[32] As Michele Ferri and Jonathan Lurie explained in a January 10, 2019 article published by the *Solari Report*, the advisory board responsible for establishing federal accounting principles has recently enacted a new Federal Accounting Standard, Standard 56, which allows the government to hide data about funds and hiring expenses that would, if made public, threaten national security.[33] Essentially, Standard 56 is a blanket that can be legally thrown over any accounting information the government does not want to become public.

Censored 2020 #25

Google Screenwise: Consenting to Surveillance Capitalism

Sydney Li and Jason Kelley, "Google Screenwise: An Unwise Trade of All Your Privacy for Cash," Electronic Frontier Foundation, February 1, 2019, https://www.eff.org/deep-links/2019/02/google-screenwise-unwise-trade-all-your-privacy-cash, republished by Common Dreams, February 4, 2019, https://www.commondreams.org/views/2019/02/04/google-screenwise-unwise-trade-all-your-privacy-cash.

Dami Lee, "Google Also Monitored iPhone Usage with a Private App," The Verge, January 30, 2019, https://www.theverge.com/2019/1/30/18204064/apple-google-monitoring-phone-usage-screenwise-meter.

Student Researcher: Fabrice Nozier (Drew University)

Faculty Evaluator: Lisa Lynch (Drew University)

As highlighted by the final story on *Censored 2020*'s Top 25 list, Google's introduction of Opinion Rewards, a survey app for Android and iOS users that allows them to earn "rewards," has raised serious new concerns about the tech giant's invasion of users' privacy. In exchange for very modest cash awards, which can earn users roughly $50–100 per year, Google gains access to app users' phone screens and web browser windows. Rather than fooling users into acceding to secretive corporate "research" behind lengthy terms and conditions, Google disguises the monitoring function of Opinion Rewards as "metering"—a "funny word for surveillance," as Sydney Li and Jason Kelley of the Electronic Frontier Foundation (EFF) pointed out.

Opinion Rewards is segmented into two distinct services, "Surveys App" and "Audience Measurement." The first is an app that prompts users to complete surveys ranging "from opinion polls, to hotel reviews, to merchant satisfaction surveys." The second, more invasive option requires registered households to install the Screenwise Meter mobile app and web extension which monitor internet usage. Google also encourages the installation of their "TV Meter," which monitors television consumption through a built-in mic.

In January 2019, Google disabled the iOS version of the app because it violated Apple's distribution policies; but Google Opinion Rewards continues to be available to Android users, who had installed it more than ten million times as of July 2019.

In February 2019, the *New York Times* published an editorial that reported on Google and Facebook paying people to download apps that track their phone activity and usage habits, and called for the Federal Trade Commission to "become the privacy watchdog that this era so desperately needs."[34] Apart from this piece, the corporate media at the time largely neglected to cover how Google's push to "meter" the market contributes to mass surveillance.

Update

Even prior to the publication of *Censored 2020* in October 2019, there were some important developments related to this story.

To begin with, just a few days after The Verge and the Electronic Frontier Foundation exposed Google's monitoring of its Screenwise app users, three US senators—Richard Blumenthal (D-CT), Ed Markey (D-MA), and Josh Hawley (R-MO)—sent a letter to Hiroshi Lockheimer, Google's senior vice president of platforms and ecosystems, demanding more information about the app.[35] As reported in a February 7, 2019 article in *Wired*, the senators' letter expressed concern that "Screenwise Meter was originally open to users as young as 13 years old, and continued to be available to the teenagers if they were registered as a part of a family group on Google Play." The senators demanded to know what measures Google had in place to ensure that underaged participants in the Screenwise program had "verified parental consent." They also requested an explanation for why Google had bypassed Apple's App Store review process to distribute and run their monitoring program and wanted to know if the company had bypassed the App Store's review process for any other non-internal apps.

Perhaps just as significant, the privacy concerns raised by the Screenwise Meter have been at the center of an ongoing and very public squabble between Google and Apple since early February 2019. On May 7, 2019 Google CEO Sundar Pichai published an op-ed in the *New York Times* pledging that the company "will never sell any personal information to third parties" and promising that users "get to decide how [their] information is used." He also expressed support for "comprehensive privacy legislation" and claimed that Google has urged Congress to pass just such a law. In the process, though, Pichai took a thinly-veiled swipe at Apple, implying that the enhanced protections on iOS devices which prevent unauthorized harvesting of user data were transforming privacy into "a luxury good offered only to people who can afford to buy premium products and services."[36]

It is interesting to note that in his recent public pronouncements on the issue, Google's CEO defines the company's promise to protect user privacy as a promise not to sell users' personal data, rather than as a promise not to gather such data in the first place. Yet what was objectionable about Screenwise—and what got it booted out of Apple's App Store—was not the selling of data to third parties but Google's invasive tracking of users' online (and offline) activities.

STEVE MACEK is professor of communication and chair of the Department of Communication and Media Studies at North Central College in Naperville, Illinois. He is the author of *Urban Nightmares: The Media, the Right, and the Moral Panic over the City* (University of Minnesota Press, 2006). His op-eds and essays about the media, politics, academic freedom, and free speech issues have been published in a wide range of magazines and newspapers, including *Z Magazine*, *St. Louis Journalism Review*, *Atlanta Journal-Constitution*, *Columbus Dispatch*, and *News & Observer*.

ZACH MCNANNA is a recent graduate of North Central College recognized as the outstanding major in philosophy for 2020. He intends to craft a diverse career working with nonprofit and humanitarian organizations, and he is determined to put his passion for writing and philosophical thought to good use.

Notes

1. Sara Flounders, "Add Climate Havoc to War Crimes: Pentagon's Role in Global Catastrophe," International Action Center, December 18, 2009, https://web.archive.org/web/20091224075919/http://www.iacenter. org/o/world/climatesummit_pentagon121809.

2. Joshua Cho, "Major Media Bury Groundbreaking Studies of Pentagon's Massive Carbon Bootprint," Fairness & Accuracy In Reporting (FAIR), October 10, 2019, https://fair.org/home/major-media-bury-groundbreaking-studies-of-pentagons-massive-carbon-bootprint/.

3. Neta C. Crawford, "Pentagon Fuel Use, Climate Change, and the Costs of War," Watson Institute for International and Public Affairs, Brown University, June 2019, https://watson.brown.edu/costsofwar/papers/ClimateChangeandCostofWar.

4. Oliver Belcher, Patrick Bigger, Ben Neimark, and Cara Kennelly, "Hidden Carbon Costs of the 'Everywhere War': Logistics, Geopolitical Ecology, and the Carbon Boot-Print of the US Military," *Transactions of the Institute of British Geographers*, Vol. 45 No. 1 (March 2020), 65–80, https://doi.org/10.1111/tran.12319 [first published online June 19, 2019].

5. Jamie McIntyre, "Iranian Threat to Shipping is Real and Growing, as US 'Smoking Gun' Video Evidence Shows," *Washington Examiner*, June 14, 2019, https://www.washingtonexaminer.com/policy/defense-national-security/iranian-threat-to-shipping-is-real-and-growing-as-u-s-smoking-gun-video-evidence-shows; Allegra Harpootlian, "The New Anti-War Movement," *The Nation*, June 25, 2019, https://www.thenation.com/article/archive/tom-dispatch-new-anti-war-movement-iraq-iran/; Dharna Noor, interview with Patrick Bigger and Neta C. Crawford, "The Pentagon's Carbon Boot Print," The Real News Network, July 10, 2019, https://therealnews.com/stories/the-pentagons-carbon-boot-print; James Pero, "The US Military is Among the World's Biggest Contributors to Climate Change and is Responsible for More Emissions Than Some Entire Countries, Study Says," *Daily Mail*, June 20, 2019, https://www.dailymail.co.uk/sciencetech/article-7163857/New-study-shows-military-bigger-contributor-climate-change-countries.html; and Lancaster University, "US Military Consumes More Hydrocarbons Than Most Countries—Massive Hidden Impact on Climate," ScienceDaily, June 20, 2019, https://www.sciencedaily.com/releases/2019/06/190620100005.htm.

6. Alexandra Ossola, "Guam's Ecological Fate is in the Hands of the U.S. Military," *National Geographic*, December 27, 2018, https://www.nationalgeographic.com/environment/2018/12/guam-endangered-species-ecology-threatened-us-military-base-expansion/.

7. Chris Gelardi and Sophia Perez, "'Biba Guåhan!': How Guam's Indigenous Activists are Confronting Military Colonialism," *The Nation*, October 21, 2019, https://www.thenation.com/article/guam-colonialism/; and Nina Finley, "'To Save a Forest You Have to Destroy a Nicer One': U.S. Marines Target Forest in Guam," Mongabay, May 8, 2019, https://news.mongabay.com/2019/05/to-save-a-forest-you-have-to-destroy-a-nicer-one-u-s-marines-target-forest-in-guam/.

8. Eric Lipton and Julie Turkewitz, "Pentagon Pushes for Weaker Standards on Contaminating Drinking Water," *New York Times*, March 14, 2019, https://www.nytimes.com/2019/03/14/us/politics/chemical-standards-water-epa-pentagon.html.

9. Berhan Taye, "The State of Internet Shutdowns Around the World: The 2018 #KeepItOn Report," Access Now, July 8, 2019, https://www.accessnow.org/cms/assets/uploads/2019/07/KeepItOn-2018-Report.pdf.

See also Kevin Collier, "Governments Loved to Shut Down the Internet in 2016—Here's Where," Vocativ, December 23, 2016, http://www.vocativ.com/386042/internet-access-shut-off-censorship/.

10. Berhan Taye, "Targeted, Cut Off, and Left in the Dark: The #KeepItOn Report on Internet Shutdowns in 2019," Access Now, February 24, 2020, https://www.accessnow.org/cms/assets/uploads/2020/02/KeepItOn-2019-report-1.pdf.

11. Melissa Etehad and Ramin Mostaghim, "When Iran Blocked the Internet, Tech Experts in the U.S. Tried to Hack a Solution. Here's Why They Couldn't," *Los Angeles Times*, December 17, 2019, https://www.latimes.com/world-nation/story/2019-12-17/iran-blocked-internet-tech-experts-hack-solution; Rashi Varshney, "Internet Shutdowns in India Caused a Loss of $3.04 Billion between 2012–2017," Medianama, April 26, 2018, https://www.medianama.com/2018/04/223-internet-shutdown/; Niha Masih, Shams Irfan, and Joanna Slater, "India's Internet Shutdown in Kashmir is the Longest Ever in a Democracy," *Washington Post*, December 15, 2019, https://www.washingtonpost.com/world/asia_pacific/indias-internet-shutdown-in-kashmir-is-now-the-longest-ever-in-a-democracy/2019/12/15/bb0693ea-1dfc-11ea-977a-15a6710ed6da_story.html; and James Griffiths, "Internet Shutdowns aren't Just Africa's Problem. They're Happening Worldwide," CNN, January 17, 2019, https://www.cnn.com/2019/01/17/africa/internet-shutdown-zimbabwe-censorship-intl/index.html.

12. Farnaz Fassihi, "Iran Blocks Nearly All Internet Access," *New York Times*, November 17, 2019, updated December 5, 2019, https://www.nytimes.com/2019/11/17/world/middleeast/iran-protest-rouhani.html; Masih, Irfan, and Slater, "India's Internet Shutdown in Kashmir"; Etehad and Mostaghim, "When Iran Blocked the Internet"; and "Iran Internet Outage First to Effectively Isolate Entire Nation," *Chicago Tribune*, November 22, 2019, http://digitaledition.chicagotribune.com/tribune/article_popover.aspx?guid=c3cd164d-d3e8-4166-8c79-f5e8cea52ddb.

13. "Internet Shutdown Tracker," Internet Shutdowns, undated, https://internetshutdowns.in/ [accessed February 11, 2020].

14. Ibid.

15. Jeremy Hsu, "How India, The World's Largest Democracy, Shuts Down the Internet," IEEE Spectrum, January 27, 2020, https://spectrum.ieee.org/tech-talk/telecom/internet/how-the-worlds-largest-democracy-shuts-down-the-internet.

16. Masih, Irfan, and Slater, "India's Internet Shutdown in Kashmir." See also Ifat Gazia and Tara Dorabji, "Kashmir Uncensored: Tortured by the World's Largest Democracy," in *Censored 2020: Through the Looking Glass*, eds. Andy Lee Roth and Mickey Huff with Project Censored (New York: Seven Stories Press, 2019), 173–83.

17. John Schwartz, "Judges Gives Both Sides Grilling in Youth Climate Case Against the Government," *New York Times*, June 4, 2019, https://www.nytimes.com/2019/06/04/climate/climate-lawsuit-juliana.html; Steve Kroft, "The Climate Change Lawsuit that Could Stop the U.S. Government from Supporting Fossil Fuels," *60 Minutes*, CBS News, March 3, 2019, https://www.cbsnews.com/news/juliana-versus-united-states-the-climate-change-lawsuit-that-could-

stop-the-u-s-government-from-supporting-fossil-fuels-60-minutes/; Rick Noack and A. Odysseus Patrick, "Climate-Change Activists Worldwide Look to Courts as a Powerful New Ally," *Washington Post*, April 24, 2019, https://www.washingtonpost.com/world/europe/climate-change-activists-worldwide-look-to-courts-as-a-powerful-new-ally/2019/04/23/b4403420-5e1d-11e9-98d4-844088d135f2_story.html; Becky Jacobs, "Environmental Advocates Rally in Hammond to Support Youth Suing Government over Climate Change," *Chicago Tribune*, October 29, 2018, https://www.chicagotribune.com/suburbs/post-tribune/ct-ptb-climate-change-case-rally-st-1027-story.html; and William Brangham, "Youth Climate Action Marches Draw Millions Around the World," *PBS NewsHour*, PBS, September 20, 2019, https://www.pbs.org/video/global-walkout-1569004984/.

18. Schwartz, "Judges Gives Both Sides Grilling."

19. Brit McCandless Farmer, "Federal Appeals Court Dismisses Young People's Climate Lawsuit," *60 Minutes*, CBS News, January 23, 2020, https://www.cbsnews.com/news/juliana-v-united-states-federal-appeals-court-dismisses-young-peoples-climate-lawsuit-60-minutes-2020-01-23/.

20. John Schwartz, "Court Quashes Youth Climate Change Case Against Government," *New York Times*, January 17, 2020, https://www.nytimes.com/2020/01/17/climate/juliana-climate-case.html; Madeleine Carlisle, "A Federal Court Threw Out a High Profile Climate Lawsuit. Here's What It Might Mean for the Future of Climate Litigation," *Time*, January 17, 2020, updated January 19, 2020, https://time.com/5767438/climate-lawsuit-kids/; Robinson Meyer, "A Climate-Lawsuit Dissent That Changed My Mind," *The Atlantic*, January 22, 2020, https://www.theatlantic.com/science/archive/2020/01/read-fiery-dissent-childrens-climate-case/605296/; and Steven P. Dinkin, "Youth Bring Their Voices to Climate Change Conversation," *San Diego Union-Tribune*, January 26, 2020, https://www.sandiegouniontribune.com/a-path-forward/story/2020-01-26/youth-bring-their-voices-to-climate-change-conversation.

21. Kroft, "The Climate Change Lawsuit."

22. Arun Gupta, "Life, Liberty and a Stable Climate: These Kids are Arguing for a New Constitutional Right," *In These Times*, June 24, 2019, http://inthesetimes.com/article/21935/life-liberty-stable-climate-trial-youth-juliana-trump-constitution.

23. Donald J. Kochan, "Keep Courts Off of the Climate Policy Playground," *The Hill*, August 13, 2019, https://thehill.com/opinion/energy-environment/457314-keep-courts-off-of-the-climate-policy-playground.

24. "Youth Plaintiffs in *Juliana v. United States* File Petition with Ninth Circuit Court of Appeals Seeking Full Court Review of Their Case," Our Children's Trust, March 3, 2020, https://static1.squarespace.com/static/571d109b04426270152febe0/t/5e5e6bf0df133120a5b53f9c/1583246321420/Juliana+Press+Release+3-3-20.pdf.

25. "National and Global Experts File Briefs in Support of *Juliana v. United States* Youth-Led Climate Change Litigation," Our Children's Trust, March 13, 2020, https://static1.squarespace.com/static/571d109b-04426270152febe0/t/5e6c0ae9a53943154a6de234/1584138985726/2020.03.13.Juliana+Amicus.pdf.

26.   Project Censored has highlighted the disarray in the Defense Department's bookkeeping practices before. See story #12 of the *Censored 2015* Top 25, "Pentagon Awash in Money Despite Serious Audit Problems," by Jeannette Acevedo and Peter Phillips, in *Censored 2015: Inspiring We the People*, eds. Andy Lee Roth and Mickey Huff with Project Censored (New York: Seven Stories Press, 2014), 59–60.

27.   Laurence Kotlikoff [with Mark Skidmore], "Is Our Government Intentionally Hiding $21 Trillion in Spending?" *Forbes*, July 21, 2018, https://www.forbes.com/sites/kotlikoff/2018/07/21/is-our-government-intentionally-hiding-21-trillion-in-spending/#6a69b2d14a73; Laurence Kotlikoff [with Mark Skidmore], "Holding U.S. Treasurys? Beware: Uncle Sam Can't Account for $21 Trillion," *Forbes*, January 9, 2019, https://www.forbes.com/sites/kotlikoff/2019/01/09/holding-u-s-treasuries-beware-uncle-sam-cant-account-for-21-trillion/#6ce7e95a7644; Bill Chappell, "Pentagon Announces First-Ever Audit of the Department of Defense," NPR, December 8, 2017, https://www.npr.org/sections/thetwo-way/2017/12/08/569394885/pentagon-announces-first-ever-audit-of-the-department-of-defense; and Mary Louise Kelly, interview with Bryan Bender, "Pentagon Audit Shows Logistical Arm of Military Can't Explain Where $800 Million Went," *All Things Considered*, NPR, February 8, 2018, https://www.npr.org/2018/02/08/584335323/pentagon-audit-shows-logistical-arm-of-military-cant-explain-where-800-million-w.

28.   Alexandria Ocasio-Cortez (@AOC), Twitter post, December 2, 2018, 2:08 p.m., https://twitter.com/aoc/status/1069307293752279040.

29.   Salvador Rizzo, "Alexandria Ocasio-Cortez's $21 Trillion Mistake," *Washington Post*, December 4, 2018, https://www.washingtonpost.com/politics/2018/12/04/alexandria-ocasio-cortezs-trillion-mistake/.

30.   Dave Lindorff, "Exclusive: The Pentagon's Massive Accounting Fraud Exposed," *The Nation*, November 27, 2018, https://www.thenation.com/article/pentagon-audit-budget-fraud/.

31.   Idrees Ali and Mike Stone, "Pentagon Fails Its First-Ever Audit, Official Says," Reuters, November 15, 2018, https://www.reuters.com/article/us-usa-pentagon-audit/pentagon-fails-its-first-ever-audit-official-says-idUSKCN1NK2MC. See also Kotlikoff, "Holding U.S. Treasurys? Beware."

32.   The lone exception to the corporate media blackout about this new development was reporter Matt Taibbi's January 2019 article in *Rolling Stone*. See Matt Taibbi, "Has the Government Legalized Secret Defense Spending?" *Rolling Stone*, January 16, 2019, https://www.rollingstone.com/politics/politics-features/secret-government-spending-779959/.

33.   Michele Ferri and Jonathan Lurie, "FASAB Statement 56: Understanding New Government Financial Accounting Loopholes," *Solari Report*, December 29, 2018, posted January 10, 2019, https://constitution.solari.com/fasab-statement-56-understanding-new-government-financial-accounting-loopholes/. For the complete text of the new standard, see "FASAB Issues Statement of Federal Financial Accounting Standards 56, *Classified Activities*," Federal Accounting Standards Advisory Board, October 4, 2018, http://files.fasab.gov/pdffiles/sffas_56_nr.pdf.

34. The Editorial Board, "How Silicon Valley Puts the 'Con' in Consent," *New York Times*, February 2, 2019, https://www.nytimes.com/2019/02/02/opinion/internet-facebook-google-consent.html.
35. Issie Lapowsky, "Senators Grill Facebook, Google, and Apple over Invasive Apps," *Wired*, February 7, 2019, https://www.wired.com/story/senators-project-atlas-facebook-google-apple/.
36. Sundar Pichai, "Google's Sundar Pichai: Privacy Should Not be a Luxury Good," *New York Times*, May 7, 2019, https://www.nytimes.com/2019/05/07/opinion/google-sundar-pichai-privacy.html.

CHAPTER 3

Capitalism, Celebrity, and Consuming Corona
Junk Food News in 2019–2020

IZZY SNOW and SUSAN RAHMAN,
with CATANIA AYALA, SHAINAH CONAWAY,
PERRY KINDEL, OLIVIA PAGE, JOAN PALACIOS,
LESLIE RIVERA, EDITH VALENCIA,
and STEFAN WERBA

And the people stayed home.

And they listened, and read books, and rested, and exercised, and made art, and played games, and learned new ways of being, and were still.

And they listened more deeply. Some meditated, some prayed, some danced. Some met their shadows. And the people began to think differently.

And the people healed.

And, in the absence of people living in ignorant, dangerous, and heartless ways, the earth began to heal.

And when the danger passed, and the people joined together again, they grieved their losses, and made new choices, and dreamed new images, and created new ways to live and heal the earth fully, as they had been healed.

—KITTY O'MEARA, "In the Time of Pandemic," March 16, 2020

As of the writing of this chapter, we find ourselves in trying times amidst a global pandemic. The world watches as people die of an illness hitherto unknown to humankind. As cultures decide how best to respond to the pandemic, marked differences emerge in the ways in which each nation reacts. Who knew that when the "Hot Girl Summer" of 2019 conclusively matriculated into "Studious Girl Fall," it would be the end of so many things that our corporate media overlords had taken for granted: summer, taco trucks, bars, pool parties, Hujis, Lizzo—but of course not now, not ever, not even in an international crisis, hot girls. As the fall of 2019 eased into winter and the new year began, a pandemic began to take hold, first appearing in Wuhan, China, before rapidly spreading across the world. Hot girls, having hibernated in their winter throws, climbed out of formfitting Uniqlo turtlenecks to find TikTok fame, the perfect sourdough starter recipe, quarantine fitness tutorials, and mask fashion statements. Corporate opportunists lurked in the corner as social upheaval has rattled the globe, promoting the newest buying trends and how to rock your "quarantine chic."

Even as millions lose their loved ones and their jobs, legacy media finds ways to monetize tragedy. By March 2020, the United States had taken multiple approaches to combating the virus, which involved major shutdowns of most institutions nationwide. The capitalist machine was forced to take a pause, and as time went on both the bourgeoisie and the proletariat have been impacted, yet late-stage capitalism memes remain potent. Class, status, and privilege are central to how the coronavirus is experienced by humankind. As soon as it became clear to everyday Americans and their insta-famous, Tummy Tea–sporting Tinseltown avatars that this pandemic would strike the motherland of Big Macs and tornado-strength AK-47s, one urgent question rose above all others for the US corporate media: Does Costco have enough toilet paper? In the face of existential panic, Americans did what they do best—they bought in bulk.

The 24/7 news cycle followed suit, shifting from *Keeping Up with the Kardashians* to *Keeping Up with the Joneses*. Vending machines filled with personal protective equipment (PPE) were spotted in US airports. *The Purge* played out in every local mall and betwixt and between two-cart-apart shoppers at Trader Joe's. Stimulus checks and meat and PPE, oh my! And as long as there are products to sell, there will always be hot girls selling them. Soon, news outlets placed their field reporters amongst empty grocery store shelves, interviewing locals who stockpiled hand sanitizer, Clorox wipes, toilet paper, and medical masks, with the intent of peddling them at marked-up prices on Amazon.

President Trump's administration resisted national stay-at-home orders in favor of daily televised presidential press conferences, which played out as *Shark Tank* pitches to the American public for get-rich-quick coronavirus cure schemes. Trump treated the novel coronavirus as novelty, enlisting the corporate news media to broadcast his thoughts about injectable bleach or UV rays that he believed could cure the disease. Thus Americans stuck at home with a lifetime supply of Chex Mix get to pile on their quarantine fifteen with a steady diet of both kinds of junk food—snacks and news.

The term "Junk Food News" was coined by the late

Project Censored founder Carl Jensen in 1983 to identify how corporate media was beginning to profiteer from headline-grabbing, sensationalist news stories in lieu of traditional investigative journalism. As we've traded in *Singles in Your Area* for *Kraft Singles* under shelter-in-place ordinances, it has become clear how empty-calorie infotainment has replaced information. CNN town halls and BuzzFeed roundups of *The Best Memes to Get You Through Your Quaranteens* expose how the news media now values view counts over truth, and censorship over the kind of reporting essential to an effective democracy.

As we grapple with this reality and prepare to hopefully climb our way back out of a recession, we are reminded of the days post-9/11 and the propaganda that then went along with coming together as a nation. What we find that is similar to the post-9/11 reality is a capitalist society that will never stop hawking its wares in whatever shape or form possible. This conception that Americans can buy their way back to prosperity has its roots in post–World War II consumerism, but it was renewed and compounded by the Bush administration's response to the tragedy of 9/11. The false belief that purchasing power equals stability—and the even more sinister false hope that mere assertion can overcome a mortal threat—is a phenomenon David L. Altheide addressed in an article titled "Consuming Terrorism."

Altheide's "Consuming Terrorism" was a sociological analysis of the ways that the corporate news media, the Bush administration, and the financial markets propagated the message that Americans should use their money to showcase their patriotism and refute terrorism. Just as soup cans, hand sanitizers, and toilet paper stocks were sold out at the big-box chains in the spring of 2020, American flags sold out in October 2001. This strategy ascribed to grief a dollar amount, the same price as a brand-new flat-screen TV and surround-sound speaker set that could play "America the Beautiful."[1]

This buy-back-your-freedom model has arisen again, now out of the desperation of the coronavirus pandemic, in which the lower and middle classes, most affected by the tragedies of the crisis, are the most pressured to reopen and re-conform to the economic systems that oppress them. While buying American was once promoted as the way to defeat the terrorists, in the time of COVID-19, toilet paper seems to be the new favored commodity in wiping out the bad guys. Witness as the corporate media dare to ask the truly hard-hitting questions: If we hoard the Charmin, does that make us good or bad Americans? In many ways the corporate media allowed the government to use the 9/11 crisis as a way to instill fear to more easily institute restrictive policies that not only reduced our freedoms but invaded our privacy. As we remain mid-pandemic, we can only wonder what is still to come of the virus and the government's halfhearted attempts to contain it, as well as what types of policies are being quietly put in place as we all focus in on the continuing crisis that is Junk Food News.

THE CLASSIC CASE OF CLASS AND ACCESS CORONA-FIED

The beginning months of 2020 saw the proliferation of COVID-19 all across the globe, manifesting in at least 185 countries and territories. With cases climbing past five million infections into the summer of 2020, people throughout the world were confined to their homes under strict quarantine orders.[2] This fundamental shift of the status quo was brought on in merely a few months. In December 2019 China informed the World Health Organization that they were experiencing several cases of pneumonia from an unknown cause throughout the city of Wuhan. On January 7, 2020, the new virus was identified and isolated, and on January 11 China reported the first death from the new coronavirus.[3] From there the novel coronavirus continued to spread, baffling scientists and doctors alike with its unique blend of symptoms and fluctuating infection rates while effectively inducing mass hysteria, fear, and uncertainty.

By early May of 2020, the pandemic had spread to millions and the United States had joined the international community in enforcing shelter-in-place orders. With almost everyone bound to their homes, Netflix, TikToks, and Twitter feeds, fearmongering news alerts or celebrity-groveling updates became the pinnacle of pandemic content. The corporate press showcased quarantining and coronavirus-diagnosed celebrities, with selfies from Hollywood's finest and star-studded lip sync battles, each message underlining the importance of staying at home while the self-appointed messengers basked in the sun beaming down on the poolside chairs of their Calabasas mansions. While celebrities spread messages that "we're all getting through this together" and that these are "uncertain times," their only uncertainties lie in whether their local Whole Foods will be restocked with vegan toilet paper. In the meantime, Americans reckon with how quarantine has impacted their careers, home lives, and finances. The corporate media is actively and consistently choosing to focus on the famed icons who are still able to share their lived perfection even during times of hardship. Slide open the phone or turn on the TV and what do we see? We gape at Arnold Schwarzenegger getting comfy with his two miniature horses, Selena Gomez adopting a puppy, and Tom Hanks and his wife Rita Wilson on the front cover of practically every tabloid magazine after they tested positive for COVID-19.[4]

On March 17 even Al Jazeera was guilty of celebs-gone-viral trending, publishing a continuously-updated article that included all the names of infected celebrities and those in power, as if it were vital for civilians to be aware of which rich and famous people have been infected.[5] What would we do if we didn't know which Hollywood stars to write "get well soon" notes to? Because we surely need to focus our attention on those lucky few with access to testing just because they *thought* they were exposed—and have their fourth home in the country to retreat to when times get tough. It has left us questioning: Who is considered important and worthy of coverage during this pandemic? On March 23, *USA Today* wrote a head-lining article under their National Basketball Association (NBA) section: "Charles Barkley says he tested negative for coronavirus."[6] Congratulations, Charles! Phoning in to the show *Inside the NBA* broadcast on TNT earlier that month, Barkley had said, "I haven't been feeling great and they didn't want me to take any chances."[7] Thank goodness for *USA Today* notifying us of Mr. Barkley's reasoning behind getting tested, and his good news! It's obviously of utmost importance for us to be aware of which celebrities have been tested, and their results. Since they're superior to us all and good at sports it's naturally also vital that they receive immediate testing. In the eyes of the corporate media, celebrity culture is the perfect justification for social Darwinism when it comes to access to healthcare treatment. That same week, Sean Turner, who's considered a mere "regular person," was spending her tenth day in hospital isolation with no test kits, so her symptoms were being treated as they appeared.[8] It seems like Sean should've been better at sports or had millions of listeners on Spotify if she wanted to be tested.

This pandemic has taken its toll on every American, but middle-class and lower-income families are the ones struggling the most. *The New York Times* published an article about how families were already facing financial hardships in a "good" economy before the crisis, and how, with the arrival of the pandemic, these struggles have skyrocketed.[9] The newly-unemployed are quick to file for benefits, lines are stretching for miles at food pantries, and tenants are pleading to landlords for extensions on rent, just as homeowners are beseeching bankers to grant extensions on mortgage payments. By the last week of May 2020, unemployment claims surpassed 38 million.[10] That is more than twice the amount of jobs that were created in the decade since the 2008 recession.[11] It certainly shows the hardship our country is facing.

It's fair to say that we won't be running into Arnold Schwarzenegger or Selena Gomez at any food pantry, even as many Americans rely on such services to make ends meet. For example, in Monmouth and Ocean Counties in New Jersey, one food pantry has seen a 40 percent spike in people accessing their services, serving 364,000 additional meals in April 2020.[12] Perhaps the media should begin to focus more on the experience of everyday Americans instead of letting us know that CNN anchor Chris Cuomo is "feeling well."[13] Those who are famous are not more important than those who are not. We are all suffering one way or another, and we would do well to shine a light on those who are facing more obstacles than those who are rich and powerful. Perhaps then those Zoom galas our media is covering in all their spectacular emptiness could be focused on and targeted to benefit the people without all the things celebrities take for granted, and we could take a step toward equity. Just an idea.

MISMANAGED MEDIA MOURNS MAMBA, MEANWHILE MISINFORMED MASSES MISS MISSILES

At the end of January 2020, the heartbreaking loss of legendary NBA player Kobe Bryant, known to fans by his self-chosen nickname "The Black Mamba," dominated the news cycle all over the world. Kobe Bryant and his daughter Gianna were killed tragically alongside several others in a helicopter crash just outside of Los Angeles while they were en route to a game Gianna would have played in, with Kobe coaching. The day following the accident, Kobe's and Gianna's names were plastered across the front pages of 23 newspapers worldwide.[14] During the weeks that followed Kobe Bryant's death, people around the world continued to follow the story while mourning his loss.[15] While a few media outlets covered the deaths with a measure of dignity, affording Bryant's grieving family and friends some privacy, there was overall a basic lack of human decency, stemming from the majorly competitive nature of the media that is fueled by the demands of everyday consumers. In the slew of articles and video reports devoted to Bryant, valorization became practically the only acceptable tone to take, ensuring little acknowledgment of any of the less-than-admirable parts of his life, such as the sexual assault accusation and charge against him from 2003. Disregarding his controversial past and commemorating him as a hero, the media managed to profit off his death for weeks by sensationalizing him and his illustrious career. For weeks, social media was a blur of purple and gold—the colors of the basketball team Bryant played for, the Los Angeles Lakers—as people voiced their love and support for the Bryant family, and appreciation for Kobe's impact on the sports world. The coverage of the tragedy was extensive, insensitive, and by the end a major distraction from other significant world events.

A few weeks prior to Kobe Bryant's death, news broke that President Trump ordered a drone strike that killed ten people, including the intended target, Iranian general Qasem Soleimani.[16] In the days following the strike, Iran retaliated by attacking two American bases in Iraq. Fortunately, no one was killed and initial reports indicated there were no injuries. Then on January 24, 2020, the Pentagon released a statement saying 34 troops were diagnosed as having sustained traumatic brain injuries from the attack.[17] Those numbers were updated five times, with the number of casualties increasing with each update in the weeks that followed. While Trump and his administration claimed that the initial attack against Soleimani was necessary, their reasoning was anything but clear. They struggled to explain their rationale and justify their abrupt and brutal decision to launch a missile strike against Soleimani and nearby Iranian and Iraqi soldiers. Trump's hubris evidently led him to make a judgment that ended lives, and changed other lives forever. The Trump administration's inability to stick to a story indicates their own misunderstanding of the incident and its consequences. While it is concerning that our current administration still cannot articulate their reasoning, it is also deeply concerning that this story did not get more critical coverage in the mass media.[18] As the number of injuries from the retaliatory attack increased, the data was left unchallenged and more or less unacknowledged by the corporate media while they fixated on the loss of Kobe Bryant. Rather than focus on the regular people caught in the crossfire of state violence, they were focused on the profitability of an accidental celebrity death.

By February 11, updated reports revealed that more than one hundred American troops suffered from brain injuries as a result of Iran's retaliatory attack.[19] The corporate media neglected to mention that the troops who were injured were only stationed at the targeted Iraqi bases as a precaution following the killings that Trump ordered.[20] While many of the injured troops have since returned to duty, those who were injured will need to be monitored for the rest of their lives. Though a traumatic brain injury can, depending on the severity, have long-term effects or even cause death, when these brain injuries were mentioned in the corporate news, they were brushed off as being very minor.[21] While there was coverage of these strikes, it was not reported on critically or promptly, typical of the corporate media's focus on headline-grabbing stories in lieu of reporting the news with integrity. Additionally, the strike and its consequences are illustrative of the lack of honor and foresight within the current administration.

Without public awareness of the problems our country is facing, there are fewer and fewer opportunities for change or resolution. While we still have not seen any public appreciation for the sacrifice of the US soldiers injured in the attacks, the "Celebration of Life" memorial for Kobe and Gianna Bryant sold out the entire Staples Center. Now, here we might ask ourselves, had those soldiers died at those bases, would they be commemorated as heroes? Would the media cover any soldier's death as extensively as they did an NBA star's? The answer is plainly no—unless the media regarded such coverage as useful in stirring up support for a new war. This disservice to troops wounded in service of the United States demonstrates how the corporate media sensationalizes the US military in action, but abandons any commitment to them once they return home as veterans. When they cease to be mere symbols and appear as real people with real struggles, they are disregarded by the governmental and media systems that once glorified them.

The media, while historically profiting off of the tragic loss of such public figures as Princess Diana or Michael Jackson, does not profit when they honestly report on the shortcomings of the bodies that govern them. Stories like Kobe Bryant's will continue to dominate news cycles because they focus our sad and negative feelings on topics we have no control over, instead of allowing us to see the greater issues happening in the world that we could come together to change.

COUNTING THE DEAD, SNAKE OIL, AND FORGOTTEN FIRST PEOPLES

Every day, the death tolls and confirmed cases of COVID-19 pass another landmark, a total beyond those who died in 9/11 or US soldiers who lost their lives in the Vietnam War. Even while addressing important information on infection rates, the corporate news media find a way to undermine the severity of this global health crisis, generating a sense of nationwide loss and hopelessness that inevitably can only be dispelled by having Americans turn out their wallets.

If you've been self-quarantining like a good citizen, you've probably tuned in to your local corporate news source and seen just how fond news channels and websites are of discussing the death toll in great detail. In the masked face of this pandemic, we see the corporate news media once again manipulating the grief of many Americans by sensationalizing the tragedies of the crisis. In the summer of 2020 one could tune in to any news station and know that within minutes they were sure to mention the words "death toll" or "confirmed cases." Morbid charts of lives lost and estimated body counts, with stock market–like speculations on what the final numbers will be, flood the various news sources and leave the average media consumer in a state of paralysis.[22] While the death toll is daunting, its coverage on corporate media is akin to that of the coverage of 9/11, which similarly sensationalized tragedy, traumatizing viewers through the unremitting repetition of grim imagery and leaving no room for any solace from grief.[23]

With a recession on the horizon, it will be the essential workers, who risk their lives to potential infection by a deadly virus, who will be thrust into a jobless environment for months. Yet just as in the aftermath of 9/11, the frenzied coverage is hyper-focused on the idea that by spending money we will prevail over a pandemic, as if COVID-19 was yet another war to throw money at. This, coupled with false claims about potential ways to prevent or test for the virus, leaves us all feeling a bit fearful and confused, looking for guidance.[24] Unfortunately, there is no solid guidance to be found from those who were charged with the job of guiding. The president of the United States suggests we inject disinfectant or take hydroxychloroquine, an antimalarial drug as of yet unproven to help, blithely telling us to "try it if you like," as he has.[25] With such a vacuum of authoritative guidance or coordinated national strategy, many Americans flock to the unregulated hucksters littering the internet with ads purporting to have reliable test kits or potential cures.[26] We are living in the wild, wild west of virus prevention and treatment and there seems to be no end in sight.

This undue focus on the exact number of people dead from the virus and the associated selling of snake oil effectively obscures the deeper issue of who is dying and why. For instance, while corporate news correspondents bicker about projected cures and body counts, five million self-identified American Indians and Alaskan Natives are suffering at a disproportionately higher rate than most.[27] The first people to inhabit this continent are turning out to be among the most vulnerable to the coronavirus. This should come as no surprise, as Indigenous Americans are some of the most economically disadvantaged populations in the country. Poverty, limited access to healthcare, densely populated households, and comorbid conditions all place this community at greater risk than the vast majority of the US populace. Experts say that entire tribes could be wiped out due to the pandemic, as households in close proximity to one another create an opportune environment for the virus to spread quickly.[28] Suggested social distancing protocol is more difficult to enforce in extended family households, which are more common among Indigenous Americans.

In addition, Native American populations have some of the country's highest rates of hypertension, asthma, cancer, and heart and cardiovascular disease—all of which put them at higher than average risk of dying from the virus. The novel coronavirus's slow slaughter of Indigenous peoples and the corporate media's indifference to their plight is reminiscent of when entire tribes were infected with smallpox during the Trail of Tears, the forced mass exodus of Native Americans from their southeastern homelands to areas west of the Mississippi River in the mid-19th century. Native Americans have a long and complicated history regarding disease; they are 600 times more likely to die of tuberculosis and close to 200 times more likely to die of diabetes than any other group in the United States.[29] The federal government historically has done little to protect these tribes, as Native American communities are often the last to receive healthcare funding. The current handling of the COVID-19 pandemic is more of the same. Speaking for the Oglala Sioux Tribe in South Dakota, President Julian Bear Runner said the federal Indian Health Service facilities "are not well equipped." There are 50,000 members of the tribe, yet there are only 24 coronavirus test kits, six ventilators, and four beds reserved for quarantine at the reservation's Pine Ridge Hospital.[30] So far, there is limited data on the number of people infected with coronavirus in Native American communities, yet the data that have been collected make it very clear that they are at very high risk.

Indigenous communities could be decimated if steps are not taken immediately to provide adequate treatment, support, and resources. Small strides have been made, and there has been marginal coverage of these developments in corporate media. For instance, the University of California, San Francisco has taken the initiative of sending a small team of doctors and nurses to serve in the Navajo Nation.[31] Yet while the opportunity exists to shine a spotlight on the urgent need to reach hard-hit Native communities before it is too late, we are presented with the "death clock," presidential suggestions that we try ingesting bleach, and encouragements to go deeper and deeper in debt in order to be good Americans. Though Native Americans are this country's first inhabitants, they tend to be last on the list of concerns among the corporate media.

CONCLUSION

The year 2020 gave way to a new kind of summer, with sweatpants tan lines, Zoom pool parties, letter writing, and swapping Spotify playlists, as millions of Americans quarantined indoors—practically everywhere but in the state of Wisconsin. As Americans settle into the uncertain norms of the future, the events of the year before our lean, mean quaranteens feel like distant memories, daydreams of crowded bars, and petty office gossip. While in the eyes of the corporate press, coronavirus defined the discourse of 2020, it wasn't the only bingeable Junk Food snack of the 2019–2020 news cycle, but it certainly felt that way. News reports focusing on climate change, human rights, and geopolitics were eclipsed by the onslaught of coronavirus content. Even as cases soared in late April, the Trump administration furthered its efforts into creating a military base on Greenland in the hopes of accessing the abundance of natural resources that lie beneath indigenous soil. Yet a story that would likely have constituted a career-ending imperial fumble in other times or administrations barely lasted one day's corporate news cycle during the pandemic.[32]

As nations throughout the world were struggling against more than 4.5 million coronavirus cases, the year-and-a-half-long Israeli elections concluded in mid-May, with a unity government between Benjamin Netanyahu and the opposition party leader, Benny Gantz. Netanyahu was sworn into office and will remain for eighteen months, in an agreement that threatens the annexation of the West Bank. Prime Minister Netanyahu is scheduled to bring the Trump administration's "vision for peace," rejected as clearly biased and dangerous by Palestinian leaders, before his cabinet in July. Yet the violent, discriminatory, Far-Right policies enforced by Israel's longest-serving prime minister, the serious corruption charges he faces, and the unconcealed cronyism between him and Trump (who appears on Netanyahu's reelection billboards, and whom Netanyahu has proposed naming an illegal settlement after) seemed to draw less attention in the corporate press than the manner in which the coronavirus crisis boosted his reelection campaign.[33]

As cities and regions throughout the United States began flirting with plans to lift quarantine orders, a major victory in the Keystone Pipeline protest movement was achieved when a federal judge in Montana revoked a Keystone XL building permit, demanding that an environmental report of the impact of the pipeline must be sufficiently completed before construction.[34] It constituted a small sliver of good news in a year in which tragedy was commercialized, GIF-ed, and memed into oblivion, though as the news came just after Trump announced he would suspend the US government's funding for the World Health Organization, it was left virtually untouched by the corporate press.[35]

In the wake of the suffering, heartbreak, and loss due to the coronavirus, American families turned to social media to spread good news. Family-made TikToks and baking Instagram stories were the perfect antidotes to our stay-at-home diets of Junk Food dysphoria. However, a craving to return to normalcy underpinned all these messages of perseverance. Social media is rife with posts that lust after the days in which people could go out to bars, restaurants, clubs, and malls, fueling the narrative that our return to normalcy should be a return to mindless spending.

While Junk Food reportage will likely increase and the commercial feedback loop return as the world re-emerges from lockdown, there is currently an opportunity to reflect on the economic and social systems that led to this pandemic—the kind of opportunity envisioned in Kitty O'Meara's poem that serves as this chapter's epigraph, where, on looking back, we could say that "the people began to think differently. And the people healed. And, in the absence of people living in ignorant, dangerous, and heartless ways, the earth began to heal." If we do not embrace that opportunity for change right now, during the heart of the crisis, those familiar Junk Food messages are sure to return: that people can replace their fears and loss with a new set of wheels, or simply buy back "Hot Girl Summer," as though Americans could consume their way out of the current crisis—only to be as uninformed and unprepared in facing the next.

IZZY SNOW is a rising senior at Barnard College of Columbia University, where she studies film, since transferring from the College of Marin, where she studied sociology and women's studies. She is a dog mom and enjoys writing satirical feminist comedy in her spare time.

SUSAN RAHMAN is a professor of sociology in Northern California. Her current work seeks to end the school-to-prison pipeline and to highlight the US injustice system that incarcerates far too many people. She is a mother and activist.

CATANIA AYALA, SHAINAH CONAWAY, PERRY KINDEL, OLIVIA PAGE, JOAN PALACIOS, LESLIE RIVERA, EDITH VALENCIA, and STEFAN WERBA are students from the College of Marin.

Notes

1. David L. Altheide, "Consuming Terrorism," *Symbolic Interaction*, Vol. 27 No. 3 (August 2004), 289–308, https://doi.org/10.1525/si.2004.27.3.289.
2. Talal Ansari and Erin Ailworth, "Coronavirus Infections Jump by More Than a Million Globally in Two Weeks," *Wall Street Journal*, May 22, 2020, https://www.wsj.com/articles/coronavirus-latest-news-05-22-2020-11590137359.
3. "Novel Coronavirus—China," World Health Organization, January 12, 2020, https://www.who.int/csr/don/12-january-2020-novel-coronavirus-china/en/.

4. Emilia Petrarca, "Self-Isolation is Very Different When You're a Celebrity," *The Cut*, March 16, 2020, https://www.thecut.com/2020/03/celebrities-coronavirus-self-isolation-instagram.html; and Chloe Melas, "Selena Gomez and Miley Cyrus Adopt Puppies While They Isolate at Home," CNN, March 26, 2020, https://www.cnn.com/2020/03/26/entertainment/selena-gomez-miley-cyrus-adopt-puppies-coronavirus-trnd/index.html.

5. "Coronavirus Pandemic: Which Politicians and Celebs are Affected?" Al Jazeera, March 17, 2020, updated June 1, 2020, https://www.aljazeera.com/news/2020/03/coronavirus-pandemic-politicians-celebs-affected-200315165416470.html.

6. Scott Gleeson, "Charles Barkley Says He Tested Negative for Coronavirus," *USA Today*, March 23, 2020, https://www.usatoday.com/story/sports/nba/2020/03/23/coronavirus-charles-barkley-announces-he-tested-negative-covid-19/2899528001/.

7. Charles Barkley via telephone, *Inside the NBA*, TNT, March 12, 2020.

8. Samantha Agate, "Do Celebrities Have It Easier during the Coronavirus Pandemic Than Regular People?" Talent Recap, March 19, 2020, https://talentrecap.com/do-celebrities-have-it-easier-during-the-coronavirus-pandemic-than-regular-people/.

9. Patricia Cohen, "Straggling in a Good Economy, and Now Struggling in a Crisis," *New York Times*, April 16, 2020, updated April 20, 2020, https://www.nytimes.com/2020/04/16/business/economy/coronavirus-economy.html.

10. Tony Romm, Jeff Stein, and Erica Werner, "2.4 Million Americans Filed Jobless Claims Last Week, Bringing Nine-Week Total to 38.6 Million," *Washington Post*, May 21, 2020, https://www.washingtonpost.com/business/2020/05/21/unemployment-claims-coronavirus/.

11. "Employment, Hours, and Earnings from the Current Employment Statistics Survey (National): All Employees, Thousands, Total Nonfarm, Seasonally Adjusted—From 2008 to 2020," U.S. Bureau of Labor Statistics, undated, https://data.bls.gov/timeseries/CES0000000001 [accessed July 2, 2020].

12. Cohen, "Straggling in a Good Economy."

13. Brian Stelter, "CNN Anchor Chris Cuomo Diagnosed with Coronavirus; He will Continue Working from Home," CNN, March 31, 2020, https://www.cnn.com/2020/03/31/media/chris-cuomo-coronavirus/index.html.

14. Connor Perrett, "How 23 of the Biggest Newspapers around the World Covered Kobe Bryant's Death," Insider, January 27, 2020, https://www.insider.com/kobe-bryant-death-newspaper-front-pages-2020-1.

15. Margaret Sullivan, "Media Coverage of Kobe Bryant's Death was a Chaotic Mess, but There were Moments of Grace," *Washington Post*, January 27, 2020, https://www.washingtonpost.com/lifestyle/style/media-coverage-of-kobe-bryants-death-was-a-chaotic-mess-but-there-were-moments-of-grace/2020/01/27/d825ade4-4106-11ea-aa6a-083d01b3ed18_story.html.

16. Julia Musto, "Brett Velicovich on the Drone that Took Down Soleimani: 'You Only Get One Shot,'" Fox News, January 4, 2020, https://www.foxnews.com/media/brett-velicovich-qassem-soleimani-drone-strike-iran; and Ryan Pickrell, "The Trump Administration is Struggling to Explain Why the US Killed Top Iranian General Soleimani—Here's All

the Shifting Explanations," Business Insider, January 13, 2020, https://
www.businessinsider.com/trump-administrations-shifting-explana-
tions-for-soleimani-killing-2020-1.

17. Bill Chappell, "109 U.S. Troops Suffered Brain Injuries in Iran
Strike, Pentagon Says," NPR, February 11, 2020, https://www.npr.
org/2020/02/11/804785515/109-u-s-troops-suffered-brain-injuries-in-iran-
strike-pentagon-says.

18. Dan Mangan, "House Foreign Affairs Chairman Blasts Trump Administration for Report on Soleimani Killing," CNBC, February 14, 2020,
https://www.cnbc.com/2020/02/14/trump-administration-issues-re-
port-on-soleimani-killing.html.

19. Chappell, "109 U.S. Troops Suffered Brain Injuries."

20. USAFacts, "How Many U.S. Troops are in the Middle East?" U.S.
News & World Report, January 9, 2020, https://www.usnews.com/news/
elections/articles/2020-01-09/after-recent-deployments-how-many-us-
troops-are-in-the-middle-east.

21. Mayo Clinic Staff, "Traumatic Brain Injury," Mayo Clinic, March
29, 2019, https://www.mayoclinic.org/diseases-conditions/traumat-
ic-brain-injury/symptoms-causes/syc-20378557.

22. Mark Abdelmalek, Chris Francescani, and Kaitlyn Folmer, "How
Accurate is the US Coronavirus Death Count? Some Experts Say It's
Off by 'Tens of Thousands,'" ABC News, April 30, 2020, https://abcnews.
go.com/Health/accurate-us-coronavirus-death-count-experts-off-tens/
story?id=70385359.

23. Ibid.; and Altheide, "Consuming Terrorism."

24. Abdelmalek, Francescani, and Folmer, "How Accurate is the US Coronavirus Death Count?"

25. Jonathan Chait, "Trump Takes Hydroxychloroquine, Does Not
Understand How Science Works," Intelligencer, May 18, 2020, https://
nymag.com/intelligencer/2020/05/trump-takes-hydroxychloro-
quine-does-not-understand-science.html.

26. "Coronavirus: Outcry after Trump Suggests Injecting Disinfectant as
Treatment," BBC News, April 24, 2020, https://www.bbc.com/news/
world-us-canada-52407177; and Rebecca Heilweil, "Coronavirus Scam-
mers are Flooding Social Media with Fake Cures and Tests," Recode
(Vox), April 17, 2020, https://www.vox.com/recode/2020/4/17/21221692/
digital-black-market-covid-19-coronavirus-instagram-twitter-ebay.

27. Dana Hedgpeth, Darryl Fears, and Gregory Scruggs, "Indian Country,
Where Residents Suffer Disproportionately from Disease, is Bracing
for Coronavirus," Washington Post, April 4, 2020, https://www.
washingtonpost.com/climate-environment/2020/04/04/native-ameri-
can-coronavirus/.

28. Ibid.

29. Ibid.

30. Ibid.

31. Scott Maier, "UCSF Health Care Workers to Serve in Navajo Nation,"
University of California, San Francisco (UCSF), April 22, 2020, https://
www.ucsf.edu/news/2020/04/417236/ucsf-health-care-workers-serve-na-
vajo-nation.

32. G. Dunkel and Paddy Colligan, "The U.S. Aims at Greenland, Targets the Arctic," *Workers World*, April 28, 2020, https://www.workers.org/2020/04/48000/.

33. Oliver Holmes, "Netanyahu Takes Office in Deal That Could See West Bank Annexation," *The Guardian*, May 17, 2020, https://www.theguardian.com/world/2020/may/17/netanyahu-takes-office-in-deal-that-could-see-west-bank-annexation; and Ephrat Livni, "The Coronavirus Crisis Has been a Huge Boon to Israel's Netanyahu," Quartz, March 30, 2020, https://qz.com/1828292/the-coronavirus-crisis-has-been-a-huge-boon-to-israels-netanyahu/.

34. Nina Lakhani, "Major Blow to Keystone XL Pipeline as Judge Revokes Key Permit," *The Guardian*, April 15, 2020, https://www.theguardian.com/environment/2020/apr/15/keystone-xl-pipeline-montana-judge-environment.

35. Cecelia Smith-Schoenwalder, "U.S. Death Toll Passes 26,000 as Trump Faces Global Pushback for Halting WHO Funds," *U.S. News & World Report*, April 15, 2020, https://www.usnews.com/news/health-news/articles/2020-04-15/us-death-toll-passes-26-000-as-trump-faces-global-pushback-for-halting-who-funds.

CHAPTER 4

Establishment Media's War Metaphors Obscure Injustices and Block Global Healing

News Abuse in 2019–2020

ROBIN ANDERSEN

Last year the earth didn't so much rotate on its axis, as it seemed to turn upside down. What sociologists once called "social unrest" broke out around the globe, from France to Lebanon and from Chile to Gaza, as people took to the streets in massive numbers demanding change, mostly against austerity measures driven by neoliberalism's inability to meet the needs of citizens. In the face of impending ecological disaster, environmental activists demanded radical change, even as the United States ruthlessly attempted to hurl the country backward into extractive deregulation and to discharge global waste.[1] Against this backdrop, two earth-shattering international scientific reports were released; one warned that the planet's climate system would destabilize at record speed unless action to cut CO_2 concentrations was taken, while the second predicted that the world's unabated loss of biodiversity would soon reach catastrophic proportions, with one million species likely to go extinct within decades.[2]

In response, activists young and old redoubled their efforts with determination and a willingness to be arrested in large numbers. The international movement Extinction Rebellion, exuberantly costumed, burst onto the streets of London, shutting down parts of the city by blocking roads, trains, passageways, and bridges. While most US corporate media ignored their actions, news of these events managed to reach and inspire the US public through independent media.

As government forces responded to global citizen actions, US media used their own template to cover global protests and established the pattern for News Abuse that can be identified throughout the year's reporting. "News Abuse" is a term coined nearly twenty years ago by former Project Censored director, sociologist Peter Phillips, who saw that it was important to understand how corporate media not only ignore crucial stories, but spin and frame news in ways that distract, distort, and sensationalize reporting. In addition, by employing interpretive frames, media serve to present familiar narratives that fit seamlessly into official, establishment positions that shape and alter the significance of global events. Phillips understood that without historical context, crucial perspectives, or meaningful follow-up reporting, corporate news produced a subtle yet sophisticated form of propaganda, and he called the practice "News Abuse."

This past year, from the denial of global injustice and environmental collapse to the framing of the COVID-19 pandemic, war and its metaphors guided coverage, and can be consistently identified among prominent examples of News Abuse in 2019–2020. As the ethos, belligerencies, and protocols of war were celebrated, establishment media took us further away from peace and global unity, and worked to obscure the visions and practices so necessary to heal the planet and its peoples.

ENDLESS WAR

As the second decade of the 21st century came to a close, endless war, launched by the George W. Bush administration in 2001 with the infamous "War on Terror," seems now to suffuse the air we breathe. The military–media mergers of these decades have come to define a militarized culture and its economic priorities, as the United States spends more on defense than the next ten countries combined.[3] The Trump administration currently carries out clandestine military maneuvers that actively destabilize the governments of Iran and Venezuela for the purposes of seizing geopolitical power and control of global resources.[4] US militarism includes 800 foreign military bases paid for by the American people at a cost of $156 billion per year—as David Vine puts it, more bases "than any other people, nation, or empire in history"—in pursuit of a particular vision of American corporate–military domination.[5]

In July 2019, Global Witness reported that Latin America continues to be one of the deadliest places for environmental defenders, where killings are often the result of US military policies in the hemisphere, especially in Guatemala.[6] In addition, amidst continuing global belligerencies, journalists keep dying in numbers that attest to the ways that war and conflict lead to the loss of global press freedoms.[7] In 2020, Reporters Without Borders ranked the US 45th on its World Press Freedom

Index.[8] When whistleblowers attempt to expose the US military's criminal activities or the impact of its wars on journalism and the environment, as WikiLeaks founder Julian Assange did by releasing the classified US military video known as "Collateral Murder," they are often targeted for punishment even as the criminals they expose are not.[9] The torture and prosecution on espionage charges of Assange, and the lack of media coverage of these injustices, stand as a stunning indictment of the treatment of journalists who struggle to reveal the truth of war.[10]

As perpetual war threatens a world ever more on the brink, military actions around the globe are infrequently covered in the corporate media, and even more rarely, from a critical perspective. Yet war is a constant backdrop, a positive ethos habitually deployed to frame news coverage of all sorts, explicitly and implicitly, from global protests to the coronavirus pandemic. Corporate media outlets almost never present ongoing war in ways that expose its vicious consequences to the globe and its peoples. Burying the truth of war assigns to it the status of cultural myth, and encourages its use as a dominant metaphor that frames a wide variety of public concerns. So many social issues, from attempts to relieve poverty to ridding the country of drugs, are conceptualized as wars, framed as the cure-all, the single solution to the earth's problems. The habitual use of war metaphors was a prominent theme of News Abuse for 2019–2020.

Journalists and scholars have long understood that the domestic consequences of a warring state have been historically devastating for freedom of the press.[11] War spending also diverts federal budgets from caring for civilian populations, robbing them of social services, including education, healthcare, and a living wage.[12] Nowhere has that become more evident than in the United States, where, in addition to neoliberal policies, the resulting erosion of the middle class and increased misery nationwide also tell a sad story about how the largest economy ever to exist in the world has achieved so little to further human well-being, yet has succeeded in transferring great wealth to a small group of billionaires.

AMERICANS HAVE HAD ENOUGH

Currently, ruling elites hold power as a minority, and their goals and views are at odds with the needs and desires expressed by global publics, especially and increasingly in the United States.[13] Even a brief glimpse at polling data reveals that the American people have had enough. In surveys documenting the views of citizens throughout the United States, the evidence is overwhelming across the political spectrum. From a wealth tax to minimum wage, Americans want change. A March 2019 CNBC All-America Economic Survey illustrates these desires: support for paid maternity leave stands at 84 percent in favor, 75 percent would like to see government funding for childcare, 60 percent agree that a higher minimum wage is past due, and free college tuition is supported by 57 percent of the public.[14] Support for Medicare for All came in at 54 percent. As reported by The Hill, another recent survey conducted by American Barometer found that "70 percent [of the public] supported providing 'Medicare for all,' also known as single-payer health care."[15]

There is also broad public support for a wealth tax. According to a Reuters/Ipsos poll published in January

2020, nearly two-thirds of respondents agree that the very rich should pay more than everyone else to support public programs.[16] Seventy-seven percent of Democrats polled support such a tax, though so too do a majority—53 percent—of Republicans.[17] In addition, vast majorities of Americans, whether self-identified as liberal or conservative, support key aspects of a Green New Deal.[18]

Such popular policy demands for social services and environmental protections were articulated and promoted by presidential candidate Bernie Sanders, first throughout his 2016 run for the White House, then further amplified in his second campaign, and they were also picked up by other Democratic candidates, especially Elizabeth Warren. Though it was clear that Sanders's ideas and policies helped set the 2020 campaign agenda and debates, by the time the flawed Wisconsin primary was carried out in April 2020 as COVID-19 was in full swing, what had begun as a seemingly unstoppable movement toward real change in American politics was all but abandoned when Bernie Sanders left the race.[19]

It will come as no surprise to thinking people that something is terribly wrong with the way we've been doing things—when the demands of a clear majority of citizens are represented by neither presidential candidate from the two largest political parties and by none of the largest, most influential news outlets—and the question we must ask ourselves next is "How did it come to this?" The ideologies, values, practices, and policies of those who hold the power and wealth are not our own. The corporate media's News Abuse functions to gloss over, deny, and in general make acceptable the disconnect between the public and the powerful by framing world events in ways that obscure the causes and contexts that explain global realities and offer alternative visions.

THE ROLE OF CORPORATE MEDIA

Interrogating corporate media treatment of some of the most important issues of our time helps reveal the key role such media have played in promoting the broken policies perpetrated on the country by both major political parties for decades. For instance, how does media embed a preference for Wall Street and the extractive industries at the expense of social justice and the natural world? How does News Abuse serve to maintain the status quo, promote US belligerencies and global militarism, and economic policies that have led to such extremes of wealth and poverty? How does media discourse make acceptable the continued burning of fossil fuels in the face of planetary collapse? How does coverage of global protest hide the role of international banking institutions and the International Monetary Fund in forcing governments to shred the social safety nets of their citizenry? What biases, double standards, and decontextualized framing—all common News Abuse tactics—are applied to a myriad of news stories, from presidential candidates to global conflicts, environmental emergencies, pandemics, and so much more?

Double Standards

One of the most telling examples of double standards this year was on display during Democratic Party primary debates: when progressive candidates advocated for

Medicare for All, corporate media presenters pressured them to explain, in detail, how they intended to pay for it; yet when the US government passed a federal budget for 2020 that allocates just short of one trillion dollars to the military, journalists and pundits from those same media outlets reported it with little to no questioning, discussion, or public debate.[20]

What forces are behind the habitual obscuring of the meaning of policies and their predictable consequences, as news frames narrow public debate and refuse to place events and information within a truthful explanatory context? Reporting is so constrained that many viewers and readers never recognize the proverbial elephant hidden by the small news details of surface description. Ideas and events seem to happen in a void when news stories come from nowhere, the foundational ideologies of their framing are rarely exposed, and the bigger picture remains outside the frame. In such a corporate media environment, understanding the forces that shape our world becomes impossible. News has no history and the world spins by at a frenetic pace, the larger meanings of which are left to the fake news utterances of conspiracy theorists and politicians who lie.[21]

Global Protests

A study done by Fairness & Accuracy In Reporting (FAIR) of the press coverage of global protests in 2019 offers a striking illustration of the US corporate press's News Abuse in covering global movements for social justice, peace, and environmental healing.[22] Researcher Alan MacLeod evaluated the coverage of CNN broadcast news and *New York Times* reporting, comparing coverage of demonstrations in Hong Kong, Ecuador, Haiti, and Chile, from March to November 2019. MacLeod found staggering disparities in how the demonstrations were reported. While Hong Kong protests were the subject of 737 stories, the protests in Ecuador were covered in 12 stories, the long run of demonstrations in Haiti garnered 28 stories, and the one million Chilean citizens who went into the streets made it into those two paragons of US corporate media a grand total of 36 times. In addition, many of the stories besides those mentioning Hong Kong were simply headlined within news briefs of global protest. Both the *Times* and CNN had similar ratios of coverage.

MacLeod attributes the prominence of Hong Kong's protesters in US media to the targeting of China, an official enemy of the United States—"hence the extent and favorability of the coverage." In Hong Kong, protests flared in response to a proposed extradition treaty between the island city, the Chinese central government, and Taiwan.[23] Residents feared the treaty would be used by Beijing to arrest and persecute critics of the Chinese state. US corporate media assigned the coveted moniker "pro-democracy" to characterize Hong Kong protesters, while the Chilean demonstrations were commonly referred to as riots, and the *New York Times* reported that protests had descended into "looting and arson."[24] Unlike in Hong Kong, where police did not kill demonstrators for disrupting commerce, in Chile 27 people were killed during protests and a national strike.[25] Column inches were devoted to such vague abstractions as "The mayhem in Chile is the latest spasm of unrest in a region that has been awash in political crises this year," as well as descriptions of violence "on both sides," with police use of force always following "violence" by protesters.[26] No mention was made of human rights violations. In contrast, an Al Jazeera report titled "Chile Protest: What Prompted the Unrest?," with the subtitle "At least 20 people have been killed in protests over inequality in the worst unrest to hit the country in decades," offered straightforward, factual information, explaining why people were in the streets and the consequences they've suffered.[27] Initially the rising cost of public transportation sparked student-led demonstrations against fare hikes, but Chileans also protested "the increasing cost of living, low wages and pensions, a lack of education rights, a poor public health system and crippling inequality." Also included in Al Jazeera's report was information on UN investigators sent to Chile in response to the UN High Commissioner for Human Rights calling for "an independent investigation into the deaths and 'disturbing allegations' of excessive force used on protesters."[28]

To its credit, though very late in the news cycle, by November 1, 2019, the *New York Times* broke with its blurry "news reporting" and published an opinion piece by a poet and essayist, Daniel Borzutzky, who pointed out that Chile's Constitution, "written in 1980 during Pinochet's rule, created the legal basis for a market-driven economic model that has privatized pensions, health and education."[29] As he pointed out, "The Chilean dictatorship destroyed collective bargaining rights; decimated the public education system; and handed over social security programs, health care, utilities and public services to private enterprises." Chile's history of militarism, and attacks on Indigenous peoples fighting deforestation by the logging industry—crucial historical context from the still-recent past—were rarely included in any US reporting of the protests.[30] Even as the country had become the most unequal in the region over the previous decades, with the most profound socio-economic inequalities, Chile's economic growth was being touted by international banking and extractive industries; yet none of this background information necessary to understanding the reasons and goals driving the protests was discussed in the US corporate media.[31]

The popular protests in Ecuador and Haiti mirrored those of Chile, though as MacLeod pointed out, "the severity of the repression meted out by security services" was often greater in those countries.[32] Yet the vast majority of establishment news coverage offered no outrage, tacitly condoning the killings and human rights abuses and instead focusing on Hong Kong.

Driven by US geopolitical strategies, corporate media followed a news frame defined by US anti-China policies. Ultimately, that coverage served to reinforce the military strategies of the United States by underscoring the demonization of the Chinese government as a US enemy target. In addition, by masking the reasons for people going into the streets in other countries, as their lives have become more precarious and their livelihoods have shrunk, media coverage obviates empathy with protesters mischaracterized as "violent." Viewers watching "riots" presented without explanation fail to recognize mutual struggles and common circumstances. Painting a broader picture of the global economy and its effects on the impoverishment of global communities and regions would encourage mutual aid and solidarity, as well as heightened under-standing between global citizens. Of course, that would also make it much more difficult to present the outside world as a scary foreign "Other," and therefore would belie the sentiments that feed the xenophobic scapegoating and warmongering that accounts for most US foreign policy.

HEALTHCARE AND THE DEMOCRATIC PRIMARY CAMPAIGNS

At no time has the need for universal healthcare in the United States been more strikingly evident than in the wake of the COVID-19 pandemic. Ironically, the crisis hit the country just prior to Bernie Sanders dropping his bid for the presidency, so the United States lost the strongest progressive voice it had fighting for the American people on the national political stage at exactly the time when that voice was most needed. In less than two months the US death toll had reached 60,000, accounting for one-third of COVID-19 deaths globally.[33]

Medicare for All: Media Follow Industry Talking Points

For insight into how the world's richest country so com-pletely failed to protect its citizens that a large portion of the population was left without access to affordable healthcare in the midst of one of the largest pandemics in its history, consider the way corporate media presented policies designed to protect the well-being of its citizens in the lead-up to the crisis.

Bernie Sanders and Elizabeth Warren have been leading

the Medicare for All (M4All) movement within the progressive wing of the Democratic Party. As the popularity of a government-funded single-payer plan snowballed, insurance companies understood they would soon be out of business, and they stepped up their attacks against it.[34] Billionaire Michael Bloomberg and Wall Street–backed Joe Biden tried to put the brakes on M4All with alternative, tepid proposals, yet the diversions did little to slow the growing calls for M4All.[35] So big insurance set its sights on designing stronger, more effective messaging that would muddy the debate and instill doubt in the public mind. They erroneously claimed M4All would result in "death panels." Of course, private, for-profit insurance companies have already been making decisions about how to ration care—often with life-or-death consequences—for some time. Such decisions have ultimately been driven by the logic of the bottom line, a cost–benefit analysis guided by the insurance industry's need to produce profits.

But it was the words of Mayor Pete that started to make a difference. Buttigieg, a former mayor of South Bend, Indiana, and at the time a Democratic candidate for president, followed what one former health insurance executive recognized as corporate messaging, using "health insurance industry talking points against more progressive health care policy."[36] Buttigieg, the candidate with the second-largest contributions from pharmaceutical and health insurance companies after Biden, claimed he supported "Medicare for All Who Want It," saying he was all for adding "choice."[37] But his plan was designed to preserve private insurance. Helaine Olen also warned that Buttigieg was using health industry talking points when he claimed that thousands of jobs would be lost in changing to a M4All healthcare system. That is, of course, a nonsensical assertion because a workforce will have to administer any program that replaces the current state of the industry. Olen went on to charge Buttigieg with "cherry-picking facts" to make the industry's case: "He's pitting the needs of those who, in many cases, benefit from making the health-care system more difficult to navigate against the moral imperative of making it better for everyone."[38]

Despite the public's overwhelming support for M4All in the face of the for-profit healthcare industry's weak excuses for perpetuating itself, NPR's Mara Liasson asserted that the vast majority of Bernie Sanders's policies were unpopular with the American people, and that "[e]ven a majority of Democrats don't want to end private health insurance."[39] Clearly the sentiments that guided that response were not those of the American people, but were invented by corporate message designers and repeated by establishment media.

Media Treatment of the Bernie Sanders Campaign and Policies

If it were possible to identify the single topic this past year most egregiously distorted by corporate media News Abuse, subjected to deliberately misinformed coverage written by biased reporters and presented without even a hint of meaningful context, that topic would undoubtedly be Bernie Sanders's presidential campaign. In fact, writing in Truthout, Nolan Higdon and Mickey Huff identified a news blackout of Sanders's campaign at the height of his popularity, and reported that "Sanders was covered three to four times less than Joe Biden in 2019 despite being neck and neck in the polls."[40]

The Washington Post's News Abuse was among the most blatant. As Julie Hollar points out, "there's a clear antipathy at the paper to many of Sanders' signature policy plans, like Medicare for All."[41] In March 2019, Michael Corcoran charged the *Post* with having taken a "hard-line stance against Medicare for All," throwing back at the paper its charge that "hard-line liberal groups and unions" and "advocates on the far left" were promoting M4All.[42] Corcoran writes,

> Among the "hard-line liberal groups and unions" the article refers to in its headline and lead is the Consortium of Citizens with Disabilities, a coalition of approximately 100 national disability organizations. The "hard-line" groups include much of the grassroots movements for healthcare justice in the country: National Nurses United, Social Security Works and the Center for Popular Democracy. These orgs—described elsewhere in the piece as "advocates on the far left"—are devoted to such "hard-line" positions as universal healthcare, protecting senior citizens and empowering voters and activists.[43]

As noted above, the majority of the American public want universal healthcare, which is enjoyed by citizens in many countries throughout the world.[44] As Corcoran points out, "[W]hat the *Post* describes as 'hard-line' and 'far left' is actually a very popular position."[45]

The New York Times and MSNBC

The New York Times assigned Sydney Ember, a reporter whose resumé was limited to the finance industry, to cover Bernie Sanders. Ember was formerly an analyst for BlackRock, the biggest global investment management corporation and the largest investor in coal plant developers in the world. Though she's credited as reporting news, not op-eds, in the more than two dozen pieces she penned she consistently depicted Sanders in a bad light. Ember went so far as to hide the conflicts of interest among corporate and political sources she relied on, which FAIR drew attention to when reviewing her biased reporting. As Katie Halper noted, Ember's hire "makes sense, given the *New York Times*' documented anti-Sanders bias, which can be found among both editors and reporters alike."[46]

MSNBC is another media outlet with a well-documented bias against Sanders, an outlet arguably highly influential in its appeal to liberal viewers and its popularity as the second-most-watched cable network. *In These Times* analyzed the network's coverage of the Democratic Party's leading candidates, Sen. Bernie Sanders, former vice president Joe Biden, and Sen. Elizabeth Warren, focusing on the network's six flagship primetime shows. The study found that over a two-month period, from August and September 2019, the programs "focused on Biden, often to the exclusion of Warren and Sanders."[47] Sanders received not only the least total coverage (less than one-third of Biden's), but also the most negative. "As to the substance," Branko Marcetic noted, "MSNBC's reporting revolved around poll results and so-called electability."

Corporate Democrats, the Media, and "Electability"

Though polls consistently showed that Bernie Sanders would beat Trump, corporate media and elite Democrats continued to claim he was *unelectable*. The day of the Iowa caucuses, NPR's Mara Liasson asserted that Democrats were "paralyzed by indecision," and that none of the candidates seemed like "a sure thing to defeat" Trump.[48] Such handwringing was not founded in facts or survey data. An NBC/*Wall Street Journal* poll published the day before found that Trump was trailing the top four 2020 Democratic candidates in theoretical head-to-head matchups.[49] Looking more broadly at polling, Bernie Sanders had by that date beaten Trump in 62 out of 67 such matchups.[50] Nevertheless, Bernie Sanders's supposed lack of "electability" solidified into a media obsession in mid-April of 2019, when Obama's former campaign manager, Jim Messina, now a political strategist for corporate Democrats, announced on the *Powerhouse Politics* podcast that Sanders couldn't beat Trump.[51] After that the *unelectability* trope was adopted by pundits as a self-evident platitude. Vox was one of the few media outlets to point out a few days later that Sanders actually had a very good electability record, having "consistently run ahead of Democratic Party presidential campaigns in Vermont" when he ran for reelection as a US representative.[52] But *unelectable* became the endless refrain for the purveyors of News Abuse, and that biased messaging pushed by centrist Democrats and corporate media had its effects. Nevertheless, as Bernie Sanders noted when he suspended his campaign, even in the states he didn't win there was still strong majority support for Medicare for All.[53]

COVID-19

By April 2020, 26 million Americans had lost their jobs, with more to come. Many were left without health coverage or any way to pay their rent.[54] At the same time, a vast amount of federal dollars were given to bail out US corporations, yet money for the American people has been woefully inadequate, compared especially to the amounts European governments have allocated to their citizens through direct payments, business loans, and expanded social services.[55] As *Jacobin* put it, "Congress offers corporate America a massive and larcenous bailout" while "American workers facing looming layoffs are still waiting."[56] In addition, COVID-19 has exacerbated a national crisis of water insecurity, where an estimated fifteen million Americans do not have access to running water in their homes, mainly because they can't afford to pay for it.[57] Though ABC News covered the hardship of those struggling without water, missing from those stories are the reasons behind it.[58] No mention was made of resource privatization, or the long, sordid history of Nestlé stealing water from California to Maine, and from myriad other countries throughout the world. That reporting was left to the UK newspaper *The Guardian*.[59]

Yet even in the midst of a raging pandemic, record unemployment, and widespread lack of access to basic resources, the US addiction to military spending seems insatiable. Environmentalists Against War reported that the defense industry was using the pandemic as an excuse to twist more taxpayer money from Congress. By the end of April, Arkansas senator Tom Cotton—a recipient of tens of thousands of dollars in campaign contributions from the arms industry—introduced a bill proposing at least $14 billion be given to weapons dealers, on top of the hundreds of billions of taxpayer dollars already budgeted for the defense industry.[60] So engrained is the military ethos in American culture, it must have seemed natural to pull from the cultural firmament the ever-popular metaphors of war and apply them to the pandemic.

Of Wars and Pandemics

Eric Levenson on CNN noticed that media was framing the battle against the virus as a war, and he claimed the metaphor "fit smoothly" in a number of ways.[61] After all, it's a front-line battle with an enemy that can strike at any time. CNN and others recast doctors and nurses as soldiers.[62] In xenophobic language, Trump identified the enemy, decrying the "China Virus," which he later described in more virulent terms as "Kung Flu."[63]

Drawing out the war analogy, the enemies in wars are always dehumanized, positioned on the other side of a wall between us and them. They are part of a vision of a world divided in conflict, a vision that runs completely contrary to the only effective way of dealing with a pandemic: that is, collectively, at the local and global levels. Trump as a "war president" uses violence in words and deeds, and still targets his declared enemies, sanctioning Iran and Venezuela and exacerbating the humanitarian crises in both countries.[64] War separates the United States from the global community and is used to justify the failure of the United States to join international efforts to contain the pandemic. As the World Health Organization organized an international consortium called Solidarity to advance global research as quickly as possible, the Trump administration announced plans to entirely cut its funding for the WHO.[65]

Trump's Messaging

With hospitals swamped by COVID-19 patients, and health professionals struggling with inadequate personal protective equipment and other necessary supplies, the President of the United States refused to respond to the virus in any compassionate or rational way. As precious lives were lost and bodies filled temporary trailer morgues in New York, or were laid to rest in mass graves in the potter's field on Hart Island, corporate media allowed an unhinged egomaniac to occupy television screens spewing nonsense, recommending that viewers inject disinfectant or irradiate their bodies with UV light, in rambling press conferences that should have been considered violations of health and safety laws.[66]

As COVID-19 swept the country, Trump, as well as Republicans in Congress, again called upon enemy demonization to deflect criticism from the US government's botched response to the pandemic and the resultant escalating death toll. They called COVID-19 the "Wuhan virus" or the "Chinese virus," and Trump used the free platform provided by the corporate media to blame Chinese leadership for the US outbreak, chiding the foreign leaders for "not telling him soon enough."[67] Throughout April 2020 right-wing messaging became more disciplined, offering a strong narrative with a clear storyline about who was to blame for the virus—China, and more generally people of Asian descent. Christian mega-church leader Jack Hibbs, a Trump supporter, proclaimed, "I absolutely believe that this is biological warfare launched by China."[68] The Trump administration's use of 'strategic racism' was amplified by right-wing propagandists, and, as Erin Heaney points out, "it has been effective in channeling the anxieties, insecurities and anger of millions of whites into blaming communities of color inside the U.S. and 'foreigners' for the troubles and hardships they face."[69]

The anti-China narrative has directed attention away from the failings of the Trump administration and the greed of corporations that supported Trump's rise to power. Combined with a "Democratic Party strategy still heavily influenced by the losing politics of the Democratic Leadership Council, established to pull the party to the right" toward corporate priorities, Erin Heaney writes, the Republicans' strategic racism presents "a perfect storm for covering up the problems created by capitalism and exacerbated" by Trump.[70] The only way to counter this narrative is to engage in a fundamental critique of the US economy, distorted as it's become under militarism and capitalist market domination—yet calls for real change as articulated by Bernie Sanders and other progressive presidential candidates were not tolerated by establishment media.[71] These factors—racist deflections, context-free reporting of catastrophes, deliberate obfuscation of the actual roots of societal problems, and the silencing of viable grassroots alternatives to a deadly status quo—all come together and reinforce one another in the regrettably potent implementation of News Abuse.

A Call to Arms

In Trump's racialized rhetoric, we can see the connections between xenophobia as a diversion from failed policies, and the way violence, belligerencies, and conflict are celebrated. The mounting protests staged by white supremacists organizing against stay-at-home orders during the pandemic, like the dumbfounding and despicable spectacles of swastikas, rifles, Confederate flags, and signs that proclaimed "Make treason punishable by hanging" on display at the Michigan statehouse, were amplified by media coverage that offered little context and often included Trump's incitement efforts.[72] Trump spoke directly to armed groups when he tweeted "Liberate" to anti-lockdown protests in states with Democratic governors.[73] Trump's tweets signaled that the White House itself backed the rifle-carrying groups, and his administration's support was immediately embraced with a surge in Twitter posts about the "boogaloo," a term meaning armed insurrection to the conspiracy-theory-infused Far Right. The rallies were part of a coordinated campaign anchored by a number of state-based conservative policy groups and a coalition that received funding from the Koch Brothers organization and the DeVos family.[74] Attorney General William Barr also threw in the support of the Justice Department, and from Fox News to talk radio, right-wing corporate media promoted the anti-lockdown protesters' dangerous actions.[75]

A "GROTESQUE SPECTACLE"

In the *Irish Times*, Fintan O'Toole gave voice to what many others around the world must have been thinking: "It is one thing to be powerless in the face of a natural disaster, quite another to watch vast power being squandered in real time—willfully, malevolently, vindictively. It is one thing for governments to fail … quite another to watch a ruler and his supporters actively spread a deadly virus. Trump, his party and Rupert Murdoch's Fox News became vectors of the pestilence." He went on to remark upon Trump's "grotesque spectacle" of "openly inciting people … to oppose the restrictions that save lives." Trump's daily briefings on the crisis, he noted, had been used "merely to sow confusion and division. They provide a recurring horror show in which all the neuroses that haunt the American subconscious dance naked on live TV."[76]

On April 28, 2020, after 58,000 coronavirus deaths and more than one million infections, a US corporate media outlet finally acknowledged what the rest of the world had been witnessing all along: Margaret Sullivan, in the pages of the *Washington Post*, wrote that "Trump has played the media like a puppet," admitting that for nearly five years "the story has been Trump," and the corporate media cover him "on the terms he dictates."[77] Outlets like the *Post* provide "far too much attention to the daily circus he provides." It is certainly true that corporate media have normalized Trump, allowing him to distract and disgust—but far worse, they have enabled the harm he has caused, by ignoring the worst aspects of an emergent fascism that seeks to scapegoat people of color, and all those "Othered," for the failures and neoliberal dismantling of the common good that US politicians continue to inflict.

In an opinion piece published in *The Guardian*, George Monbiot wrote an eloquent appeal to governments, enjoining them to resist throwing a lifeline to the biggest industrial polluters hemorrhaging money during the coronavirus pandemic:

> Do Not Resuscitate. This tag should be attached to the oil, airline and car industries. Governments should provide financial support to company workers while refashioning the economy to provide new jobs in different sectors. They should prop up only those sectors that will help secure the survival of humanity and the rest of the living world.[78]

Few writers, and ever fewer publishers, offer such creative, linguistic bonds able to connect social justice strategies, economic restructuring, government actions, and environmental imperatives so nimbly and persuasively. His words demonstrate how easy it can be to reveal a larger picture and provide the scope needed for a new vision of a future world. They lay bare the distortions and obfuscation of the News Abuse so often propagated by corporate, so-called "mainstream" media reporting.

Corporate news media habitually marginalize or discredit popular movements that aim to promote peace, social justice, economic equality, or environmental sustainability. These narrow "mainstream" narratives foreclose meaningful public debate and offer no alternative visions for a society based on racial justice, economic equality, or global peace and security. Calling out and opposing News Abuse is thus an important and necessary step for nurturing the burgeoning social and environmental movements to halt planetary collapse and to create a more equitable society.

ROBIN ANDERSEN is an author and professor of communication and media studies at Fordham University. She has written dozens of book chapters and journal articles, and she serves as a Project Censored judge. Her book *A Century of Media, A Century of War* won the Alpha Sigma Nu Book Award in 2007. She is currently co-editor of the Routledge Focus Book Series on Media and Humanitarian Action, and the volume she co-edited in the series, *Routledge Companion to Media and Humanitarian Action*, was published in 2018. Her latest book is *Media, Central American Refugees, and the U.S. Border Crisis*. She writes media criticism for FAIR, Common Dreams, and other online publications.

Notes

1.   Not only did Trump pull out of the Paris Agreement, he rolled back Environmental Protection Agency protections. See Nadja Popovich, Livia Albeck-Ripka, and Kendra Pierre-Louis, "95 Environmental Rules being Rolled Back under Trump," *New York Times*, December 21, 2019, updated May 20, 2020, and retitled "The Trump Administration is Reversing 100 Environmental Rules. Here's the Full List," https://www.nytimes.com/interactive/2019/climate/trump-environment-rollbacks.html.

2.   "Landmark United in Science Report Informs Climate Action Summit," Intergovernmental Panel on Climate Change (IPCC), September 22, 2019, https://www.ipcc.ch/2019/09/22/united-in-science-report-climate-summit/; and "UN Report: Nature's Dangerous Decline 'Unprecedented'; Species Extinction Rate 'Accelerating,'" United Nations, May 6, 2019, https://www.un.org/sustainabledevelopment/blog/2019/05/nature-decline-unprecedented-report/.

3.   Robin Andersen and Tanner Mirrlees, eds., *Democratic Communiqué*, Vol. 26 No. 2 (Fall 2014), https://journals.flvc.org/demcom/issue/view/4047; and "U.S. Defense Spending Compared to Other Countries," Peter G. Peterson Foundation, May 13, 2020, https://www.pgpf.org/chart-archive/0053_defense-comparison.

4.   As Gareth Porter writes, "The architects of the drive to war [with Iran], Mike Pompeo and Benjamin Netanyahu, have relied on a series of cynical provocations to force Trump's hand," in "Pompeo and Netanyahu Paved a Path to War with Iran, and They're Pushing Trump Again," The Grayzone, March 20, 2020, https://thegrayzone.com/2020/03/20/pompeo-netanyahu-war-iran-trump/; and Madeleine Freeman, "The US is Using Coronavirus to Push Regime Change in Venezuela," *Left Voice*, April 5, 2020, https://www.leftvoice.org/the-u-s-is-using-coronavirus-to-push-regime-change-in-venezuela.

5.   David Vine, "The United States Probably Has More Foreign Military Bases Than Any Other People, Nation, or Empire in History," *The Nation*, September 14, 2015, https://www.thenation.com/article/archive/the-united-states-probably-has-more-foreign-military-bases-than-any-other-people-nation-or-empire-in-history/.

6.   Last year, "Guatemala recorded the sharpest rise in murders, which jumped more than fivefold to make it the deadliest country per capita." "Enemies of the State? How Governments and Businesses Silence Land and Environmental Defenders," Global Witness, July 30, 2019, https://www.globalwitness.org/en/campaigns/environmental-activists/enemies-state/. See also Robin Andersen and Adrian Bergmann, *Media, Central American Refugees, and the U.S. Border Crisis* (New York: Routledge, 2020), Chapter 4: "Guatemala and the Extractive Industries."

7.   The 2019 World Press Freedom Index compiled by Reporters Without Borders (RSF) shows "how hatred of journalists has degenerated into violence, contributing to an increase in fear. The number of countries regarded as safe, where journalists can work in complete security, continues to decline, while authoritarian regimes continue to tighten their grip on the media." "2019 World Press Freedom Index—A Cycle of Fear," Reporters Without Borders (RSF), April 18, 2019, https://rsf.org/en/2019-world-press-freedom-index-cycle-fear.

8.   "United States: Trump-Era Hostility Toward Press Persists," Reporters Without Borders (RSF), undated, https://rsf.org/en/united-states [accessed May 30, 2020].

9.   See "Collateral Murder," WikiLeaks, recorded July 12, 2007, published April 5, 2010, https://collateralmurder.wikileaks.org.

10.   "UN Expert on Torture Sounds Alarm Again That Julian Assange's Life May be at Risk," Office of the United Nations High Commissioner for Human Rights (OHCHR), November 1, 2019, https://www.ohchr.org/en/NewsEvents/Pages/DisplayNews.aspx?NewsID=25249.

11.   Steve Rendall, "Amplifying Officials, Squelching Dissent," Fairness & Accuracy In Reporting (FAIR), May 1, 2003, https://fair.org/extra/amplifying-officials-squelching-dissent/.

12.   Pierre Guerlain, "The Social and Economic Consequences of US Militarism," *Revue LISA/LISA e-journal*, November 22, 2013, http://journals.openedition.org/lisa/5371.

13.   Peter Phillips, *Giants: The Global Power Elite* (New York: Seven Stories Press, 2018).

14.   Steve Liesman, "Majority of Americans Support Progressive Policies such as Higher Minimum Wage, Free College," CNBC, March 27, 2019, https://www.cnbc.com/2019/03/27/majority-of-americans-support-progressive-policies-such-as-paid-maternity-leave-free-college.html.

15.   Julia Manchester, "70 Percent of Americans Support 'Medicare for All' Proposal," The Hill, October 22, 2018, https://thehill.com/hilltv/what-americas-thinking/412545-70-percent-of-americans-support-medicare-for-all-health-care.

16.   Howard Schneider and Chris Kahn, "Majority of Americans Favor Wealth Tax on Very Rich: Reuters/Ipsos Poll," Reuters, January 10, 2020, https://www.reuters.com/article/us-usa-election-inequality-poll/

majority-of-americans-favor-wealth-tax-on-very-rich-reuters-ipsos-poll-idUSKBN1Z9141.

17. In 2014, economist Thomas Piketty's book *Capital in the Twenty-First Century*, tr. Arthur Goldhammer (Cambridge, Massachusetts: Harvard University Press, 2014 [French orig. 2013]) argued that a wealth tax is necessary to address economic inequality. It became an internationally bestselling book.

18. Eliza Relman and Walt Hickey, "More Than 80% of Americans Support Almost All of the Key Ideas in Alexandria Ocasio-Cortez's Green New Deal," Business Insider, February 14, 2019, https://www.businessinsider.com/alexandria-ocasio-cortez-green-new-deal-support-among-americans-poll-2019-2.

19. Asma Khalid, "Bernie Sanders Leaves 2020 Presidential Race," *All Things Considered*, NPR, April 8, 2020, https://www.npr.org/2020/04/08/830205848/bernie-sanders-leaves-2020-presidential-race.

20. Total US military spending from October 1, 2020, through September 30, 2021, is estimated at $934 billion. See Kimberly Amadeo, "US Military Budget, Its Components, Challenges, and Growth," The Balance, March 3, 2020, https://www.thebalance.com/u-s-military-budget-components-challenges-growth-3306320

21. Nolan Higdon and Mickey Huff, *United States of Distraction: Media Manipulation in Post-Truth America (and What We Can Do about It)* (San Francisco: City Lights Books, 2019).

22. Alan MacLeod, "With People in the Streets Worldwide, Media Focus Uniquely on Hong Kong," Fairness & Accuracy In Reporting (FAIR), December 6, 2019, https://fair.org/home/with-people-in-the-streets-worldwide-media-focus-uniquely-on-hong-kong/.

23. Ming-Sung Kuo, "Hong Kong's Extradition Bill and Taiwan's Sovereignty Dilemma," The Diplomat, June 26, 2019, https://thediplomat.com/2019/06/hong-kongs-extradition-bill-and-taiwans-sovereignty-dilemma/.

24. Pascale Bonnefoy, "After Fare Hike Stirs Violent Unrest in Chile, President Suspends It," *New York Times*, October 19, 2019, updated October 21, 2019, https://www.nytimes.com/2019/10/19/world/americas/chile-protests-emergency.html.

25. "Death Toll in Chile Protests since October Rises to 27," Associated Press, December 28, 2019, https://apnews.com/89bd348e9e10a0edf4f2bdcc29b66a50.

26. See Bonnefoy, "After Fare Hike Stirs Violent Unrest." News coverage frequently depicts attacks by security forces on demonstrators in foreign lands as retaliatory. In narrative sequencing, force is applied only after protesters initiate it, yet most of the time snipers or police shoot first. This type of reporting is used to justify police repression and human rights violations when state security forces murder demonstrators. See Robin Andersen, *A Century of Media, A Century of War* (New York: Peter Lang Publishing, 2006), Chapter 5: "Visions of Instability: Telling Stories on Television News."

27. Charis McGowan, "Chile Protests: What Prompted the Unrest?" Al Jazeera, October 30, 2019, https://www.aljazeera.com/news/2019/10/chile-protests-prompted-unrest-191022160029869.html.

28. "Press Briefing Note on Haiti Unrest," Office of the United Nations High Commissioner for Human Rights (OHCHR), November 1, 2019, https://www.ohchr.org/EN/NewsEvents/Pages/DisplayNews.aspx-?NewsID=25247&LangID=.

29. Daniel Borzutzky, "Chile is in Danger of Repeating Its Past," *New York Times*, November 1, 2019, https://www.nytimes.com/2019/11/01/opinion/chile-is-in-danger-of-repeating-its-past.html.

30. One notable exception to this trend in News Abuse reporting on the protests in Chile is Rodrigo Espinoza-Truncoso and Michael Wilson-Becerril, "What is Behind State Violence in Chile?" Al Jazeera, December 4, 2019, https://www.aljazeera.com/indepth/opinion/state-violence-chile-191202110752549.html.

31. Dario Hidalgo, "What Chile's Protests Reveal about the Country's Transport Inequalities," World Resources Institute, November 1, 2019, https://www.wri.org/blog/2019/11/what-chile-s-protests-reveal-about-country-s-transport-inequalities.

32. MacLeod, "With People in the Streets Worldwide."

33. David Matthews, "U.S. Passes 60,000 Coronavirus Deaths," *New York Daily News*, April 29, 2020, https://www.nydailynews.com/coronavirus/ny-coronavirus-us-death-toll-surpasses-60000-20200429-pg-foleblafeqtomexigwinwqcm-story.html.

34. Indeed, in August 2018 a Reuters/Ipsos survey found that a stunning 85 percent of Democrats supported Medicare for All, and a majority of Republicans—a full 52 percent—were in favor of it as well. See Letitia Stein, Susan Cornwell, and Joseph Tanfani, "Inside the Progressive Movement Roiling the Democratic Party," Reuters, August 23, 2018, https://www.reuters.com/investigates/special-report/usa-election-progressives/.

35. Maggie Severns, "New York Power Set Comes Off the Sidelines to Back Biden," *Politico*, January 25, 2020, https://www.politico.com/news/2020/01/25/biden-takes-the-lead-in-nyc-donor-chase-104108.

36. Tess Bonn, "Former Health Insurance Executive: Buttigieg Uses Industry Talking Points Against Progressive Health Care Policy," The Hill, December 24, 2019, https://thehill.com/hilltv/rising/475844-former-health-insurance-executive-says-buttigieg-uses-industry-talking-points-against-progressive-health-care-policy.

37. Victoria Knight, "Sanders' Claim That Buttigieg is 'Favorite of the Health Care Industry' is Broad and Needs Context," Kaiser Health News (KHN), February 19, 2020, https://khn.org/news/sanders-claim-that-buttigieg-is-favorite-of-the-health-care-industry-is-broad-and-needs-context/.

38. Helaine Olen, "Pete Buttigieg's Disingenuous Attack on Medicare-for-All," *Washington Post*, December 12, 2019, https://www.washingtonpost.com/opinions/2019/12/12/pete-buttigiegs-disingenuous-attack-medicare-for-all/.

39. Robin Andersen, "Factchecking NPR's Attempted Takedown of Bernie Sanders," Fairness & Accuracy In Reporting (FAIR), February 18, 2020, https://fair.org/home/factchecking-nprs-attempted-takedown-of-bernie-sanders/.

40. Nolan Higdon and Mickey Huff, "The Bernie Blackout is Real, and These Screenshots Prove it," Truthout, January 30, 2020, https://truthout.org/articles/the-bernie-blackout-is-real-and-these-screenshots-prove-it/.

41. Julie Hollar, "Here's the Evidence Corporate Media Say is Missing of WaPo Bias Against Sanders," Fairness & Accuracy In Reporting (FAIR), August 15, 2019, https://fair.org/home/heres-the-evidence-corporate-media-say-is-missing-of-wapo-bias-against-sanders/.

42. Paige Winfield Cunningham, "The Health 202: Jayapal's Medicare-for-All Bill Reflects Influence of Hard-Line Progressive Groups," *Washington Post*, March 11, 2019, https://www.washingtonpost.com/news/powerpost/paloma/the-health-202/2019/03/11/the-health-202-jayapal-s-medicare-for-all-bill-reflects-influence-of-hard-line-progressive-groups/5c82a8d61b326b2d177d6037/.

43. Michael Corcoran, "WaPo's 'Hard-Line' Stance Against Medicare for All," Fairness & Accuracy In Reporting (FAIR), March 20, 2019, https://fair.org/home/wapos-hard-line-stance-against-medicare-for-all/.

44. For the long list of countries that provide their citizens with some form of free, or very inexpensive, care, see "Countries with Universal Healthcare 2020," World Population Review, undated, https://worldpopulationreview.com/countries/countries-with-universal-healthcare/ [accessed May 31, 2020].

45. Corcoran, "WaPo's 'Hard-Line' Stance."

46. Katie Halper, "Sydney Ember's Secret Sources," Fairness & Accuracy In Reporting (FAIR), June 28, 2019, https://fair.org/home/sidney-embers-secret-sources/.

47. Branko Marcetic, "MSNBC is the Most Influential Network Among Liberals—and It's Ignoring Bernie Sanders," *In These Times*, November 13, 2019, https://inthesetimes.com/features/msnbc-bernie-sanders-coverage-democratic-primary-media-analysis.html.

48. Mara Liasson, "Where Iowa Falls in the Big Picture of the 2020 Election," *All Things Considered*, NPR, February 3, 2020, https://www.npr.org/2020/02/03/802392319/where-iowa-falls-in-the-big-picture-of-the-2020-election.

49. Mark Murray, "NBS/WSJ Poll: Country Remains Divided over Trump's Impeachment Trial," NBC News, February 2, 2020, https://www.nbcnews.com/politics/meet-the-press/nbc-wsj-poll-country-remains-divided-over-trump-s-impeachment-n1128326.

50. "General Election: Trump vs. Sanders," RealClearPolitics, undated, https://www.realclearpolitics.com/epolls/2020/president/us/general_election_trump_vs_sanders-6250.html#polls [accessed May 31, 2020].

51. Annika Merrilees, "Bernie Sanders Can't Beat Donald Trump in 2020: Obama Campaign Manager Jim Messina," ABC News, April 17, 2019, https://abcnews.go.com/Politics/bernie-sanders-beat-donald-trump-2020-obama-campaign/story?id=62455986.

52. Matthew Yglesias, "The Democratic Establishment Should Chill Out about Bernie Sanders," Vox, April 24, 2019, https://www.vox.com/policy-and-politics/2019/4/24/18510756/bernie-sanders-2020-democrats-neoliberals-chill.

53. Isabella Grullón Paz, "Read Bernie Sanders's Full Speech on Ending His Campaign," *New York Times*, April 8, 2020, https://www.nytimes.com/2020/04/08/us/politics/bernie-sanders-concession-speech.html. A transcription of Sanders's speech on leaving the Democratic presidential race is included in full.

54. Sara R. Collins, "Did You Lose Your Health Insurance Because of the Coronavirus Pandemic? Coverage Options for Laid-Off Workers and Others," Commonwealth Fund, April 24, 2020, https://www.commonwealthfund.org/blog/2020/coverage-options-laid-off-workers.

55. "Coronavirus Bailouts: Which Country Has the Most Generous Deal?" BBC News, May 8, 2020, https://www.bbc.com/news/business-52450958.

56. Luke Savage, "Corporate America is Getting a Bailout. Its Workers are Getting Screwed," *Jacobin*, March 28, 2020, https://www.jacobinmag.com/2020/03/corporate-america-bailout-stimulus-package-coronavirus.

57. "Sign Now: Stop Water Shutoffs During COVID-19 Pandemic and Restore Water Access Immediately," Action Network, undated, https://actionnetwork.org/petitions/sign-now-stop-water-shutoffs-during-covid-19-pandemic-and-restore-water-access-immediately [accessed May 31, 2020].

58. Briana Stewart, "For Some, the Quest for Clean Water Complicates Life amid the Coronavirus," ABC News, April 21, 2020, https://abcnews.go.com/Politics/quest-clean-water-complicates-life-amid-coronavirus/story?id=70171622.

59. Tom Perkins, "The Fight to Stop Nestlé from Taking America's Water to Sell in Plastic Bottles," *The Guardian*, October 29, 2019, https://www.theguardian.com/environment/2019/oct/29/the-fight-over-water-how-nestle-dries-up-us-creeks-to-sell-water-in-plastic-bottles.

60. As the organization pointed out, this would add to its nearly one-trillion-dollar budget, which is "15 times [the] annual U.S. contributions to the World Health Organization and the budgets of the Centers for Disease Control and National Institutes of Health, *combined*." Win Without War, "Billionaire Merchants of Death Want a Bailout," Environmentalists Against War, May 2, 2020, http://www.envirosagainstwar.org/2020/05/02/action-alert-billionaire-merchants-of-death-want-a-bailout/.

61. Eric Levenson, "Officials Keep Calling the Coronavirus Pandemic a 'War.' Here's Why," CNN, April, 2, 2020, https://www.cnn.com/2020/04/01/us/war-on-coronavirus-attack/index.html.

62. Robin Andersen, "A Pandemic is Not a War," Fairness & Accuracy In Reporting (FAIR), April 30, 2020, https://fair.org/home/a-pandemic-is-not-a-war/.

63. "Donald Trump Calls COVID-19 'Kung Flu' at Rally," Al Jazeera, June 29, 2020, https://www.aljazeera.com/programmes/newsfeed/2020/06/donald-trump-calls-covid-19-kung-flu-rally-200629091258959.html.

64. Porter, "Pompeo and Netanyahu Paved a Path to War with Iran"; and Sam Husseini, "During Pandemic, U.S. Trying to Overthrow Venezuela Government," Institute for Public Accuracy, May 5, 2020, http://accuracy.org/release/during-pandemic-u-s-trying-to-overthrow-venezuela-government/.

65. Ignacio López-Goñi, "Coronavirus Treatments and Vaccines—Research on 3 Types of Antivirals and 10 Different Vaccines is being Fast-Tracked," The Conversation, March 26, 2020, https://theconversation.com/coronavirus-treatments-and-vaccines-research-on-3-types-of-antivirals-and-10-different-vaccines-is-being-fast-tracked-134613.

66. Alan Feuer and Andrea Salcedo, "New York City Deploys 45 Mobile Morgues as Virus Strains Funeral Homes," *New York Times*, April 2, 2020, updated April 10, 2020, https://www.nytimes.com/2020/04/02/nyregion/coronavirus-new-york-bodies.html; Jody Rosen, "How COVID-19 Has Forced Us to Look at the Unthinkable," *New York Times*, April 29, 2020, https://www.nytimes.com/2020/04/29/magazine/covid-hart-island.html; and "Coronavirus: Outcry after Trump Suggests Injecting Disinfectant as Treatment," BBC News, April 24, 2020, https://www.bbc.com/news/world-us-canada-52407177.

67. Erin Heaney, "Echo Chamber Could Hand Win to Trump . . . Again," Organizing Upgrade, April 24, 2020, https://organizingupgrade.com/echo-chamber-could-hand-win-to-trump-again/.

68. Ibid.

69. Ibid.

70. Ibid.

71. Higdon and Huff, *United States of Distraction*.

72. Craig Mauger, "Protesters, Some Armed, Enter Michigan Capitol in Rally against COVID-19 Limits," *Detroit News*, April 30, 2020, https://www.detroitnews.com/story/news/local/michigan/2020/04/30/protesters-gathering-outside-capitol-amid-covid-19-restrictions/3054911001/. It was progressive news analyses that drew parallels between the orchestrated COVID-19 protests now and the Tea Party movement from 2014. In both cases, what were ostensibly grassroots uprisings were orchestrated behind the scenes by elites. See Mickey Huff, interview with Anthony DiMaggio, *The Project Censored Show*, KPFA (Pacifica Radio), May 4, 2020, https://www.projectcensored.org/special-guests-nicholas-baham-iii-anthony-dimaggio/ [interview begins at 29 minutes 30 seconds].

73. Max Elbaum, "Trump and the Militias Consummate Their Marriage," Portside, May 4, 2020, https://portside.org/2020-05-04/trump-and-militias-consummate-their-marriage.

74. Igor Derysh, "Conservative Group Linked to DeVos Family Organizes Protest of Coronavirus Restrictions in Michigan," Salon, April 16, 2020, https://www.salon.com/2020/04/16/conservative-grouplinked-to-devos-familyorganizes-protest-of-coronavirus-restrictions-in-michigan/; and Lisa Graves, "Who's Behind the 'Reopen' Protests?" *New York Times*, April 22, 2020, https://www.nytimes.com/2020/04/22/opinion/coronavirus-protests-astroturf.html.

75. Elbaum, "Trump and the Militias Consummate Their Marriage."

76. Fintan O'Toole, "Donald Trump Has Destroyed the Country He Promised to Make Great Again," *Irish Times*, April 25, 2020, https://www.irishtimes.com/opinion/fintan-o-toole-donald-trump-has-destroyed-the-country-he-promised-to-make-great-again-1.4235928.

77. Tucker Reals, Sarah Lynch Baldwin, Victoria Albert, and Justin Carissimo, "Coronavirus Updates from April 28, 2020," CBS News, April 28, 2020, updated April 29, 2020, https://www.cbsnews.com/live-updates/coronavirus-latest-updates-2020-04-28/; and Margaret Sullivan, "Trump Has Played the Media Like a Puppet. We're Getting Better—But History Will Not Judge Us Kindly," *Washington Post*, April 28, 2020, https://www.washingtonpost.com/lifestyle/media/trump-has-played-the-media-like-a-puppet-were-get-

ting-better--but-history-will-not-judge-us-kindly/2020/04/28/
e709b1cc-88c6-11ea-ac8a-fe9b8088e101_story.html.

78.　　George Monbiot, "Airlines and Oil Giants are on the Brink. No Government Should Offer Them a Lifeline," *The Guardian*, April 29, 2020, https://www.theguardian.com/commentisfree/2020/apr/29/air-lines-oil-giants-government-economy.

CHAPTER 5

Going Remote

Our community college classroom is now a diaspora, tethered loosely together for a few hours a week by online tools...

STATE OF THE FREE PRESS | 2021 **207**

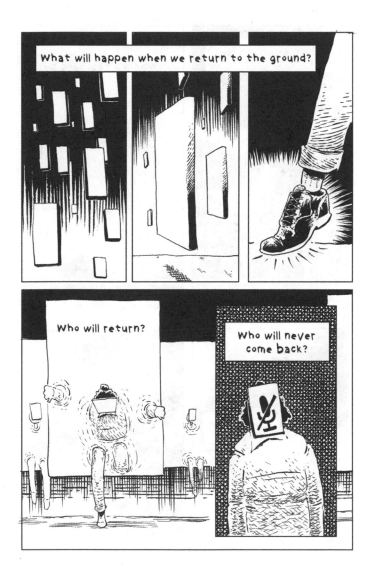

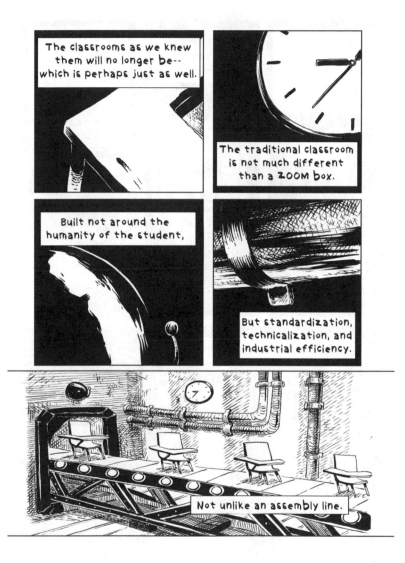

The classrooms as we knew them will no longer be-- which is perhaps just as well.

The traditional classroom is not much different than a ZOOM box.

Built not around the humanity of the student,

But standardization, technicalization, and industrial efficiency.

Not unlike an assembly line.

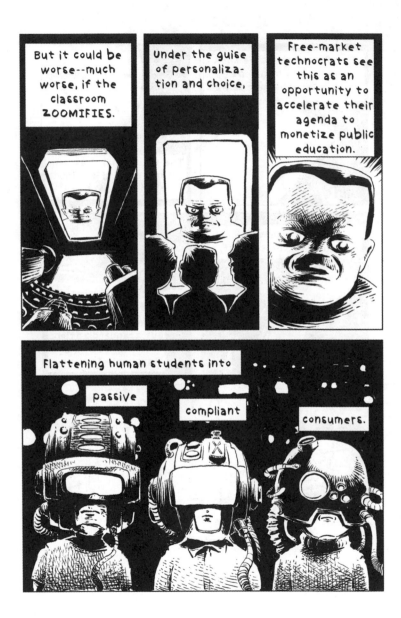

But this vision doesn't have to pass.

When we return to the ground,

We can design around students,

Developing expansive classrooms

For imaginative creators and critical citizens.

Page 207
Widdicombe, Lizzie. "The Great Zoom-School Experiment." The New Yorker. April 2, 2020.
Casey, Nicholas. "College Made Them Feel Equal. The Virus Exposed How Unequal Their Lives Are." New York Times. April 4, 2020. Updated May 5, 2020.

Page 208
Postman, Neil. Technopoly: The Surrender of Culture to Technology. Alfred A. Knopf. 1992.

Page 209
Lanier, Jaron. You are Not a Gadget: A Manifesto. Alfred A. Knopf. 2010.

Page 210
Higdon, Nolan and Huff, Mickey. "Zooming Past Equity in Higher Education: Technocratic Pedagogy Fails Social Justice Test." ProjectCensored.org. May 20, 2020.

Page 211
Spiegelman, Art. The Complete Maus. Pantheon. 1996.

Page 212
Sousanis, Nick. Unflattening. Harvard University Press. 2015.

Page 213
McCloud, Scott. Understanding Comics: The Invisible Art. Tundra Publishing. 1993.

Page 214
Giroux, Henry A. Neoliberalism's War on Higher Education. Haymarket Books. 2014.

Page 217
Bessie, Adam and Archer, Dan. The Disaster Capitalism Curriculum: The High Price of Education Reform. Truthout. May 31, 2012.

Bessie, Adam. "The Answer to the Great Question of Education Reform? The Number 42." Truthout. October 15, 2013.

Page 218
Klein, Naomi. "Screen New Deal." The Intercept. May 8, 2020.
Klein, Naomi. The Shock Doctrine: The Rise of Disaster Capitalism. Picador. 2007.

Page 219
Ware, Chris. Building Stories. Pantheon Books. 2012.

Ravitch, Diane. Slaying Goliath: The Passionate Resistance to Privatization and the Fight to Save America's Public Schools. Alfred A. Knopf. 2020.

Adam Bessie teaches community college English in the Bay Area and writes comics. See more of his work at AdamBessie.com.

Peter Glanting is a cartoonist and illustrator in Portland, OR (how original). See more of his work at PeterGlantingDraws.com.

CHAPTER 6

Media Democracy in Action

Contributions by
KRISTINA BORJESSON (*The Whistleblower Newsroom*),
MILES KENYON (Citizen Lab), REINA ROBINSON
(Center for Urban Excellence), JEFF SHARE (UCLA),
FRED BROWN (Society of Professional Journalists),
and VICTOR PICKARD (Media, Inequality,
and Change Center)

Edited and introduced by
ANDY LEE ROTH and MICKEY HUFF

*It is your ability to discern facts that makes you an
individual, and our collective trust in common knowledge
that makes us a society. The individual who investigates
is also the citizen who builds.*
—TIMOTHY SNYDER, *On Tyranny*[i]

In his 2017 bestseller *On Tyranny*, the historian Timothy
Snyder drew on his expertise about Nazi Germany and the
Soviet Union to reflect on current authoritarian threats to
democracy in the United States. He advised that one way
to preempt the rise of authoritarianism is to "stand out."
Noting that it is "easy to follow along," Snyder wrote, "[i]t
can feel strange to do or say something different." But this
unease, he advised, is necessary to freedom, and standing
out can break "the spell of the status quo."[2]

This spell of the status quo is reflected in the dismal

reporting that passes for journalism when corporate news media succumb to profit-driven logic. That logic reduces news to just another commodity to be hawked and consumed, and the mind-numbing effects of poor journalism (as illustrated in previous chapters on Junk Food News and News Abuse) can aid and abet authoritarianism.

In bright contrast, the contributors to this year's Media Democracy in Action chapter "stand out" by rejecting the status quo in favor of cultivating our individual capacities to discern facts and our shared need for trustworthy knowledge about the world. From a Toronto-based research group that tracks links between developing technologies and digital censorship, to a media literacy program in Oakland that empowers youth impacted by incarceration and violence, this year's Media Democracy in Action chapter provides inspiring examples of how to build a (more) civil society.

As the contributors here demonstrate, these goals entail the establishment of clear ethical guidelines for journalists, new platforms and protections for whistleblowers who risk their reputations and livelihoods to call out abuses of power, and educational settings in which young people can question the politics of media representations and develop their identities as conscientious community members and global citizens.

Power, Snyder writes, "wants your body softening in your chair and your emotions dissipating on the screen."[3] Exemplifying what Project Censored means by media democracy in action, the individuals and organizations spotlighted here call on each of us to engage, together, in building a more inclusive, equitable, and democratic society.

The Whistleblower Newsroom:
A Radio Show for Whistleblowers,
by Whistleblowers, and about
Whistleblowers

KRISTINA BORJESSON

New York University's media professor Mark Crispin Miller unwittingly catalyzed the creation of *The Whistleblower Newsroom* when he invited three investigative reporters—Celia Farber, Stephen Jimenez, and me—to come enlighten his students about extreme forms of press censorship and retaliation for reporting the truth.

Celia Farber is an exacting investigative journalist who had drawn the abject wrath of AIDS researchers and activists by writing "Out of Control: AIDS and the Corruption of Medical Science" for *Harper's Magazine*, in which she exposed human experimentation, murder, and corruption in AIDS research.[4]

Farber's article "ignited a blaze of condemnation," according to NPR media critic Brooke Gladstone in her introduction to an interview with Farber's editor, Roger Hodge, on her radio show *On the Media*.[5] Citing a group of scientists who, "on behalf of a South African treatment advocacy organization, issued a 35-page fact-by-fact rebuttal of the scientific material in the piece," Gladstone challenged Hodge; "And so I wonder," she said, "in a case where the author's thesis depends so much on medical specifics, how do you reassure yourself that the factchecking is good enough?" Gladstone had accepted the account of an AIDS group in South Africa called Treatment Action Campaign (TAC) that has been accused of taking donations from Big Pharma. TAC issued a rebuttal to Farber's reporting with the dubious claim that her article contained 56 errors.[6] Gladstone was not alone in believing TAC; other major press including *The Nation* and the *New York Times* had gullibly run with TAC's allegations while also reporting how "shocked" and "betrayed" AIDS researchers felt because *Harper's* had published an "AIDS denier."[7] *Harper's Magazine*'s response was that the article had been thoroughly fact-checked, and they continued to stand by it. "The fact that [Farber]'s been covering this story," Hodge said, "does not make her a crackpot—it makes her a journalist. She's a courageous journalist, I believe, because she has covered the story at great personal cost."[8] The AIDS research community's virulent attacks on Farber continued, leaving her with post-traumatic stress disorder and a shattered career.

Stephen Jimenez described his run into a hurricane of rage after the publication of his investigation, *The Book of Matt: Hidden Truths about the Murder of Matthew Shepard*.[9] Shepard was a 21-year-old gay student at the University of Wyoming who was killed in the winter of 1998. The brutal killing—Shepard was tied to a fence, pistol-whipped, and set on fire—was determined to be an anti-gay hate crime, and it sparked national outrage. "As a result of Matthew's death," *Guardian* reporter Julie Bindel wrote, "many good things have happened for the gay community. . . . Politicians and celebrities pledged support and funding to combat anti-gay hate crime. . . . There have been numerous documentaries, dramas, books and events based on the story."[10] Enter Jimenez, who blew up the story in his book, reporting that Shepard was a meth dealer and had been killed for $10,000 worth of crystal by people he knew, including a gay sex partner. "This does not make the perfect poster boy for the gay-rights movement," Jimenez told *The Guardian*'s Bindel, "[w]hich is a big part of the reason my book has been so trashed." Bindel reported that Jimenez's enraged critics accused him of being "a revisionist, a criticism usually reserved for extreme rightwing ideologues that deny the Holocaust," and Bindel noted that he had been labeled "a homophobe."

I told my story about being hired and fired three times by three networks: twice while working on the story of the explosion of TWA Flight 800 off the coast of Long Island, New York, and once while working on a story about who was responsible for pushing the United States into the Iraq War on false pretenses. I, too, saw my work attacked in the mainstream corporate press and shunned by fellow journalists. I described my experiences as "being buzzsawed." But I bit back, publishing a book in which well more than a dozen journalists, including me, detailed our run-ins with censorship. I am still proud of *Into the Buzzsaw: Leading Journalists Expose the Myth of a Free Press.*[11]

After the panel discussion in Miller's class, Farber and I became fast friends. I told her I had been thinking about doing a podcast called "The Whistleblower Newsroom" that would provide a platform for whistleblowers. We could do it together, I suggested. She agreed, then called Progressive Radio Network founder Gary Null, and *The Whistleblower Newsroom* was born.

Our first show, "Russiagate Debunked," featured Ray McGovern, a retired Central Intelligence Agency analyst and co-founder of Veteran Intelligence Professionals for Sanity (VIPS), talking about forensic evidence which showed there was no "hack" of the Democratic National

Committee (DNC)'s computers. McGovern was part of a team of VIPS experts who had discovered that the speed at which the data was removed from the DNC computer indicated a *download*, not a hack. This finding should have been of extreme interest to Special Counsel Robert Mueller and his team of investigators. It wasn't. Scant attention was paid to the VIPS report, even though other key experts working with McGovern were elite National Security Agency (NSA) techno-geniuses: William Binney, former NSA technical director for world geopolitical and military analysis; J. Kirk Wiebe, ex–senior analyst at the NSA's Signals Intelligence Automation Research Center; and Edward Loomis Jr., former technical director in the NSA's Office of Signals Processing.

The only major outlet that did cover the VIPS report was *The Nation*. Patrick Lawrence's piece, "A New Report Raises Big Questions about Last Year's Hack," came out on August 9, 2017.[12] The backlash from powerful progressive quarters was immediate. Lawrence was attacked and *The Nation*'s editor, Katrina vanden Heuvel, responded by gathering a group of "dissenters" to counter the VIPS report. "A Leak or a Hack? A Forum on the VIPS Memo" may have mollified the baying critics but it was hardly a forum.[13] The exchange between the VIPS researchers and the dissenters was far too limited and inconclusive to be worthy of the term. We invited Patrick Lawrence on our show two years later. A highly accomplished journalist with a distinguished career, he was clearly still reeling from his experience at *The Nation*. We understood. We'd run the gauntlet for our truth-telling too.

Celia Farber and I continued to cover the disintegration of the official Russiagate narrative that the establishment press clung to with pathological tenacity. We conducted a series of interviews with financial analyst Ed Butowsky and his lawyer, Ty Clevenger. Butowsky is suing NPR and other press outlets for defamation after they claimed he fabricated a news story to eliminate "suspicions that the Russians had a hand in President Trump's election."[14] Butowsky had told several Fox News hosts and then–press secretary Sean Spicer that he had been asked by a friend, news analyst Ellen Ratner, to call the parents of murdered DNC staffer Seth Rich and relay a message from Julian Assange. The message: WikiLeaks had published the DNC documents after receiving them not from a Russian source, but from Seth Rich. Seth Rich's parents, Butowsky says, when confronted with this information which could be important to the investigation of their son's murder, told him they already knew their sons (plural) had leaked the DNC documents to WikiLeaks. Subsequent to Butowsky's going public with the story, Ratner quickly backed away from Butowsky and has all but disappeared. Unfortunately for Ratner, says Butowsky's lawyer, Butowsky still has his email exchanges with her. And on YouTube, there's footage of Ratner saying that she had met with Assange for three hours at the Ecuadorian Embassy in London and that he had told her the DNC leaks "were not from the Russians, they were [from] an internal source from the Hillary [Clinton] campaign or from somebody that knew Hillary—an enemy."[15]

Instead of covering a different story every week, Celia Farber and I often drill down on the same story for months. Besides Russiagate, we've done a series of shows on Jeffrey Epstein and other pedophile rings in powerful circles and government agencies; on vaccines and viruses; and on the biggest unresolved crime of all—9/11.

Co-hosting with Celia has been magical. She's a master of the unexpected question or comment that comes out of nowhere and persuades a guest to bare their soul. Guests are always saying things they didn't intend to on our show in response to her. Her reporting wheelhouse is the medical industry and science, particularly viruses. My guest interaction style is frontal, direct. I'm obsessed with hard and forensic evidence. My wheelhouse is high-level malfeasance and the mechanics of major cover-ups. Both of us are completely ourselves on the show. That we can actually be that and be of service to whistleblowers and our audience at the same time is the greatest blessing of all.

KRISTINA BORJESSON, an investigative reporter, became internationally known for blowing the whistle on corruption in the US press following publication of her landmark books, *Into the Buzzsaw: Leading Journalists Expose the Myth of a Free Press* and *Feet to the Fire: The Media After 9/11, Top Journalists Speak Out.* Her groundbreaking documentary, *TWA Flight 800* (2013, Epix Premium Cable Channel), featured high-level whistleblowers from inside the US government's official investigation into the jetliner's explosion, revealing a massive, multi-agency cover-up and almost two decades of false reporting on the subject. A veteran network television and radio producer, Borjesson currently co-hosts *The Whistleblower Newsroom* on the Progressive Radio Network.

Digital Repression and Resistance: Citizen Lab Research on Tracking and Exposing Human Rights Violations

MILES KENYON

Advances in technology are inseparable from their implications for human rights: the same tools that can spark a revolution can quell dissent. Understanding how technology and human rights intersect in society is integral in ensuring that free expression grows unabated and autocrats are held accountable for censorship and the dampening of free expression.

Based at the University of Toronto's Munk School of Global Affairs and Public Policy, the Citizen Lab is an interdisciplinary research group. We bring together computer scientists, political scientists, legal advisors, and subject area experts to focus on research at the intersection of information and communication technologies, human rights, and global security. This often positions us at the center of stories involving censorship, technology, and members of civil society.

Journalists form a key part of our research strategy, helping to translate highly technical reports into language easily understood by general audiences. They also provide a direct link to some of our most important stories, as they are often targets of authoritarian governments with access to powerful tools of suppression.

In May 2019, WhatsApp identified a vulnerability that allowed attackers to inject spyware onto phones simply by calling up a target's device. More than 1400 individuals were believed to be targets, representing a serious breach of the popular app. After the incident, Citizen Lab volunteered to help WhatsApp identify cases in which the suspected targets of this attack were members of civil society, including journalists.[16]

WhatsApp has since traced this targeting to spyware created by the Israeli technology firm NSO Group and launched legal claims against them. NSO Group's Pegasus spyware is a powerful tool of espionage, granting high-paying operators access to everything on a target's phone, including secure chats. Attackers can even turn on an infected phone's camera and microphone to capture activity in the user's vicinity, transforming the phone into a near-omnipotent spy device.

While NSO Group claims that their powerful spyware is sold exclusively to governments for the sole purpose of tracking terrorists and other criminals, Citizen Lab research has shown otherwise. In Mexico it's been used to target journalists, public health officials, human rights lawyers, and anti-corruption advocates. Closer to the Lab's home in Canada, Omar Abdulaziz, a Saudi Arabian dissident and YouTube satirist, was targeted.[17] Abdulaziz was a friend and confidant of slain journalist Jamal Khashoggi. Given their connection, the nature of their conversations, and the access that spyware operators had to his phone, Abdulaziz suspects it was the presence of spyware that led to Khashoggi's execution.

Citizen Lab's analysis of Abdulaziz's device traced the operator to Saudi Arabia. The same operator also targeted Ben Hubbard, Beirut bureau chief of the *New York Times*. He was targeted in June 2018 but only decided to disclose the incident publicly in January 2020.[18] Given his experience reporting on Saudi Arabia and Crown Prince Mohammed bin Salman, one could surmise why he might be a target of digital reprisal.

There is clearly reason for journalists to be wary of powerful and targeted digital threats. But research has shown that even the suspicion that government surveillance might be taking place has a chilling effect on free speech, thus infringing on a bevy of human rights for everyone.[19] While digital attacks often target specific individuals, Pegasus spyware and similar technologies potentially impact anyone with, or even near, a smartphone.

Information controls—actions conducted in or through information and communication technologies that seek to deny, disrupt, secure, or monitor information for political ends—shape how we are able to view the world around us.[20] Consider the influence of internet filtering products, tools deployed by network managers to determine which websites users are allowed to access and which ones will be blocked. Canadian company Netsweeper has created one such product.[21] In the hands of well-meaning librarians, it can be used to block student access to pornography or websites containing hate speech. But in the hands of authoritarian governments, it can be used to limit access to dissenting beliefs and place unnecessary restrictions on public discourse. Citizen Lab research investigated how Netsweeper was used in ten countries with histories of human rights abuses, finding the blocking of religious content in Bahrain, political campaigns in the United Arab Emirates, and media websites in Yemen.

Among our findings was that Netsweeper had created a category called 'Alternative Lifestyles' that served no purpose other than blocking access to non-pornographic LGBTQ2+ websites, including some that provide life-saving HIV/AIDS information. After a public campaign and critical media attention, Netsweeper acquiesced in

January 2019 and removed the filtering function, signaling a victory in a long and continued fight for free expression.[22]

While Citizen Lab will continue to document foundationless attacks on free expression, authorities must be willing to resolutely address the dangers of an unregulated environment that allows spyware to be sold to countries with egregious human rights records. If spyware sales are allowed to continue unabated, human rights defenders will continue to be targeted, critical media will be silenced, and our collective rights will be vitiated.

To keep up to date about Citizen Lab's ongoing research, see https://citizenlab.ca/.

MILES KENYON is a former journalist and current communications specialist at the Citizen Lab, where he studies how LGBTQ2+ content is censored online.

Digital and Social Media Literacy as Critical Aspects of Justice-Involved Youth Success

REINA ROBINSON

Working with justice-involved youth in the San Francisco Bay Area, I've witnessed the ways criminalized activity is displayed and surveilled on social media. Problematic content discovered on cell phones and/or social media accounts perpetually causes young people to violate courts' probation terms. As the intersection of urban youth violence and digital media attracts more and more attention from law enforcement and the judicial system, activists, advocates, and educators must demand critical digital and social media literacy education for underprivileged populations, in alternative education programs and schools for incarcerated and marginalized youth.

The digital sphere enables us to manipulate and create our social identities. YouTube, Instagram, and Snapchat social media platforms currently dominate youth attention. A 2019 Pew Research Center study found that at least 90 percent of 18- to 24-year-olds use some form of social media.[23] Social media encourages oversharing, and the typical consumer is unaware of the potential consequences. In 2018, seeing the general lack of understanding among young people of the risks posed by their social media use motivated me to establish a nonprofit organization, the Center for Urban Excellence (CUE), and to create a free critical digital and social media literacy educator resource guide.

CUE is specifically aimed at supporting youth affected by incarceration and violence. CUE encourages safe, critical media praxis by providing trainings, event coordination, and a youth-focused curriculum that pushes past conversation. For the first Urban Excellence Convention at Oakland's Museum of Children's Arts in March 2019, panel-style discussions and performances supported the theme "digital and social media literacy as a critical aspect of justice-involved Black youth success (life, freedom, and social and economic opportunity)." CUE's digital and social media literacy curriculum has been implemented in Bay Area juvenile justice institution schools and youth organizations, and in April 2019 Dr. Colleen Mihal began using the CUE educator guide in her classes with Project L.A.'s San Quentin Prison program.

We collaborate with nonprofits such as SHIFT Inc., Contra Costa County Independent Living Skills Program, Museum of Children's Arts, and Vallejo Girls Youth Empowerment Group to provide free community events, trainings, and supportive services for justice-involved youth. To date, nearly 450 young people have participated in or benefited from CUE's programs and services.

Justice-Involved Youths' Problematic Reproduction of Social Norms

Youth create digital content grounded in their life experiences and the norms of their elected social groups. The intersection of high rates of adverse childhood experiences (ACEs) and limitations on opportunities to expand social identity forces justice-involved youth into a social undercaste.[24] Some youth use digital media to capture problematic scenes of their reality to share online. These images and posts document experiences that are outside of "mainstream" norms but are normalized within their social circles, such as content involving alcohol, drugs, sex, or weapons.

To target specific consumer markets, social media giants like Instagram (owned by Facebook) use algorithms to sift through user profile data and analyze them for users' interests, preferences, and traits. This overt stereotyping and automated categorizing for advertisers is just the most obvious consequence of unprecedented digital surveillance, but other consequences—including the exploitation of user data by law enforcement and the justice system—are far more insidious. While over-policing of Black and Latinx communities is well documented throughout history, dehumanizing "stop and frisk" tactics have been restructured and expanded in the digital age to a degree almost unimaginable to today's youth.[25] Developing youths' critical digital and social media literacy, as well as their ability to create advantageous experiences to capture and share, has the potential to aid them in escaping social media silos and expand their social identity through new and safer group memberships.

About the Educator Resource Guide

The Digital and Social Media Literacy Educator Resource Guide is a tool for educators within underprivileged, alternative, and incarcerated education settings whose students face issues of violence and problematic behaviors. The guide uses a social identity perspective to reconceive of digital and social media and the types of content that users share. Social identity theory posits that people's perception of themselves is based on the groups they are part of. Creating alternative visions for oneself through digital media can assist with liberation from problematic social norms. Digital and social media literacy education can help students

- develop critical questioning and thinking skills;

- reflect on how digital media messages shape society;

- identify target marketing strategies;

- recognize bias, misinformation, and fake news; and

- advocate for positive change in the digital sphere.

The guide provides socially relevant readings, videos, and activities. It is organized into five units and can be modularized. The guide invites conversation on racially biased media, social identification, and social comparison. It is organized as follows:

Unit 1: What is the internet?	A simplified explanation of the internet, the World Wide Web, and web browsers. We discuss basic understanding of the internet, accessing information on the internet, and spotting misinformation (fake news).
Unit 2: What is a digital footprint?	Discover how digital lives leave forever searchable footprints on the internet.
Unit 3: What is social media?	Develop an understanding of social media and how it is used.
Unit 4: What is social media literacy and why is it important?	Discuss oversharing (identity), safety (security), and responsibility (agency).
Unit 5: What is social media etiquette ("netiquette") and how is social media used for good?	Explore the ways to display social media etiquette and how social media is used for online activism, spreading awareness, and connecting to opportunities.

Critical digital and social media literacy education allows for social media subversion and social identity transformation. While there are limitations to social justice in education and juvenile justice institutional spaces—such as navigating strict zero-tolerance policies, instruction time tables, and bureaucratic approval systems—the Digital and Social Media Literacy Educator Resource Guide acts as a practical starting point for essential transformative discourse between educators and students. Request a free copy of the guide by visiting https://www.centerforurbanexcellence.org/contact.

REINA ROBINSON, MA, is the executive director of the Center for Urban Excellence (CUE), a certified Community Resiliency Model (CRM) trainer, and a coordinator of services for San Francisco Bay Area justice-involved youth. Her work focuses on digital media literacy, spectrum thinking, and social and economic opportunity development.

Teaching Critical Media Literacy at UCLA

JEFF SHARE

In the education department at the University of California, Los Angeles (UCLA), students are critically engaging with media, information, and technology to interrogate the role of these tools in society—the positive contributions that inform, entertain, connect, and empower, as well as the negative influences that mislead, distract, exploit, surveil, and oppress. Through interactive lessons that involve analysis and production, students question dominant ideologies, misrepresentations, biases, stereotypes, and possibilities for creating alternative messages that support social and environmental justice. When students learn to critically analyze and create images, sounds, multimedia, and text, they deepen their critical thinking skills to question the social construction of media, the politics of representation, and the inequalities of power, and they develop their identities as conscientious and empowered global citizens.

The pervasiveness of social media and digital tools is analyzed through critical lenses, such as Shoshana Zuboff's theory of *surveillance capitalism*.[26] A quiz about the function and purpose of Google's search engine helps students rethink the tool that more than 90 percent of internet users go to for answers. The quiz asks students to think through the lens of surveillance capitalism and answer: What is the purpose of Google's search engine? What is the raw product they extract? What is the finished product they create? Who are the customers? Who are the workers? What is the ultimate goal?[27]

The critical media literacy course explores the development of media education, defined less as a specific body of knowledge or set of skills and more as a framework of *conceptual understandings*.[28] Much of the theory that informs critical media literacy has evolved from cultural studies, a field of critical inquiry that incorporates an understanding of political economy, textual analysis, and audience theory.[29]

Every class begins by reviewing the critical media literacy framework to analyze media texts through asking questions that support the six conceptual understandings of media shown in Table 1. Researchers at UCLA constructed this framework based on decades of work from cultural studies scholars and media educators throughout the world.[30]

TABLE 1

Critical Media Literacy Framework

1. SOCIAL CONSTRUCTIVISM
All information is constructed by individuals and/or groups of people who make choices within social contexts.

WHO are all the possible people who made choices that helped create this text?

2. LANGUAGES/SEMIOTICS
Each medium has its own language with specific grammar and semantics.

HOW was this text constructed and delivered/accessed?

3. AUDIENCE/POSITIONALITY
Individuals and groups understand media messages similarly and/or differently depending on multiple contextual factors.

HOW could this text be understood differently?

4. POLITICS OF REPRESENTATION
Media messages and the medium through which they travel always have a bias and support and/or challenge dominant hierarchies of power, privilege, and pleasure.

WHAT values, points of view, and ideologies are represented or missing from this text or influenced by the medium?

5. PRODUCTION/ INSTITUTIONS
All media texts have a purpose (often commercial or governmental) that is shaped by the creators and/or systems within which they operate.

WHY was this text created and/or shared?

6. SOCIAL AND ENVIRONMENTAL JUSTICE
Media culture is a terrain of struggle that perpetuates or challenges positive and/or negative ideas about people, groups, and issues; it is never neutral.

WHOM does this text advantage and/or disadvantage?

A series of assignments require students to work collaboratively to create a variety of media projects such as photographs, podcasts, memes, Validated Independent News stories (VINs), social media posts, and advertisements.[31] One example from the critical media literacy class is a lesson in which students in teams take photographs to visually communicate a word. This lesson begins by comparing two different photographs of the same person. Through a whole group discussion, students deconstruct the techniques that the photographers used to create the two images. Their ideas are charted on the board and are then reconceived as visual literacy skills for the others to employ when taking their photographs.[32] Students then leave the classroom in teams to create a single photograph that will communicate their assigned vocabulary word. After taking their pictures, they choose one image to be projected for the entire class to see and attempt to guess the word.

Photograph to illustrate the word "overwhelmed."
The student pictured is Rogelio Pizano.
PHOTOGRAPH BY RUOSHI HUANG

Throughout the process, students are encouraged to be metacognitive about their learning and reflect on their conceptual understandings of the critical media literacy framework. For example: Concept #1—The process they engaged in to create the photographs demonstrates how media messages are socially constructed through every decision they had to make (such as choice of camera angle, lighting, composition, etc.); Concept #2—The techniques of photography they used are the codes and conventions of visual language that they applied to create the pictures; Concept #3—The variety of responses to each other's photographs show how audiences can read the same message differently; Concept #4—Their choices of *what* to photograph (or what to leave out) and *how* to take the pictures are influenced by their positionalities and context that contribute to the bias of the photographs; Concept #5— Everyone's photograph had a clear purpose since the task required that they illustrate a specific word; and Concept #6—Each photograph they took required students to consider if they were perpetuating a stereotype or creating an image that could have a negative effect (unintended or otherwise).

The process of analysis, production, and reflection is part of all assignments because learning is enhanced when students can demonstrate their understandings through applying analytical concepts in the creation process. However, simply creating media does not promote critical thinking if the process does not encourage students to critically question the representations, context, and process. Therefore, this class incorporates critical analysis and practice with all activities. Students use the critical media literacy framework to guide their inquiry while they are analyzing and creating alternative media messages. It is essential for everyone to deepen their critical capacity to question all information, to analyze the context in which it is constructed and shared, and to act responsibly with that knowledge, because society requires critical thinkers to participate in the process of shaping democracy.

JEFF SHARE has worked as an award-winning photojournalist, bilingual elementary school teacher, and since 2007 as a teacher in the Teacher Education Program at UCLA. His research and practice focuses on preparing educators to teach critical media literacy in K–12 education, for the goals of social and environmental justice. He now teaches critical media literacy to undergraduate students as well.

Society of Professional Journalists—Code of Ethics

Introduction and Brief History by FRED BROWN,
former president of SPJ

For journalism to fulfill its purpose of producing and distributing well-researched information with honesty, clarity, and precision, its practitioners must follow a code of ethics. It's one thing that separates responsible, informed journalism from random spurts of tweeting or blogging.

Ethics has been one of the principal missions of the Society of Professional Journalists for decades, but SPJ didn't actually have an ethics code until seventeen years after it was founded as a fraternity called Sigma Delta Chi (SDX). In 1926, SDX essentially borrowed the American

Society of Newspaper Editors's canons of journalism, which served SDX until it drafted its own code in 1973 in the aftermath of Watergate.

The 1973 code underwent modest changes in 1987 but still adhered to the basic principles—truth and accuracy at the top of the list, along with preserving freedom of the press, avoiding conflicts of interest, and striving for fairness and objectivity.

There was continuing debate over whether there should be some sort of enforcement clause, as other professions like law and medicine have in their codes. Instead, the 1973 and 1987 codes had a pledge at the end, in which journalists were asked to promise that they would uphold the standards of the profession. The 1973 code said journalists should "actively censure" violations of the standards; the "censure" language was replaced in 1987 with a pledge to "encourage" adherence.

In 1996 the ethics code was rewritten more extensively, to confront what even then seemed to be a growing public mistrust of journalism and its perceived negativity. So the 1996 code added a major section headed "Minimize Harm," comprising several principles in the previous code but with a clear message that journalists should consider the consequences of what they're doing—not to stop them from telling the truth, hurtful though it may be, but to emphasize that they should at least be aware of what might happen.

Instead of any attempt at enforcement or even a "pledge," there was an admonition that journalists had a responsibility to be accountable for their actions and to call attention to any ethical missteps they might encounter.

After that code had been around for more than a

decade, it became apparent that changing technologies and changing marketplaces were having a profound effect on how journalism was practiced. Anyone with access to the internet could profess to be doing real journalism.

But rather than try to keep up with rapidly evolving delivery systems for information, SPJ decided to adapt its code of ethics for more general application, allowing for any medium of communication through which journalism is conveyed. The Society's 2014 code eliminates any reference to specific technologies and techniques and focuses instead on what the code's drafters hope are abiding principles.

Those principles are the four spelled out in the 1996 code, with language only slightly updated to account for the influence of the crowded, sometimes careless world of reportage steeped in the fast-moving realm of the internet: Seek Truth and Report It; Minimize Harm; Act Independently; and Be Accountable and Transparent.

Preamble

Members of the Society of Professional Journalists believe that public enlightenment is the forerunner of justice and the foundation of democracy. Ethical journalism strives to ensure the free exchange of information that is accurate, fair and thorough. An ethical journalist acts with integrity.

The Society declares these four principles as the foundation of ethical journalism and encourages their use in its practice by all people in all media.

Seek Truth and Report It

Ethical journalism should be accurate and fair. Journalists should be honest and courageous in gathering, reporting and interpreting information.

Journalists should:

—Take responsibility for the accuracy of their work. Verify information before releasing it. Use original sources whenever possible.

—Remember that neither speed nor format excuses inaccuracy.

—Provide context. Take special care not to misrepresent or oversimplify in promoting, previewing or summarizing a story.

—Gather, update and correct information throughout the life of a news story.

—Be cautious when making promises, but keep the promises they make.

—Identify sources clearly. The public is entitled to as much information as possible to judge the reliability and motivations of sources.

—Consider sources' motives before promising anonymity. Reserve anonymity for sources who may face danger, retribution or other harm, and have information that cannot be obtained elsewhere. Explain why anonymity was granted.

—Diligently seek subjects of news coverage to allow them to respond to criticism or allegations of wrongdoing.

—Avoid undercover or other surreptitious methods of gathering information unless traditional, open methods will not yield information vital to the public.

—Be vigilant and courageous about holding those with

power accountable. Give voice to the voiceless.

—Support the open and civil exchange of views, even views they find repugnant.

—Recognize a special obligation to serve as watchdogs over public affairs and government. Seek to ensure that the public's business is conducted in the open, and that public records are open to all.

—Provide access to source material when it is relevant and appropriate.

—Boldly tell the story of the diversity and magnitude of the human experience. Seek sources whose voices we seldom hear.

—Avoid stereotyping. Journalists should examine the ways their values and experiences may shape their reporting.

—Label advocacy and commentary.

—Never deliberately distort facts or context, including visual information. Clearly label illustrations and re-enactments.

—Never plagiarize. Always attribute.

Minimize Harm

Ethical journalism treats sources, subjects, colleagues and members of the public as human beings deserving of respect.

Journalists should:

—Balance the public's need for information against potential harm or discomfort. Pursuit of the news is not a license for arrogance or undue intrusiveness.

—Show compassion for those who may be affected by news coverage. Use heightened sensitivity when dealing with juveniles, victims of sex crimes, and sources or subjects who are inexperienced or unable to give consent. Consider cultural differences in approach and treatment.

—Recognize that legal access to information differs from an ethical justification to publish or broadcast.

– Realize that private people have a greater right to control information about themselves than public figures and others who seek power, influence or attention. Weigh the consequences of publishing or broadcasting personal information.

—Avoid pandering to lurid curiosity, even if others do.

—Balance a suspect's right to a fair trial with the public's right to know. Consider the implications of identifying criminal suspects before they face legal charges.

—Consider the long-term implications of the extended reach and permanence of publication. Provide updated and more complete information as appropriate.

Act Independently

The highest and primary obligation of ethical journalism is to serve the public.

Journalists should:

—Avoid conflicts of interest, real or perceived. Disclose unavoidable conflicts.

—Refuse gifts, favors, fees, free travel and special treatment, and avoid political and other outside activities that may compromise integrity or impartiality, or may damage credibility.

—Be wary of sources offering information for favors or money; do not pay for access to news. Identify content provided by outside sources, whether paid or not.

—Deny favored treatment to advertisers, donors or any other special interests, and resist internal and external pressure to influence coverage.

—Distinguish news from advertising and shun hybrids that blur the lines between the two. Prominently label sponsored content.

Be Accountable and Transparent

Ethical journalism means taking responsibility for one's work and explaining one's decisions to the public.

Journalists should:

—Explain ethical choices and processes to audiences. Encourage a civil dialogue with the public about journalistic practices, coverage and news content.

—Respond quickly to questions about accuracy, clarity and fairness.

—Acknowledge mistakes and correct them promptly and prominently. Explain corrections and clarifications carefully and clearly.

—Expose unethical conduct in journalism, including within their organizations.

—Abide by the same high standards they expect of others.

The SPJ Code of Ethics is a statement of abiding principles supported by additional explanations and position papers that address changing journalistic practices. It is not a set of rules, rather a guide that encourages all who engage in journalism to take responsibility for the information they provide, regardless of medium. The code should be read as a whole; individual principles should not be taken out of context. It is not, nor can it be under the First Amendment, legally enforceable.

FRED BROWN, retired political reporter, editor, and colum-
nist for the *Denver Post*, teaches media ethics at the University
of Denver. He is a former national president of the Society of
Professional Journalists and recently completed editing the fifth
edition of the SPJ's *Journalism Ethics: A Casebook of Professional
Conduct for News Media.*

Media, Inequality, and Change: Market Censorship and the Ongoing Struggle for Media Democracy

VICTOR PICKARD

The notion of censorship typically evokes fear of oppressive
governments or corporate media policing the bounds of
acceptable discourse and constricting the range of political
opinion. A long history—including many cases carefully documented by Project Censored over the decades—shows that
we *should* be concerned about such abuses. However, a deeper,
more systemic form of censorship warps our media, one we
too often neglect. This subtle—but no less malignant—filtering process is a byproduct of toxic commercialism, a set
of values that systematically privilege entertainment over
information, treat audiences as consumers not citizens, and
consistently marginalize progressive arguments and issues.
Resulting in a truncated public sphere and an impoverished
imagination of what is possible, this profit-driven logic structures much of our news and information. We might refer to
such patterns of omission and emphasis—where some voices
and views are elevated and others muffled according to commercial values, profit accumulation, and corporate power—as
"market censorship."

Against Market Censorship

The idea of market censorship has received only passing attention in media scholarship over the years. Sue Curry Jansen offers what is perhaps the best definition: "Market censorship points to practices that routinely filter or restrict the production and distribution of selected ideas, perspectives, genres or cultural forms within mainstream media of communication based upon their anticipated profits and/or support for corporate values and consumerism."[33] C. Edwin Baker rightly observes that much of this power to filter or restrict ideas traces back to the influence of advertisers, who act as the "most consistent and the most pernicious 'censors' of media content."[34] Other models shed light on various aspects of the filtering that takes place, but too rarely draw linkages to a commercial media system's structural characteristics.[35]

Much to their disadvantage, progressives must try to politically organize and communicate their messages within this inhospitable media landscape. Their arguments seldom receive a fair hearing by a system so stacked against them. The treatment of Bernie Sanders's presidential campaigns in our establishment news media could serve as exhibit A.

Progressives cannot compete because their issues rarely sell advertising. What sells advertising? Fear sells advertising. Hate sells advertising. Simplistic soundbites—and anything that captures our attention—sells advertising. That is, after all, what ratings are all about: baiting and selling our attention to advertisers. It is what led the now-disgraced CEO of CBS, Les Moonves, to acknowledge that Donald Trump might be bad for America, but he is "damn good for CBS."[36]

Corporate television outlets, owned by gigantic media conglomerates, make obscene amounts of money from these relationships, and we can never shame them into better behavior. To counter market censorship, therefore, we must combat the commercial logic driving it. As much as possible, we must remove news and information from the market altogether. But this will not happen if we misdiagnose the root of the problem. Our media-related challenges exceed the bad behavior of right-wing journalists, run-amok corporations, and an overbearing government. These are all problems, of course, but they are symptoms of deeper pathologies—they reflect the values of a commercial or capitalistic media system.

Commercialism drives many of the negative attributes that we rightly decry in our news and information systems, from social media to news media. It is what incentivizes Facebook and other platform monopolies to practice surveillance capitalism. It drives corporate outlets to routinely trivialize, ignore, or sensationalize life-and-death issues such as hyper-inequality, mass incarceration, and climate change. In a truly democratic system, journalists would maintain a laser-like focus on these issues to help find practical, community-driven policy solutions.

Market values also are culpable for driving journalism into the ground. Public service journalism was always in a precarious position within a commercial system. Now that the 150-year-old print advertising model has fallen apart, these preexisting fissures have blown wide open. Because any hope for a democratic society requires a free and functional press, we need non-market alternatives. The journalism crisis is an opportunity for imagining something bold and new to replace the failing commercial model that is now collapsing beneath the weight of its own contradictions.[37]

Since structural critiques of capitalism have been beaten out of the discourse over the years, we often miss the forest for the trees and fail to understand the systemic biases at work. To correctly diagnose the core impediment to a democratic media system, this commercial censoring of our news and information deserves far more attention—an essential task in building structural alternatives to the corporate, heavily commercialized, and barely regulated media system that we have inherited in the United States.[38]

Imagining Structural Alternatives

Nicholas Johnson, former commissioner of the Federal Communications Commission, famously argued that whatever your first political priority is, your second should be media reform—otherwise you will not make progress on your first issue.[39] A market-driven media system will almost always champion the status quo, which means that working toward social change should also include de-commercializing and democratizing our media. Ultimately, we should treat news and access to information as public services that should not be left entirely to the mercy of capitalist logic. We must build systemic and sustainable alternatives.

Working toward such structural alternatives inspired Todd Wolfson and me in 2018 to launch the Media, Inequality, and Change (MIC) Center, a partnership between the University of Pennsylvania and Rutgers University.[40] We see MIC as not just a traditional academic research center but also an activist center—one that moves from theory to praxis. We deliberately set out to not just better describe the world but to change it. Our research is dedicated to social justice and to creating a more democratic society.

At the theory level, MIC serves as a policy workshop to imagine and advocate for alternative structures of ownership and control over core systems in society. At the praxis level, we assist activists, journalists, and workers who are trying to create a more just and equitable world. In particular, we are trying to actualize visions of a progressive future for work and for media. This project includes creating new systems for a truly publicly owned and democratically governed local journalism. Toward these objectives, we are collaborating with gig workers, labor journalists, and policy advocates on a variety of projects to envision a better society. We aim to craft counter-narratives to the market fundamentalism and neoliberalism that has misguided so much of our society for so long and we strive to broaden our political imaginary about what is possible. We call on progressive academics and intellectuals—especially media scholars—to join our endeavors. The struggle before us all is a long one. Reimagining and restructuring society looks far beyond Trump and the pandemic crisis. History is open-ended and we can seize these opportunities if we organize accordingly.

VICTOR PICKARD is an associate professor at the University of Pennsylvania's Annenberg School for Communication, where he co-directs the Media, Inequality, and Change (MIC) Center.

He has authored or edited six books, including *America's Battle for Media Democracy*, *Will the Last Reporter Please Turn Out the Lights* (with Robert W. McChesney); *After Net Neutrality* (with David Elliot Berman); and, most recently, *Democracy Without Journalism?*

Notes

1. Timothy Snyder, *On Tyranny: Twenty Lessons from the Twentieth Century* (New York: Tim Duggan Books, 2017), 73.
2. Ibid., 51.
3. Ibid., 83.
4. Celia Farber, "Out of Control: AIDS and the Corruption of Medical Science," *Harper's Magazine*, March 2006, 37–52.
5. Brooke Gladstone, interview with Roger Hodge, "Harper's Bizarre?" *On the Media*, WNYC Studios, May 5, 2006, https://www.wnycstudios.org/podcasts/otm/segments/128750-harpers-bizarre.
6. Robert Gallo et al., "Errors in Celia Farber's March 2006 Article in Harper's Magazine," Treatment Action Campaign, March 4, 2006, https://web.archive.org/web/20060318155138/https://tac.org.za/Documents/ErrorsInFarberArticle.pdf.
7. Richard Kim, "Harper's Publishes AIDS Denialist," *The Notion* blog (*The Nation*), March 2, 2006, https://www.thenation.com/article/archive/harpers-publishes-aids-denialist/; and Lia Miller, "An Article in Harper's Ignites a Controversy Over H.I.V.," *New York Times*, March 13, 2006, https://www.nytimes.com/2006/03/13/business/media/an-article-in-harpers-ignites-a-controversy-over-hiv.html.
8. Miller, "An Article in Harper's."
9. Stephen Jimenez, *The Book of Matt: Hidden Truths about the Murder of Matthew Shepard* (Hanover, New Hampshire: Steerforth Press, 2013).
10. Julie Bindel, "The Truth behind America's Most Famous Gay-Hate Murder," *The Guardian*, October 26, 2014, https://www.theguardian.com/world/2014/oct/26/the-truth-behind-americas-most-famous-gay-hate-murder-matthew-shepard.
11. Kristina Borjesson, ed., *Into the Buzzsaw: Leading Journalists Expose the Myth of a Free Press* (Amherst, New York: Prometheus Books, 2002/2004).
12. Patrick Lawrence, "A New Report Raises Big Questions about Last Year's DNC Hack," *The Nation*, August 9, 2017, https://www.thenation.com/article/archive/a-new-report-raises-big-questions-about-last-years-dnc-hack/.
13. Various Contributors, "A Leak or a Hack? A Forum on the VIPS Memo," *The Nation*, September 1, 2017, https://www.thenation.com/article/archive/a-leak-or-a-hack-a-forum-on-the-vips-memo/.
14. David Folkenflik, "The Man Behind the Scenes in Fox News' Discredited Seth Rich Story," *Morning Edition*, NPR, August 16, 2017, https://www.npr.org/2017/08/16/543830392/the-role-of-ed-butowsky-in-advancing-retracted-seth-rich-story.

15. Ellen Ratner with John LeBoutillier, "Speaker Series: John LeBoutillier and Ellen Ratner," YouTube video of the "Left to Right after Election Day" event at Embry-Riddle Aeronautical University on November 9, 2016, posted by "EmbryRiddleUniv" on November 15, 2016, https://www.youtube.com/watch?v=gdtkACCxdnc [quote begins at 1 hour 2 minutes 25 seconds].

16. "NSO Group / Q Cyber Technologies: Over One Hundred New Abuse Cases," Citizen Lab, October 29, 2019, https://citizenlab.ca/2019/10/nso-q-cyber-technologies-100-new-abuse-cases/.

17. Bill Marczak, John Scott-Railton, Adam Senft, Bahr Abdul Razzak, and Ron Deibert, "The Kingdom Came to Canada: How Saudi-Linked Digital Espionage Reached Canadian Soil," Citizen Lab, October 1, 2018, https://citizenlab.ca/2018/10/the-kingdom-came-to-canada-how-saudi-linked-digital-espionage-reached-canadian-soil/.

18. Bill Marczak, Siena Anstis, Masashi Crete-Nishihata, John Scott-Railton, and Ron Deibert, "Stopping the Press: New York Times Journalist Targeted by Saudi-Linked Pegasus Spyware Operator," January 28, 2020, https://citizenlab.ca/2020/01/stopping-the-press-new-york-times-journalist-targeted-by-saudi-linked-pegasus-spyware-operator/.

19. See, for example, Jon Penney, "Chilling Effects: Online Surveillance and Wikipedia Use," *Berkeley Technology Law Journal*, Vol. 31 No. 1 (2016), 117–82, https://papers.ssrn.com/sol3/papers.cfm?abstract_id=2769645; and Shelby Meyers and Mickey Huff, "Fear of Government Spying is 'Chilling' Writers' Freedom of Expression," in *Censored 2016: Media Freedom on the Line*, eds. Mickey Huff and Andy Lee Roth with Project Censored (New York: Seven Stories Press, 2015), 57–58, reposted online at https://www.projectcensored.org/7-fear-of-government-spying-is-chilling-writers-freedom-of-expression/.

20. Jakub Dalek, Ron Deibert, Sarah McKune, Phillipa Gill, Adam Senft, and Naser Noor, "Information Controls during Military Operations: The Case of Yemen during the 2015 Political and Armed Conflict," Citizen Lab, October 21, 2015, https://citizenlab.ca/2015/10/information-controls-military-operations-yemen/.

21. Jakub Dalek, Lex Gill, Bill Marczak, Sarah McKune, Naser Noor, Joshua Oliver, Jon Penney, Adam Senft, and Ron Deibert, "Planet Netsweeper: Executive Summary," Citizen Lab, April 25, 2018, https://citizenlab.ca/2018/04/planet-netsweeper/.

22. "Netsweeper: Stop Censoring LGBT+ Content Now!" All Out, December 13, 2018, updated January 21, 2019, https://go.allout.org/en/a/netsweeper/.

23. Andrew Perrin and Monica Anderson, "Share of U.S. Adults Using Social Media, Including Facebook, is Mostly Unchanged since 2018," Pew Research Center, April 10, 2019, https://www.pewresearch.org/fact-tank/2019/04/10/share-of-u-s-adults-using-social-media-including-facebook-is-mostly-unchanged-since-2018/.

24. Adverse childhood experiences (ACEs) refer to ten experiences that researchers have identified as risk factors for adult chronic diseases: emotional abuse, physical abuse, sexual abuse, emotional neglect, physical neglect, family violence, household substance abuse, household mental illness, parental separation or divorce, and having an incarcerated house-

hold member. A study of 64,329 juvenile offenders in Florida revealed that 73 percent of the youth had lived with at least three ACE factors. See Michael T. Baglivio, Nathan Epps, Kimberly Swartz, Mona Sayedul Huq, Amy Sheer, and Nancy S. Hardt, "The Prevalence of Adverse Childhood Experiences (ACE) in the Lives of Juvenile Offenders," *OJJDP Journal of Juvenile Justice*, Vol. 3 No. 2 (Spring 2014), 1–23, https://web.archive. org/web/20140905115936/http://www.journalofjuvjustice.org/JOJJ0302/ article01.htm. On social undercastes, see Michelle Alexander, *The New Jim Crow: Mass Incarceration in the Age of Colorblindness* (New York: The New Press, 2010/2012).

25. Desmond Upton Patton, Douglas-Wade Brunton, Andrea Dixon, Reuben Jonathan Miller, Patrick Leonard, and Rose Hackman, "Stop and Frisk Online: Theorizing Everyday Racism in Digital Policing in the Use of Social Media for Identification of Criminal Conduct and Associations," *Social Media + Society*, Vol. 3 No. 3 (July–September 2017), https:// doi.org/10.1177/2056305117733344.

26. Shoshana Zuboff, *The Age of Surveillance Capitalism: The Fight for a Human Future at the New Frontier of Power* (New York: PublicAffairs, 2019).

27. Google Surveillance Capitalism Quiz, with accompanying answers: *1. What is the purpose of Google's search engine?* To be a supply route for the product. *2. What is the raw product they extract?* Behavioral data about us. *3. What is the finished product they create?* Predictions about our behavior. *4. Who are the customers?* Advertisers and governments wanting predictive power. *5. Who are the workers?* Us. *6. What is the ultimate goal?* Make money through modifying behavior.

28. David Buckingham, *Media Education: Literacy, Learning and Contemporary Culture* (Cambridge, UK: Polity Press, 2003).

29. Rhonda Hammer and Douglas Kellner, eds., *Media/Cultural Studies: Critical Approaches* (New York: Peter Lang, 2009).

30. Douglas Kellner and Jeff Share, *The Critical Media Literacy Guide: Engaging Media and Transforming Education* (Leiden, The Netherlands: Brill | Sense, 2019).

31. For a detailed description of the course, see Kellner and Share, *The Critical Media Literacy Guide.*

32. For a more thorough explanation of this lesson and other educational uses of photography, see Jeff Share, "Cameras in Classrooms: Photography's Pedagogical Potential," in *Essentials of Teaching and Integrating Visual and Media Literacy: Visualizing Learning*, eds. Danilo M. Baylen and Adriana D'Alba (New York: Springer, 2015), 97–118.

33. Sue Curry Jansen, "Ambiguities and Imperatives of Market Censorship: The Brief History of a Critical Concept," *Westminster Papers in Communication and Culture*, Vol. 7 No. 2 (October 2010), 12–30, 13, https://www. westminsterpapers.org/articles/abstract/10.16997/wpcc.141/.

34. C. Edwin Baker, *Advertising and a Democratic Press* (Princeton, New Jersey: Princeton University Press, 1994), 3.

35. One great exception is the five filters of the Propaganda Model in Edward S. Herman and Noam Chomsky, *Manufacturing Consent: The Political Economy of the Mass Media* (New York: Pantheon Books, 1988/2002).

36.   Eliza Collins, "Les Moonves: Trump's Run is 'Damn Good for CBS,'" *Politico*, February 29, 2016, https://www.politico.com/blogs/on-media/2016/02/les-moonves-trump-cbs-220001.

37.   I expand on this project in Victor Pickard, *Democracy Without Journalism? Confronting the Misinformation Society* (New York: Oxford University Press, 2020).

38.   For a history of how this system developed, see Victor Pickard, *America's Battle for Media Democracy: The Triumph of Corporate Libertarianism and the Future of Media Reform* (New York: Cambridge University Press, 2015).

39.   See, for instance, Nicholas Johnson, *Your Second Priority: A Former FCC Commissioner Speaks Out* (Morrisville, North Carolina: Myrtle Orchard Press/Lulu.com, 2007/2008).

40.   For more information, visit the MIC Center website: https://www.miccenter.org/.

Acknowledgments

Many people contributed to *State of the Free Press | 2021*. Here we are pleased to acknowledge some of this year's most important contributors and supporters.

We are blessed to work with an extraordinary editor, Michael Tencer. His deep knowledge, keen vision, and crisp editing enhanced every page in this book.

At Seven Stories Press, we thank Sam Brown, intern; Stewart Cauley, art director; Jon Gilbert, operations director; Lauren Hooker, senior editor; Allison Paller, senior publicist and web coordinator; Shayan Saalabi, production editor; Dan Simon, publisher and editorial director; Eva Sotomayor, publicist; Silvia Stramenga, rights director and editor of foreign literature; Elisa Taber, assistant editor and academic manager; Jordan Taylor-Jones, publicity manager at Seven Stories Press UK; and Ruth Weiner, publicity director of Seven Stories Press and co-publisher of Triangle Square Books for Young Readers—all of whom have our respect and gratitude for their steadfast commitment to publishing Project Censored's research.

Anson Stevens-Bollen provided the striking cover art for this year's book.

Jason Bud, Ama Cortes, Mischa Geracoulis, Sierra Kaul, Gavin Kelley, Juliana Moreno, Troy Patton, Matthew Phillips, and Spencer Wilkinson assisted in proofreading the manuscript.

Vital financial support from donors sustains the Project. This year, we are especially thankful to Cooper Atkinson,

Sharyl Attkisson, Margli and Phil Auclair, John Boyer, Allison Butler, Sandra Cioppa, James Coleman, Dwain A. Deets, Jan De Deka, Dmitry Egorov, Arlene Engelhardt, Martha Fleischman, Larry Gassan, Michael Hansen, Elizabeth Hegeman, Louise Johnston, Neil Joseph, Sheldon Levy, Robert Manning, James March, Sandra Maurer, Harry Mersmann, Nate Mudd, David Nelson, Christopher Oscar, Richard and Janet Oscar, Edwin Phillips, Allison Reilly, Lynn and Leonard Riepenhoff, John and Lyn Roth, Katherine Schock, T.M. Scruggs, Bill Simon, Mark Squire, David Stanek, Roger Stoll, Sal Velasco, Elaine Wellin, Barbara Wells, Derrick West and Laurie Dawson, David Winkler, and Montgomery Zukowski.

The Media Freedom Foundation board of directors, whose members are identified below, provide invaluable counsel and crucial organizational structure. Peter Phillips continues to be an inspiration and one of the Project's most stalwart supporters.

Without Adam Armstrong, almost no one in this digital era would know about the Project. Adam deftly manages our website, social media channels, and related audio and video content, including the Project's weekly radio program and podcast.

Christopher Oscar and Doug Hecker of Hole in the Media Productions provide ongoing support. We are especially grateful to Richard and Janet Oscar for their generous financing of the Project's newest documentary film, which is highlighted on the last page of this volume.

Anthony Fest and Dennis Murphy provide critical production assistance for the Project's weekly public affairs program. Bob Baldock and Ken Preston at KPFA continue to support the Project.

For amplifying the Project's voice, we thank Nolan Higdon; John Bertucci; John Crowley and the Aqus community; Jen Jensen, Larry Figueroa, and the crew at Lagunitas Brewing Company; Chase and Marco Palmieri and family at Risibisi; Raymond Lawrason and all at Copperfield's Books; Kevin Herbert at Common Cents; James Preston Allen, Paul Rosenberg, Terelle Jerricks, and the team at *Random Lengths News*, as well as the Association of Alternative Newsmedia; the Mount Diablo Peace and Justice Center; the Peace and Justice Center of Sonoma County; the Sociology Social Justice and Activism Club at Sonoma State University; Jason Houk at KSKQ, and the folks behind Independent Media Week, including Kathleen Gamer at Southern Oregon University in Ashland, Oregon; our allies in the Union for Democratic Communications and the Action Coalition for Media Education; Davey D and Hard Knock Radio; Abby Martin of *The Empire Files* and Media Roots; Mnar Muhawesh and the team at MintPress News; Eleanor Goldfield of *Act Out!*; Kevin Gosztola and Rania Khalek at Shadowproof and the *Unauthorized Disclosure* podcast; The Real News Network; Lee Camp and *Redacted Tonight*; Sharyl Attkisson of *Full Measure*; Arlene Engelhardt and Mary Glenney, hosts of *From a Woman's Point of View*; Eric Draitser and *CounterPunch Radio*; James Tracy and everyone at the Howard Zinn Book Fair in San Francisco; Chris Carosi, Greg Ruggiero, Elaine Katzenberger, and City Lights Publishers; David Talbot; Peter Kuznick; Michael Welch of *The Global Research News Hour*; Theresa Mitchell of *Presswatch* on KBOO; Jon Gold; John Collins and the team at Weave News; Chase Palmieri and all at Credder; Betsy Gomez and the Banned Books

Week Coalition, including Christopher Finan and our allies at the National Coalition Against Censorship and the American Library Association's Office for Intellectual Freedom; Ralph Nader and the Center for Study of Responsive Law; and Peter Ludes, Hektor Haarkötter, Daniel Müller, and Marlene Nunnendorf at the German Initiative on News Enlightenment.

At Diablo Valley College, Mickey thanks Lisa Martin and History program co-chair Matthew Powell, as well as the people who have supported the Journalism Revitalization Committee, including Adam Bessie, Mark Akiyama, Steve Johnson, Rayshell Clapper, Alan Haslam, Katy Agnost, Maria Dorado, Robert Hawkins, Nolan Higdon, Lisa Smiley-Ratchford, John Freytag, Ann Patton-Langelier, Terence Elliott, Albert Ponce, Sangha Niyogi, and everyone involved in the Social Justice Studies program and the Faculty Senate; and Dean of English and Social Sciences, Obed Vazquez; Vice President of Instruction, Mary Gutierrez; as well as college president Susan Lamb. Thanks also to current research assistants and Project interns including Troy Patton, Sierra Kaul, Veronica Vasquez, and Matthew Phillips. Mickey would also like to thank all of his students for the inspiration they provide, as they are a constant reminder of the possibilities of the future.

Mickey thanks his family, especially his wife, Meg, for her amazing work, counsel, and care; and their children, for patience, moral support, sense of humor, and their love of a good argument. Andy remembers Jessica Mae Orozco (1987–2018), whose passion for botany and life inspired everyone who knew her. He is grateful beyond words for Elizabeth Boyd, whose love sustains him.

Finally, we thank you, our readers, who continue to cherish a truly free press. Together, we make a difference.

Media Freedom Foundation/Project Censored Board of Directors

Adam Armstrong, Nicholas Baham III, Ben Boyington, Kenn Burrows, Allison Butler, Mary Cardaras, Doug Hecker, Mickey Huff (president), Christopher Oscar, Susan Rahman (vice president), Andy Lee Roth, T.M. Scruggs, and Elaine Wellin; with bookkeeper Michael Smith.

Project Censored 2019–20 Judges

ROBIN ANDERSEN. Professor of Communication and Media Studies, Fordham University. She has written dozens of scholarly articles and is author or co-author of four books, including *A Century of Media, A Century of War* (2006), winner of the Alpha Sigma Nu Book Award. She recently published *The Routledge Companion to Media and Humanitarian Action* (2017), and *HBO's* Treme *and the Stories of the Storm: From New Orleans as Disaster Myth to Groundbreaking Television* (2017). Writes media criticism and commentary for the media watch group Fairness & Accuracy In Reporting (FAIR), The Vision Machine, and the *Antenna* blog.

APRIL ANDERSON. Electronic Resources Librarian at Macalester College. A member and advocate of the LGBTQI+ community researching LGBTQ censorship, in print and online. Recent publications include "Queer Erasure" in the Spring 2020 issue of *Index on Censorship* and "Stonewalled: Establishment Media's Silence on the Trump Administration's Crusade against LGBTQ People," featured in *Censored 2020*.

JULIE ANDRZEJEWSKI. Professor Emeritus, St. Cloud State University. Served as director of the Social Responsibility master's program, and president of the faculty union. Publications include *Social Justice, Peace, and Environmental Education* (co-edited, 2009) and, most recently, a book chapter, "The Roots of the Sixth Mass Extinction" (2017). She is currently co-chair of Indivisible Tacoma and organizer of the WA Indivisible Town Hall Series.

OLIVER BOYD-BARRETT. Professor Emeritus of Media and Communications, Bowling Green State University and California State Polytechnic University, Pomona. Most recent publications include *News Agencies in the Turbulent Era of the Internet* (2010), *Hollywood and the CIA: Cinema, Defense, and Subversion* (2011), *Western Mainstream Media and the Ukraine Crisis* (2017), *RussiaGate and Propaganda* (2020), and *Media Imperialism: Continuity and Change* (2020).

KENN BURROWS. Faculty member at the Institute for Holistic Health Studies, Department of Health Education, San Francisco State University. Founder and director of the Holistic Health Learning Center and producer of the biennial conference, Future of Health Care.

ERNESTO CARMONA. Journalist and writer. Chief correspondent, teleSUR Chile. Director, Santiago Circle of Journalists. Executive Secretary of the Investigation Commission on Attacks Against Journalists, Latin American Federation of Journalists (CIAP-FELAP).

ELLIOT D. COHEN. Professor of Philosophy and chair of the Humanities Department, Indian River State College. Editor and founder of the *International Journal of Applied Philosophy*. Recent books include *Making Peace with Imperfection* (2019), *Counseling Ethics for the 21st Century* (2018), *Logic-Based Therapy and Everyday Emotions* (2016), and *Technology of Oppression: Preserving Freedom and Dignity in an Age of Mass, Warrantless Surveillance* (2014).

BRIAN COVERT. Independent journalist, author, and educator based in Japan. Worked for United Press International (UPI) news service in Japan, as staff reporter and editor for English-language daily newspapers in Japan, and as contributing writer to Japanese and overseas newspapers and magazines. Contributing author to past *Censored* editions. Teaches journalism/media studies at Doshisha University in Kyoto.

GEOFF DAVIDIAN. Investigative reporter, war correspondent, legal affairs analyst, editor, photojournalist, data analyst, and educator. Founding publisher and editor of the *Putnam Pit*, *Milwaukee Press*, and ShorewoodNewsroom. Contributor to Reuters, magazines, newspapers, and online publications.

ROBERT HACKETT. Professor Emeritus of Communication, Simon Fraser University, Vancouver. Co-founder of NewsWatch Canada (1993), Media Democracy Days (2001), and OpenMedia.ca (2007). Publications include *Remaking Media: The Struggle to Democratize Public Communication* (with W.K. Carroll, 2006) and *Journalism and Climate Crisis: Public Engagement, Media Alternatives* (with S. Forde, S. Gunster, and K. Foxwell-Norton, 2017). He blogs at rabble.ca.

KEVIN HOWLEY. Professor of Media Studies, DePauw University. His work has appeared in the *Journal of Radio Studies*, *Journalism: Theory, Practice and Criticism*, *Social Movement Studies*, and *Television and New Media*. He is the author of *Community Media: People, Places, and Communication Technologies* (2005), and editor of *Understanding Community Media* (2010) and *Media Interventions* (2013). His latest book is *Drones: Media Discourse and the Public Imagination* (2018).

NICHOLAS JOHNSON.* Author, *How to Talk Back to Your Television Set* (1970) and nine additional titles, including *Columns of Democracy* (2018) and *Catfish Solution* (2019). Commissioner, Federal Communications Commission (1966–1973).

Former media and cyber law professor, University of Iowa College of Law. More online at nicholasjohnson.org.

CHARLES L. KLOTZER. Founder, editor, and publisher emeritus of *St. Louis Journalism Review* and *FOCUS/Midwest*. The *St. Louis Journalism Review* has been transferred to Southern Illinois University, Carbondale, and is now the *Gateway Journalism Review*. Klotzer remains active at the *Review*.

NANCY KRANICH. Lecturer, School of Communication and Information, and special projects librarian, Rutgers University. Past president of the American Library Association (ALA), and convener of the ALA Center for Civic Life. Author of *Libraries and Democracy: The Cornerstones of Liberty* (2001) and "Libraries: Reuniting the Divided States of America" (2017).

DEEPA KUMAR. Professor of Media Studies, Rutgers University. Award-winning scholar and activist. Author of *Outside the Box: Corporate Media, Globalization, and the UPS Strike* (2007), *Islamophobia and the Politics of Empire* (2012), and about 75 journal articles, book chapters, and contributions in independent and establishment media. Past president of the Rutgers AAUP-AFT faculty union.

MARTIN LEE. Investigative journalist and author. Co-founder of Fairness & Accuracy In Reporting, and former editor of FAIR's magazine, *Extra!*. Director of Project CBD, a medical science information nonprofit. Author of *Smoke Signals: A Social History of Marijuana—Medical, Recreational, and Scientific* (2012), *The Beast Reawakens: Fascism's Resurgence from Hitler's Spymasters to Today's Neo-Nazi Groups and Right-Wing Extremists* (2000), and *Acid Dreams: The Complete Social History of LSD: The CIA, the Sixties, and Beyond* (with B. Shlain, 1985).

PETER LUDES. Professor of Mass Communication, Jacobs University, Bremen, 2002–2017. Visiting Professor, University of Cologne, 2018–2021. Founder of the German Initiative on News Enlightenment (1997) at the University of Siegen (Project Censored, Germany). Recent publications include *Brutalisierung und Banalisierung Asoziale und soziale Netze* (Brutalization and Banalization in Asocial and Social Networks) (2018), and, as co-editor, *Collective Myths and Decivilizing Processes* (with Stefan Kramer, 2020) and *Contact Zones in China: Multidisciplinary Perspectives* (with Merle Schatz and Laura De Giorgi, 2020).

WILLIAM LUTZ. Professor Emeritus of English, Rutgers University. Former editor of the *Quarterly Review of Doublespeak.* Author of *Doublespeak: From Revenue Enhancement to Terminal Living: How Government, Business, Advertisers, and Others Use Language to Deceive You* (1989), *The Cambridge Thesaurus of American English* (1994), *The New Doublespeak: Why No One Knows What Anyone's Saying Anymore* (1996), and *Doublespeak Defined* (1999).

CONCHA MATEOS. Professor of Journalism, Department of Communication Sciences, Universidad Rey Juan Carlos, Spain. Journalist for radio, television, and political organizations in Spain and Latin America. Coordinator for Project Censored research in Europe and Latin America.

MARK CRISPIN MILLER. Professor of Media, Culture, and Communication, Steinhardt School of Culture, Education, and Human Development, New York University. Author, editor, and activist.

DANIEL MÜLLER. Head of the Postgraduate Academy at the University of Siegen, in Germany. Researcher and educator in journalism and mass communication studies and history at public universities for many years. Has published extensively on media history, media–minority relations in Germany, and on nationality policies and ethnic relations of the Soviet Union and the post-Soviet successor states, particularly in the Caucasus. Jury member of the German Initiative on News Enlightenment.

JACK L. NELSON.* Distinguished Professor Emeritus, Graduate School of Education, Rutgers University. Former member, Committee on Academic Freedom and Tenure, American Association of University Professors. Recipient, Academic Freedom Award, National Council for Social Studies. Author of seventeen books, including *Critical Issues in Education: Dialogues and Dialectics*, 9th ed. (with S. Palonsky and M.R. McCarthy, 2020) and *Human Impact of Natural Disasters* (with V.O. Pang and W.R. Fernekes, 2010), and about 200 articles.

PETER PHILLIPS. Professor of Political Sociology, Sonoma State University, since 1994. Director, Project Censored, 1996–2010. President, Media Freedom Foundation, 2010–2016. Editor or co-editor of fourteen editions of *Censored*. Co-editor (with Dennis Loo) of *Impeach the President: The Case Against Bush and Cheney* (Seven Stories Press, 2006). Author of *Giants: The Global Power Elite* (Seven Stories Press, 2018), as well as four chapters in recent *Censored* yearbooks.

MICHAEL RAVNITZKY. Attorney, writer, editor, engineer, and Freedom of Information Act expert who has developed tools to broaden access to public records in the public interest.

T. M. SCRUGGS. Professor Emeritus (and token ethnomusicologist), University of Iowa. Published in print, audio, and/ or video format, on Central American, Cuban, and Venezuelan music and dance and US jazz. Involvement with community radio in Nicaragua, Venezuela, and the United States, including the KPFA (Berkeley, CA) Local Station Board and Pacifica National Board. Executive producer, The Real News Network, and board member, Truthout.

NANCY SNOW. Pax Mundi Professor of Public Diplomacy, Kyoto University of Foreign Studies, Japan. Professor Emeritus of Communications, California State University, Fullerton. Fellow, Temple University, Japan, Institute of Contemporary Asian Studies. Author or editor of twelve books, including *The SAGE Handbook of Propaganda* (2020) and a new edition of *The Routledge Handbook of Public Diplomacy* (with Nicholas J. Cull, 2020).

PAUL STREET. Researcher, award-winning journalist, historian, author, and speaker. Author of seven books to date: *Empire and Inequality: America and the World Since 9/11* (2004); *Segregated Schools: Educational Apartheid in Post–Civil Rights America* (2005); *Racial Oppression in the Global Metropolis: A Living Black Chicago History* (2007); *Barack Obama and the Future of American Politics* (2009); *The Empire's New Clothes: Barack Obama in the Real World of Power* (2010); *Crashing the Tea Party: Mass Media and the Campaign to Remake American Politics*, with Anthony R. DiMaggio (2011); and *They Rule: The 1% vs. Democracy* (2014). He writes regularly for Truthdig and *CounterPunch*.

SHEILA RABB WEIDENFELD.* Emmy Award–winning television producer. Former press secretary to Betty Ford and special assistant to the President; author, *First Lady's Lady*. President of DC Productions Ltd. Creator of snippetsofwisdom. com. Director of community relations of Phyto Management LLC and Maryland Cultivation and Processing LLC.

ROB WILLIAMS. Founding president of the Action Coalition for Media Education (ACME). Teaches media, communications, global studies, and journalism at the University of Vermont and Champlain College. Author of numerous articles on critical media literacy education. Publisher of the *Vermont Independent* online news journal. Co-editor of *Media Education for a Digital Generation* (with J. Frechette, 2016) and *Most Likely to Secede* (with R. Miller, 2013), about the Vermont independence movement.

*Indicates having been a Project Censored judge since our founding in 1976.

In Memoriam

With sadness, we note the passing of Hugh Downs (1921–2020). A pioneer of broadcast journalism, Downs was also an early advocate of Project Censored. He wrote the introduction to the very first *Censored* yearbook and served as one of the Project's esteemed judges. At a time when few acclaimed journalists called out censorship in their own profession, Downs courageously did so.

How to Support Project Censored

Nominate a Story

To nominate a *Censored* story, send us a copy of the article and include the name of the source publication and the date that the article appeared. For news stories published on the internet, forward the URL to mickey@projectcensored.org or andy@projectcensored.org. The deadline for nominating *Censored* stories is March 15 of each year.

Criteria for Project Censored
News Story Nominations:

1) A censored news story reports information that the public has a right and a need to know, but to which the public has had limited access.

2) The news story is recent, having been first reported no later than one year ago. For *State of the Free Press | 2021*, the Top 25 list includes stories reported between April 2019 and March 2020. Thus, stories submitted for *State of the Free Press | 2022* should be no older than April 2020.

3) The story is fact-based with clearly defined concepts and verifiable documentation. The story's claims should be supported by evidence—the more controversial the claims, the stronger the evidence necessary.

4) The news story has been published, either electronically or in print, in a publicly circulated newspaper, journal, magazine, newsletter, or similar publication from either a domestic or foreign source.

Make a Tax-Deductible Donation

We depend on tax-deductible donations to continue our work. Project Censored is supported by the Media Freedom Foundation, a 501(c)(3) nonprofit organization. To support our efforts on behalf of independent journalism and freedom of information, send checks to the address below or donate online at projectcensored.org. You can also make monthly donations through our Patreon account at patreon.com/projectcensored. Your generous donations help us to oppose news censorship and promote media literacy.

Media Freedom Foundation • PO Box 750940 • Petaluma, CA 94975
mickey@projectcensored.org; andy@projectcensored.org
Phone: (707) 241-4596

About the Editors

MICKEY HUFF is the director of Project Censored and president of the nonprofit Media Freedom Foundation. He has edited or co-edited twelve annual volumes of *Censored*. He is the co-author, with Nolan Higdon, of *United States of Distraction: Media Manipulation in Post-Truth America* (City Lights, 2019). Huff received the Beverly Kees Educator Award as part of the 2019 James Madison Freedom of Information Awards from the Society of Professional Journalists, Northern California. He is a professor of social science and history at Diablo Valley College, where he co-chairs the History program and is chair of the Journalism Department. He is also a lecturer in communications at California State University, East Bay. Huff is executive producer and co-host of *The Project Censored Show*, the Project's weekly syndicated public affairs radio program. A musician and composer, he lives with his family in Sonoma County, California.

ANDY LEE ROTH is the associate director of Project Censored and co-editor of ten previous editions of this yearbook. He coordinates the Project's Campus Affiliates Program, a news media research network of several hundred students and faculty at two dozen colleges and universities across North America. His research and writing have been published in a variety of outlets, including *Index on Censorship*, *In These Times*, *YES! Magazine*, *Media, Culture & Society*, and the *International Journal of Press/Politics*. He earned a PhD in sociology at the University of California, Los Angeles, and a BA in sociology and anthropology at Haverford College. He lives in Seattle with his sweetheart and their two wonderful cats.

For more information about the editors, to invite them to speak at your school or in your community, or to conduct interviews, please visit projectcensored.org.

Index

United States of Distraction
Fighting the Fake News Invasion

Project Censored's new documentary is now available, at no charge, from projectcensored.org and on YouTube.

UNITED STATES OF DISTRACTION:

FIGHTING THE FAKE NEWS INVASION

A FILM SHOT AND PRODUCED BY STUDENTS
WITH PROJECT CENSORED
EDITED AND NARRATED BY ABBY MARTIN

Hole in the Media Productions, LLC
Media Freedom Foundation

Filmed by students, edited and narrated by Abby Martin of *The Empire Files*, and produced by Project Censored, "United States of Distraction: Fighting the Fake News Invasion" chronicles critical media literacy with faculty experts, students, and media makers who provide contextual analysis for understanding the current rise of "fake news." In addition to deconstructing this phenomenon, the film reminds us that fake news is nothing new, but rather an age-old form of propaganda. The film's interviewees offer solutions to forestall the pernicious influence of fake news on America's democratic institutions.

Selected as an entry for the 2020 Sonoma International Film Festival, the documentary provides a comprehensive account of the current media landscape, making it a valuable teaching tool. To arrange a screening with discussion by the filmmakers, contact mickey@projectcensored.org.